international review of social history

Special Issue 26

Transportation, Deportation and Exile: Perspectives from the Colonies in the Nineteenth and Twentieth Centuries

Edited by Christian G. De Vito, Clare Anderson, and Ulbe Bosma

Published by the Press Syndicate of the University of Cambridge
The Pitt Building, Trumpington Street, Cambridge, CB2 1RP
1 Liberty Plaza, Floor 20, New York, NY 10006, USA
10 Stamford Road, Oakleigh, Melbourne 3166, Australia

© Internationaal Instituut voor Sociale Geschiedenis

*A catalogue record for this book is available
from the British Library*

Library of Congress Cataloguing-in-Publication Data applied for

ISBN 9781108727617 (paperback)

Printed in the UK by Bell & Bain Ltd, Glasgow, UK.

CONTENTS

Transportation, Deportation and Exile: Perspectives from the Colonies in the Nineteenth and Twentieth Centuries

Edited by
Christian G. De Vito, Clare Anderson, and Ulbe Bosma

IRSH 63 (2018), Special Issue, pp. 1–24 doi:10.1017/S0020859018000196
© 2018 Internationaal Instituut voor Sociale Geschiedenis

Transportation, Deportation and Exile: Perspectives from the Colonies in the Nineteenth and Twentieth Centuries*

CHRISTIAN G. DE VITO

School of History, Politics and International Relations
University of Leicester
University Road, Leicester LE1 7RH, UK

E-mail: christian.devito@gmail.com

CLARE ANDERSON

School of History, Politics and International Relations
University of Leicester
University Road, Leicester LE1 7RH, UK

E-mail: ca26@le.ac.uk

ULBE BOSMA

International Institute of Social History
PO Box 2169, 1000 CD
Amsterdam, The Netherlands

E-mail: ubo@iisg.nl

ABSTRACT: The essays in this volume provide a new perspective on the history of convicts and penal colonies. They demonstrate that the nineteenth and twentieth centuries were a critical period in the reconfiguration of empires, imperial governmentality, and punishment, including through extensive punitive relocation and associated extractive labour. Ranging across the global contexts of Africa, Asia, Australasia, Japan, the Americas, the Pacific, Russia, and Europe, and exploring issues of criminalization, political repression, and convict management alongside those of race, gender, space, and circulation, this collection offers a perspective from the colonies that radically transforms accepted narratives of the history of empire and the history of punishment. In this introduction, we argue that a colony-centred perspective reveals that, during a critical period in world history, convicts and penal colonies created new spatial hierarchies, enabled the incorporation of territories into

* The research leading to these results has received funding from the European Research Council under the European Union's Seventh Framework Programme (FP/2007–2013) / ERC Grant Agreement 312542.

spheres of imperial influence, and forged new connections and distinctions between "metropoles" and "colonies". Convicts and penal colonies enabled the formation of expansive and networked global configurations and processes, a factor hitherto unappreciated in the literature.

INTRODUCTION

Penal transportation, deportation, and exile have played a crucial role in the history of nations and empires. Without them, many colonial projects would not have materialized, or only at a much later stage. Punitive mobility helped to govern and manage populations, expand empires, and bring coerced labour to the peripheries of empires. It reinforced spatial hierarchies, created new circuits of imperial movement, and allowed colonial powers to deploy a repertoire of punitive measures within and beyond the criminal justice system. In addressing these themes, the articles in this special issue are situated at the intersection of the history of punishment, of labour, and the New Imperial History.[1] We focus on the modern period because more global powers employed penal transportation during the third quarter of the nineteenth century than at any other point in world history. Interestingly, this was at precisely the time when states unified their legal systems, modern prisons putatively emerged as sites of discipline and punishment, and forms of penal mobility and confinement diversified, owing in part to political factors.[2] These penal transportations, usually to territories outside the jurisdiction of imperial parliaments, allowed for politically expedient deflections from these projects of unification of the administration of justice. In the colonies, the punitive relocation of colonial subjects both enabled and enacted imperial modes of governance and population control. At the same time, the relocation of convicts served the purpose of empire-building, which, in terms of geographical reach and scale, was at its height between the late nineteenth and early twentieth centuries.

The routes of penal transportation, deportation, and exile were determined by a hierarchically ordered relationship between different parts of the empire. Colonial subjects were rarely deported to Europe, whereas hundreds of thousands of Europeans (and if we include Soviet Russia, millions) were sent to the outskirts of colonial empires. Moreover, empires

---

1. Antoinette Burton and Tony Ballantyne (eds), *World Histories From Below: Disruption and Dissent, 1750 to the Present* (London, 2016); Durba Ghosh, "Another Set of Imperial Turns?", *American Historical Review*, 117:3 (2012), pp. 772–793; Stephen Howe (ed.), *The New Imperial Histories Reader* (London, 2010); Kathleen Wilson (ed.), *A New Imperial History: Culture, Identity, and Modernity in Britain and the Empire, 1660–1840* (Cambridge, 2004).
2. Mary Gibson, "Global Perspectives on the Birth of the Prison", *American Historical Review*, 116:4 (2011), pp. 1040–1063.

moved colonially convicted imperial subjects and citizens around colonial peripheries to a remarkable degree.[3] Since these movements were crucial for the population of sparsely or non-settled territories, they were also often permanent. However, though convicts were sometimes the first choice in terms of labour supply, in some locations, at a later stage, non-punitive migration might take over. This was the result of a full incorporation of colonized spaces, the achieved independent statehood of former colonies, or the emergence of alternative strategies of colonization. It is the practices and processes that occurred within these colonized spaces that interest us primarily in this volume. By foregrounding the perspective of the colonies, rather than that of colonizing powers, this special issue highlights the dual character of convict mobility – that is to say, it proposes that it was both a means of imperial consolidation and a means of creating new forms of spatial distinction.

The volume's perspective is the culmination of a thorough transformation of the scholarship on convict transportation over the past forty years. This began with studies in the 1980s and 1990s of European transportation outwards from Europe as a means of colonization, or towards already colonized territories: from Britain to the Americas and the Australian colonies, from Spain to the Caribbean, and from China's core region to its borderlands.[4] During the same period, research was conducted on inter-imperial transportations within the British Empire, notably from the Caribbean and Cape colonies to those of Australia.[5] Then, in the early 2000s, new work stressed intra-imperial movements in other contexts. This included Timothy J. Coates' work on the Portuguese Empire (*Convicts and Orphans*), and Kerry Ward's *Networks of Empire*, which explored banishment and convict transportation in the Dutch East India Company. The focus of *Networks of Empire* on the connections between the Cape and Batavia joined Clare Anderson's *Convicts in the Indian Ocean* in pointing to the relevance of inter-colonial routes of penal transportation, and

3. Clare Anderson, "Introduction: A Global History of Convicts and Penal Colonies", in *idem* (ed.), *A Global History of Convicts and Penal Colonies* (London, 2018), pp. 1–35.

4. Ian Duffield and James Bradley (eds), *Representing Convicts: New Perspectives on Convict Forced Labour Migration* (London, 1997); Roger Ekirch, *Bound for America: The Transportation of British Convicts to the Colonies, 1718–1775* (Oxford, 1987); Steven Nicholas (ed.), *Convict Workers: Reinterpreting Australia's Past* (Cambridge, 1988); Ruth Pike, *Penal Servitude in Early Modern Spain* (Madison, WI, 1983); Joanna Waley-Cohen, *Exile in Mid-Qing China: Banishment to Xinjiang, 1758–1820* (New Haven, CT, 1991).

5. Lesley C. Duly, "'Hottentots to Hobart and Sydney': The Cape Supreme Court's Use of Transportation, 1828–38", *Australian Journal of Politics and History*, 25:1 (1979), pp. 39–50; Ian Duffield, "From Slave Colonies to Penal Colonies: The West Indian Convict Transportees to Australia", *Slavery and Abolition*, 7:1 (1986), pp. 25–45; Vertrees Canby Malherbe, "Khoikhoi and the Question of Convict Transportation from the Cape Colony, 1820–1842", *South African Historical Journal*, 17:1 (1985), pp. 19–39.

represented major shifts in the understanding of punishment, mobility, and convict experience.[6] This focus has also characterized the third, and present, generation of studies, dating from c.2010, which have stressed the significance of convict transportation in other national and imperial contexts. This body of work includes research on Germany, Italy, France, the Habsburg Empire, the Ottoman Empire, the Iberian empires, Latin America, and the empire of Denmark-Sweden, and has widened the field to studies of galley servitude, deportation, and exile. As well as expanding our knowledge of specific contexts, this, in turn, has enhanced our understanding of the larger global context for the British, French, Russian, Soviet, and Dutch cases.[7]

6. Clare Anderson, *Convicts in the Indian Ocean: Transportation from South Asia to Mauritius, 1815–53* (Basingstoke, 2000); Timothy J. Coates, *Convicts and Orphans: Forced and State-Sponsored Colonizers in the Portuguese Empire, 1550–1755* (Stanford, CA, 2001); Kerry Ward, *Networks of Empire: Forced Migration in the Dutch East India Company* (Cambridge, 2008).
7. For an overview, see Anderson, "Introduction". See also Clare Anderson and Hamish Maxwell-Stewart, "Convict Labour and the Western Empires, 1415–1954", in Robert Aldrich and Kirsten McKenzie (eds), *The Routledge History of Western Empires* (London, 2013), pp. 102–117. Regional studies include: Ricardo D. Salvatore and Carlos Aguirre, "Colonies of Settlement or Places of Banishment and Torment? Penal Colonies and Convict Labour in Latin America, c.1800–1940", in Christian G. De Vito and Alex Lichtenstein (eds), *Global Convict Labour* (Leiden, 2016), pp. 273–309; Clare Anderson, "A Global History of Exile in Asia, c.1700–1900", in Ronit Ricci (ed.), *Exile in Colonial Asia: Kings, Convicts, Commemoration* (Honolulu, HI, 2016), pp. 20–47; Timothy J. Coates, *Convict Labor in the Portuguese Empire, 1740–1932: Redefining the Empire with Forced Labor and New Imperialism* (Leiden, 2014); Timothy J. Coates, "The Long View of Convict Labour in the Portuguese Empire, 1415–1932", in De Vito and Lichtenstein, *Global Convict Labour*, pp. 144–167; Christian G. De Vito, "Convict Labor in the Southern Borderlands of Latin America (c.1750s–1910s): Comparative Perspectives", in Marcel van der Linden and Magaly Rodríguez García (eds), *On Coerced Labor: Work and Compulsion after Chattel Slavery* (Leiden, 2016), pp. 98–126; Matthew P. Fitzpatrick, *Purging the Empire: Mass Expulsions in Germany, 1871–1914* (Oxford, 2015); J.M. Gheith and K.R. Jolluck, *Gulag Voices: Oral Histories of Soviet Incarceration and Exile* (Basingstoke, 2010); A.A. Gentes, *Exile to Siberia, 1590–1822* (Basingstoke, 2008); idem, *Exile, Murder and Madness in Siberia, 1823–61* (Basingstoke, 2010); Johan Lund Heinsen, *Mutiny in the Danish Atlantic World: Convicts, Sailors and a Dissonant Empire* (London, 2017); Miranda F. Spieler, *Empire and Underworld: Captivity in French Guiana* (Cambridge, MA, 2012); Jean-Lucien Sanchez, *À perpétuité. Relégués au bagne de Guyane* (Paris, 2013); Stephan Steiner, "'An Austrian Cayenne': Convict Labour and Deportation in the Habsburg Empire of the Early Modern Period", in De Vito and Lichtenstein, *Global Convict Labour*, pp. 126–143. An important sub-field is represented by the study of penal servitude in the galleys: Marc Vigié, *Les galériens du roi, 1661–1715* (Paris, 1985); Nicole Castan, André Zysberg, and Jacques-Guy Petit, *Histoire des galères, bagnes et prisons en France de l'Ancien Régime* (Toulouse, 1991); José Luis de las Heras, "Los galeotes de la monarquía hispánica durante el antiguo régimen", *Studia histórica*, 22 (2000), pp. 283–300; Luca Lo Basso, *Uomini da remo. Galee e galeotti del Mediterraneo in età moderna* (Milan, 2003); David Wheat, "Mediterranean Slavery, New World Transformations: Galley Slaves in the Spanish Caribbean, 1578–1635", *Slavery and Abolition*, 31:3 (2010), pp. 327–344; Fariba Zarinebaf, *Crime and Punishment in Istanbul, 1700–1800* (Berkeley, CA, 2010); Manuel Martínez Martínez, *Los forzados de marina en la España del siglo XVIII (1700–1775)* (Almería, 2011).

More generally, its multi-century chronological scope, focus on a wide range of national and imperial contexts, and concern with punitive regimes associated with spatial mobility have placed the scholarship on convict transportation at the forefront of new trends in the history of unfree labour migration. This has blurred distinctions between "free" and "unfree", and incorporated military service, labour circulation, and sojourning into the analysis.[8] The enduring character of punitive relocation since the Portuguese Empire first used convicts for colonizing purposes in 1415 has also challenged the dominant narrative of the history of punishment as a story of the demise of corporal sanction and the rise of penitentiary systems. This is still largely based on Michel Foucault's Eurocentric view of a linear development that took place around the end of the eighteenth century, culminating in the "triumphant prison" of the nineteenth and twentieth centuries.[9]

The richness and diversity of the literature on convict transportation means that we are now at the stage at which we can meaningfully discuss more than their significance for the history of migration and punishment – that is to say, the connectivity and interdependence between the evolution of punitive regimes, colonial labour mobility, and empire- and nation-building.[10] This special issue comprises a set of essays on practices of administrative and penal relocations in the British, Dutch, French, Japanese, Russian, Portuguese, Spanish, US, and Italian empires during the period from the nineteenth to the mid-twentieth centuries. All the papers begin

---

8. Clare Anderson *et al.*, "Locating Penal Transportation: Punishment, Space, and Place c.1750 to 1900", in Karen M. Morin and Dominique Moran (eds), *Historical Geographies of Prisons: Unlocking the Usable Carceral Past* (London, 2016), pp. 147–167; Tom Brass and Marcel van der Linden (eds), *Free and Unfree Labour* (Berne, 1997); Ulbe Bosma, "European Colonial Soldiers in the Nineteenth Century: Their Role in White Global Migration and Patterns of Colonial Settlement", *Journal of Global History*, 4:2 (2009), pp. 317–336.

9. Michel Foucault, *Discipline and Punish: The Birth of the Prison* (London, 1977). See also David Garland, *Punishment and Modern Society: A Study in Social Theory* (Oxford, 1991), chs 6 and 7.

10. This approach was first pioneered at the University of Leicester, during the 1999 conference "Colonial Spaces, Convict Places: Penal Transportation in Comparative Global Perspective". Since 2013, Leicester has hosted the ERC-funded project "The Carceral Archipelago: Transnational Circulations in Global Perspective, 1415–1960", which has encompassed new research on penal transportation within British Asia, the Australian colonies, Bermuda, Gibraltar, Zanzibar, the British Caribbean, Cape Colony, French Guiana, New Caledonia, the Spanish Empire, Ecuador, Russia (Sakhalin), and Japan (including Hokkaido). Since 2014, the NWO project "Four Centuries of Labour Camps: War, Rehabilitation, Ethnicity", based at the International Institute of Social History (IISH) and the Institute for War, Holocaust and Genocide Studies (NIOD), Amsterdam, has focused particularly on labour camps, working on the Netherlands Indies, Hamburg, Italy and the Italian colonies, and imperial and Soviet Russia. For the Carceral Archipelago project, see http://www2.le.ac.uk/departments/history/research/grants/CArchipelago and www.convictvoyages.org; last accessed 11 March 2018. For the Labour Camps project, see https://www.nwo.nl/en/research-and-results/research-projects/i/90/10790.html; last accessed 11 March 2018.

their analysis from the colonies, and by doing so they make three crucial analytical interventions. First, they focus on how understandings of class, ethnicity, race, and gender in the colonies are influenced by the sometimes conflicting demands associated with the organization of punishment and the management of labour. They integrate discussions about the flows of convicts sentenced in the framework of criminal justice systems (penal transportation), the mobilization of individuals through special laws and orders (administrative deportation), and the relocation of military and non-military individuals by means of military courts and authorities (military deportation). It is for this reason that we refer to these flows collectively as "punitive relocations". This special issue interrogates the relationships between punitive practices and their links with legal cultures, criminological knowledge, strategies of social control, and labour extraction. It addresses the interplay between groups of individuals, types of punishment, and penal destinations.

Second, these papers address the multiple interactions between punitive relocations and modes of incarceration. The contributions in this special issue join a growing body of scholarship in highlighting the point that punishment in the colonies was only marginally, if at all, related to imprisonment, because capital and corporal punishment and penal servitude continued to play a central role.[11] Moreover, by expanding the observation from the criminal justice system to include administrative and military deportations, they point to the persistent relevance of punitive relocations not only for colonial, but also for metropolitan punitive regimes. The contributions also highlight the ongoing significance of penal *mobility* as a mode of punishment, in lieu of exclusively conflating penalty with incarceration and immobilization. From this perspective, there is more fluidity between penal transportation and incarceration than has been hitherto appreciated.

Third, this special issue points to the significant shifts that existed between early modern and modern punitive relocations, coinciding with the Age of Revolution (c.1774–1860s) and its aftermath, the rise of modern European empires, the increasingly global ambitions of the US, Russia, and Japan, and the rise of liberalism.[12] For instance, we highlight the connections between imperial governmentality and the late nineteenth-century

11. See especially Florence Bernault (ed.), *Enfermement, prison et châtiments en Afrique. Du 19e siècle à nos jours* (Paris, 1999); Frank Dikötter and Ian Brown (eds), *Cultures of Confinement: A History of the Prison in Africa, Asia, and Latin America* (London, 2007).
12. Clare Anderson, Niklas Frykman, Lex Heerma van Voss, and Marcus Rediker (eds), "Mutiny and Maritime Radicalism in the Age of Revolution: A Global Survey", *International Review of Social History*, 58: Special Issue 21 (2013); David Armitage and Sanjay Subrahmanyam, *The Age of Revolutions in Global Context, c.1760–1840* (London, 2010). On the rise of liberalism and the relationship between nation- and empire-building: Josep M. Fradera, *La nación imperial (1750–1918)*, 2 vols (Barcelona, 2015), 1; Stefan Berger and Alexei Miller (eds), *Nationalizing Empires* (Budapest and New York, 2015).

Scramble for Africa and competition in the Pacific, and the renewed importance of penal colonization. This includes Britain's use of transportation to suppress rebellion among its enslaved and colonized peoples, Russo-Japanese arguments over Sakhalin and Hokkaido, and the shift from mixed settlements of punishment and unfree labour to convict-only penal colonies. Finally, several contributions highlight the increasing impact during the period under consideration of administrative and military relocations connected to states of exception, and the "politicization" of punishment and imperial governance it implied.[13]

IN THE COLONIES

A distinctive feature of this special issue is its focus on an exceptionally wide range of national and imperial contexts, including not just the European empires but also European "internal" colonization and non-European colonies in East Asia. Ranging across locales as diverse as Indochina, Trinidad, Japan, the Philippines, Libya, Australia, Cuba, Russia, Siberia, India, Aceh, and Angola, the authors use penal transportation, deportation, and exile as lenses through which to view various modes of imperial governmentality, which in our collective understanding renders colonial and metropolitan contexts distinct from each other in important ways. These modes included the management of populations through geographically and economically extractive kinds of punishment, and the use of punishment to expropriate labour. Nations and empires used regional systems to inflict punitive relocations, and made racial and gender instrumental in the management and supervision of transportation, deportation, and exile. The relationship between convicts and other kinds of unfree labour is also important here. The centring of the colonies in our analysis enables us to glimpse snapshots of convict agency and creativity too, through effecting escapes and rebellions as well as expressing choice and identity in the most unpromising of penal circumstances.

Viewed from the colonies, empires look simultaneously more fragile and more violent than in their metropolitan blueprints. Colonial domination reveals itself as a complex exercise in governance, based on both repression and negotiation. The homogeneous colours of sovereignty on metropolitan maps turn into a rugged cartography of "corridors" and enclaves, including commercial and military outposts, urban centres, and religious missions. Clear-cut imperial "frontiers" appear as contested and porous borderlands, zones of contact and conflict with both indigenous peoples and competing imperial powers. The centre–periphery divide becomes populated, and contested, by a plethora of actors across multiple sites.[14] The view from the

13. Cf. Giorgio Agamben, *State of Exception* (Chicago, IL, 2005).
14. Michiel Baud and Willem van Schendel, "Toward a Comparative History of Borderlands", *Journal of World History*, 8:2 (1997), pp. 211–242; Christine Daniels and Michael V. Kennedy

penal colonies that we propose here makes this reconceptualization of empires even more compelling. Indeed, sites of convict transportation, deportation, and exile were often keys to the further expansion of colonization, the setting of new frontiers, and the governance of peoples: this makes them ideal vantage points to observe both the precariousness and the complexity of the fabric empires were made of. From this perspective, the repeated "failure" of penal colonization to conform to the plans of imperial centres, particularly where sites were costly or rates of morbidity and mortality were high, should not be seen as a sign of their lack of success, as it is sometimes suggested. Rather, the idea of "failed" penal sites provides an entry point into the ideal of the making of empires as an ongoing process.[15]

As the contributions to this volume show, when the destinations of punitive relocations did emerge and persist, they were frequently as vulnerable as the imperial sovereignty that they represented and constructed. For example, Coates indicates that the tight-knit image of a model prison constructed by the authorities and colonial lobbies in Lisbon around the *depósito* of convicts in Luanda had little correspondence with the reality on the ground, especially in the face of convicts' frequent escapes and high mortality. Similarly, Zhanna Popova highlights the fact that even the infamous punitive regime of imperial Siberia was the product of multiple negotiations and the sum of highly uneven local circumstances, rather than a mirror for the blueprints of the imperial centre. And although such contradictions and uncertainties often accounted for the appalling conditions in which convicts lived, they also created spaces that could be used by some

---

(eds), *Negotiated Empires: Centers and Peripheries in the Americas, 1500–1820* (New York, 2002); Serge Gruzinski, *Les Quatre Parties du monde. Histoire d'une mondialisation* (Paris, 2004); Sanjay Subrahmanyam, *Explorations in Connected History: From the Tagus to the Ganges* (Oxford, 2005); C.W.J. Withers, "Place and the 'Spatial Turn' in Geography and in History", *Journal of the History of Ideas*, 70:4 (2009), pp. 637–658; Lauren Benton, *A Search for Sovereignty: Law and Geography in European Empires, 1400–1900* (Cambridge, 2010); Wayne E. Lee (ed.), *Empires and Indigenes: Intercultural Alliance, Imperial Expansion, and Warfare in the Early Modern World* (New York, 2011); Alan Lester, "Spatial Concepts and the Historical Geographies of British Colonialism", in Andrew Thompson (ed.), *Writing Imperial Histories* (Manchester, 2013), pp. 118–142; Paul Readman, Cynthia Radding, and Chad Bryant (eds), *Borderlands in World History, 1700–1914* (Houndmills, 2014); Tamar Herzog, *Frontiers of Possession: Spain and Portugal in Europe and the Americas* (Cambridge, MA, 2015); Ernesto Bassi, *An Aqueous Territory: Sailor Geographies and New Granada's Transimperial Greater Caribbean World* (Durham, NC, 2016); Valentina Favarò, Manfredi Merluzzi, and Gaetano Sabatini (eds), *Fronteras. Procesos y practicas de integración y conflictos entre Europa y América (siglos XVI–XX)* (Madrid, 2017).
15. Discussion on the "success" or "failure" of penal colonization, considered exclusively from the perspective of the imperial authorities, is a feature of much of the historiography. See, for example, Coates, *Convict Labor in the Portuguese Empire*, pp. 125–129; Eva Maria Mehl, *Forced Migration in the Spanish Pacific World: From Mexico to the Philippines, 1765–1811* (Cambridge, 2016), pp. 258–266.

prisoners to their advantage. This was the case for the Indochinese exiles in French Guiana, as noted by Lorraine Paterson, and for revolts and escapes in the Philippines under US administration, as narrated by Benjamin Weber.

Empire-building and related punitive relocations were not just about controlling territories, but also, and primarily, about governing people. And, of course, one of the distinctive features of empires was the often multi-ethnic character of their populations, constituted of indigenous, enslaved, and migrant peoples and communities. The destinations of convict transportation, deportation, and exile, then, were contact zones among, and places of governmentality of, individuals subjected to multiple punitive regimes and with distinct ethnic, linguistic, and political backgrounds. Analysing them creates a unique opportunity to study the manifestations of individual and collective solidarity and conflict among prisoners, as well as the authorities' strategies of control and repression. As numerous historians have noted, the organization of race was funda-mental to imperial governance.[16] The question here is: did penal colonies reflect or innovate with respect to the management of empires? The answer perhaps lies in an appreciation of their role in both ways. As Anderson shows, the use of Anglo-Indian intermediaries in the Andaman Islands drew on experiences in mainland India, albeit more intensively with respect to the demography of the penal colony. The intersections with class are also important here, as highlighted by Clare Anderson, Francesca Di Pasquale, and Christian G. De Vito in relation to the differentiated destinations and treatment of elite and subaltern subjects. On the other hand, Coates' ana-lysis shows that the penal colony in Portuguese Angola produced degrees of un-separation between Europeans, Africans, and Asians that are surprising to readers used to thinking of empires as carefully organized, racially stra-tified spaces.

Though empires might have used race and gender in the organization of punitive regimes, convict subjects could use them for their own purposes. Paterson, for example, analyses the remarkable journeys of political exiles from Indochina around and beyond colonial Asia, during the French imperial era. Though the French racialized transportation practices, deciding upon the suitability of French Guiana for colonially convicted transportees only during particular periods of time, it is evident from Paterson's narrative that colonized subjects created their own means of "passing", taking on Chinese identities and thus creating routes to escape repressive regimes and forge new lives. As for gender, the large majority of the penal colonies under consideration here were either largely or completely male in character. One of the gaps in our collection is a

---

16. David Arnold, *Colonizing the Body: State Medicine and Epidemic Disease in Nineteenth-Century India* (Berkeley, CA, 1993); Frederick Cooper and Ann Laura Stoler (eds), *Tensions of Empire: Colonial Cultures in a Bourgeois World* (Berkeley, CA, 1997).

discussion of sex and sexuality, which has left few traces in the archives. Glimpses can be gained from the contributions by Paterson, Di Pasquale, and Anderson. However, it is clear that for most contexts we still lack sophisticated analyses of sexuality and gender relations like those produced by Joy Damousi and Kirsty Reid for the Australian colonies, Anderson for the Indian Ocean world, and Dan Healey for the USSR.[17]

To write of race, gender, and identity, with an attention that lies close to the concerns of New Imperial History, and to speak of punitive sites as "contact zones" is not to downplay the brutality of convict labour regimes. Indeed, in Japan up to one third of convicts died during road construction in the penal colonies of Hokkaido.[18] The repression of political prisoners could be particularly violent too, as in the case of the American Philippines (Weber). And as Matthias van Rossum shows for the Dutch East Indies, in common with many other sites of punitive relocation, penal transportation co-existed with corporal punishment and chain-gang labour, including on the roads and in the particularly harsh environment of coal mines. Moreover, the function of punishment vis-à-vis labour relations was broader than the direct production of convict labour. It played a central role in disciplining other contract and coerced workers, such as enslaved people, indentured servants (European and Asian), and *corvée* labourers.[19]

Following the traces of transported convicts implies addressing the minute geographies of colonization, and makes us aware of the importance of spatiality in managing convicts within colonies. For example, Katherine Roscoe looks closely at the islands off the coast of the Australian colonies and foregrounds their multiple functions within the imperial project. Weber provides a detailed account of how the various parts and populations of the Philippines were conceptualized during US (and Spanish) colonial rule. Popova names the specific sites of punishment within Eastern and Western Siberia – from Tobolsk to Sakhalin – instead of referring to that vast region as one uniform entity. This spatial awareness is necessary, for the unevenness of colonial geography was precisely the basis for the creation of regional systems of punishment. Indeed, translocal flows of transportation,

17. Joy Damousi, *Depraved and Disorderly: Female Convicts, Sexuality and Gender in Colonial Australia* (Cambridge, 1997); Kirsty Reid, *Gender, Crime and Empire: Convicts, Settlers and the State in Early Colonial Australia* (Manchester, 2007); Clare Anderson, *Subaltern Lives: Biographies of Colonialism in the Indian Ocean World, 1790–1920* (Cambridge, 2012); Dan Healey, *Russian Homophobia from Stalin to Sochi* (London, 2017), ch. 1. See also Abby M. Schrader, "Unruly Felons and Civilizing Wives: Cultivating Marriage in the Siberian Exile System, 1822–1860", *Slavic Review*, 66:2 (2007), pp. 230–256.
18. Minako Sakata, "Japan in the 18th and 19th Centuries", in Anderson, *A Global History of Convicts and Penal Colonies*, pp. 307–335.
19. See also Clare Anderson, "Transnational Histories of Penal Transportation: Punishment, Labour and Governance in the British Imperial World, 1788–1939", *Australian Historical Studies*, 47:3 (2016), pp. 381–397.

deportation, and exile between the colonies fed the Siberian punitive system, together with those that originated in the Western part of Russia. Intra-colonial relocations were the exclusive sources of the punitive systems in the Philippines under US rule (Weber), in the Australian colonies after the discontinuation of transportation from Britain (Roscoe), in British India (Anderson), and in the Dutch East Indies (Van Rossum). Punitive systems generated in colonized localities additionally constructed connections between colonies. Examples here include Mozambique and Angola (Coates), Cuba, Fernando Poo, and the Philippines (De Vito), and Indo-china and Gabon, Algeria, and Tahiti (Paterson). Many of the regional systems in evidence here entirely circumvented what are usually viewed as centres of political and other forms of imperial or territorially acquisitive power. In this regard, this issue adds weight to the historiography of inter-imperial transportation, taking it into new contexts and highlighting its nature, extent, and importance.

The decentring of European metropoles in the analysis proposed in this volume also pushes us to ask a key question: As a locus of imperial power, where was the metropole? Though this term is used widely in global and imperial history, its origins lie within a rather particular context: imperial France.[20] Historically, contemporaries in France and the French Empire used the term to refer to European France. In a post-colonial context in which many of the former colonies remain, politically, overseas dependencies (*départements d'outre-mer*), and thus part of the European Union, the word "metropole" remains widely used today. As a shorthand for the organization and hierarchies of all empires, does it work? We are uncertain. Up to the independence of Latin America in the early nineteenth century, the Spanish Empire is a case in point, for the system of viceroyalties was grounded in numerous imperial centres. There are similar points to be made regarding the British Empire in the later period. As Roscoe shows, the Australian colonies themselves managed the continent's carceral islands. These islands lay at the geographical peripheries of the colonies, twice removed from the Colonial Office in London, and their utility generated out of the distinctive concerns of Australian imperial governors and officials. To take another example from the British Empire, the Andaman Islands penal colony (see Anderson) received convicts from all over the mainland Indian Empire, which at the time encompassed a vast area that stretched from what is now Pakistan and Bangladesh to the southern coast of India, and around the rim of the Bay of Bengal to Myanmar (then known as Burma). Its imperial centres were located in Delhi and the Indian presidencies of Bengal, Bombay, and Madras, far from the British Isles.

---

20. The classic text is Ann Laura Stoler and Frederick Cooper, "Between Metropole and Colony: Rethinking a Research Agenda", in Cooper and Stoler, *Tensions of Empire*, pp. 1–56.

A decade ago, John Darwin attempted to capture the diffuseness of the British Empire by defining it as an imperial project, reaching into many areas of social, cultural, and economic life all over the globe, but by no means as a unified entity.[21] This issue, centred on peoples and places marginalized by empire and by punitive relocation, seeks to push this important insight further. By focusing on convicts and penal colonies, and in particular by highlighting the significance of regional systems of transportation, deportation, and exile, we show that there is no easy answer to the question of where "the metropole" lies. Certainly, from a Eurocentric perspective, the answer might be clear: in European capitals, or their equivalents in other parts of the world. From the perspective of the colonies, the answer is rather less certain. We could propose to call them "colonial metropoles" – centres of imperial power that lay beyond nation states, sometimes amorphous, often mobile, and frequently shifting.

COLONIES AND METROPOLES

The relationship between imperial centres and their colonies constitutes another important focus throughout this special issue. Several contributions make it evident that imperial centres usually avoided colony-to-centre punitive relocations, thus constituting European cities and their hinterlands as effectively separated and "protected" legal spaces (Van Rossum, Sakata, Popova, Coates, and De Vito). On the rare occasions that empires shipped colonial convicts to Europe, they almost exclusively took the form of the repatriation of white settlers accused of crimes, or the administrative deportation or exile of elites. The Italian case is the striking exception. As Di Pasquale points out in her chapter, in the Liberal period (1861–1922) judicially sentenced convicts flowed from Libya towards Italy, alongside exiles and individuals deported on military orders. This was the result of the precarious hold on the newly colonized overseas territories, and of the fact that the south of Italy and the island of Sardinia were not only conceptualized as in need of internal colonization, but also as "colonial" territories themselves.

This special issue addresses the more usual pattern of centre-to-colony punitive relocations against the background of the changes in the spatiality and conceptualization of empires in the aftermath of the Age of Revolution (c.1774–1860s). The Atlantic Revolutions of the late eighteenth and early nineteenth centuries obliged the majority of the Western empires to search for new sites of banishment, deportation, and transportation. In the transition from their "first" to "second" empires, for example, the British

---

21. John Darwin, *The Empire Project: The Rise and Fall of the British World-System, 1830–1970* (Cambridge, 2009).

largely re-routed metropolitan convicts from North America to the littorals of West Africa and then to the Australian colonies. Though before the American Revolution the French had shipped convicts to Louisiana, as they gradually occupied new overseas territories they began to send convicts to French Guiana and New Caledonia. Expelled from Brazil in the early 1820s, the Portuguese similarly sought to enhance the exploitation of their African colonies in Angola and Mozambique, and established *depósitos* of convicts. Finally, Spain struggled to replace the flows of penal transportation to the lost viceroyalties of South America with punitive relocations towards its remaining three colonies (Cuba, Puerto Rico, and the Philippines), the North African *presidios*, or military outposts, and newly acquired possessions such as Fernando Poo and the Carolina Islands.

The effects of the Age of Revolution were even deeper than those significant geographical reconfigurations of empires and related convict flows suggest. The transition from ancient to constitutional regimes in many locations meant that the characteristic legal pluralism of the ancien régime was tendentially replaced with a unified legal space. As liberalism advanced in metropolitan Europe, all Western imperial powers had to determine whether, and how far, colonial subjects should enjoy emancipation, citizenship, and/or political representation.[22] For example, with respect to the outreach of the metropolitan legal regimes: Were the overseas territories to be governed by the same constitutions and legislation as the metropole, or did their different ethnic and social composition, and their allegedly inferior level of "civilization", require exceptional laws? And should all colonies within empires be governed by the same laws? The answers to these questions differed, and a focus on nineteenth-century metropole-to-colony penal transportation offers a privileged entry point into that variation. Indeed, the transportation of judicially sentenced convicts from European nations to overseas territories was in some cases a sign of the extension of the metropolitan legal regime (including the penal code) to the whole empire. This was the choice made by French legislators, reflecting the universalistic tradition of the Revolution of 1789 and the long-standing hegemony of the principle of assimilation in French colonial policy. Therefore, once a new imperial balance was found around the mid-nineteenth century, flows of penal transportation took approximately 70,000 sentenced convicts (*transportés*) – including some 2,000 women – from France to French Guiana and New Caledonia, the last of them not repatriated until after World War II.[23] The Portuguese expressed a similar

22. See especially Fradera, *La nación imperial*; Berger and Miller, *Nationalizing Empires*.
23. Peter Redfield, *Space in the Tropics: From Convicts to Rockets in French Guiana* (Berkeley, CA, 2000); Louis-José Barbançon, *L'archipel des forçats. Histoire du bagne de Nouvelle-Calédonie (1863–1931)* (Pas-de-Calais, 2003); Danielle Donet-Vincent, *De soleil et de silences. Histoire des bagnes de Guyane* (Paris, 2003). On French colonial theory, see Raymond F. Betts,

preference through their legal codes of the 1860s and 1870s, and from the
1880s to 1932 transported 16,000 to 20,000 sentenced convicts (*degredados*)
to their possessions in Angola and Mozambique.[24]

Other imperial nations took the opposite direction. They highlighted the
legal distinction of the colonies vis-à-vis the metropole, and accordingly
discontinued or banned penal transportation from the metropole to the
colonies. Together with the colonies' opposition to new arrivals of convicts,
this was the underlying reason for the end of penal transportation from
Britain and Ireland to the Australian colonies. However, in British Asia
laws of penal transportation, largely imported from those of the British
Isles, led to the creation of the single largest penal colony in the whole
British Empire – the Andaman Islands (1793–1796, 1858–1945).[25] In the
same way, the regional character of the circuits of penal transportation in
the Dutch East Indies, addressed by Van Rossum, stemmed from the
discontinuation of metropolitan convict transportation after the shift from
the sprawling Dutch East India Company's settlements to that of the
geographically contracted Dutch East Indies. Spain, in turn, is a telling
example of the shift that occurred in the first few decades of the nineteenth
century: from universalist-inspired "imperial" constitutions to "colonial"
constitutions based on the distinct legal status of the colonies. While Cuba,
Puerto Rico, and the Philippines continued to be conceptualized as
"provinces" throughout the century, hinting at a model of full assimilation
in the metropolitan legal space, from the 1830s onwards they were subjected
to a special legal status.[26] As De Vito explains in his chapter, this led to the
discontinuation of the centuries-long practice of sending judicially
sentenced individuals from Spain to the colonies. At the turn of the nineteenth century, during intense debates in the Reichstag, the new nation state
and imperial power of Germany chose to avoid convict transportation to its
colonies.[27] Finally, the US never considered sending American citizens to
its colonies in the Philippines or Puerto Rico, and only briefly discussed the
possibility of sending US convicts to work on the Panama Canal. When a
project for the establishment of a penal colony materialized in the 1870s and
1880s, the envisaged location was Alaska, which was at once distant from
and part of metropolitan legal space. That plan was never implemented, but

---

Assimilation and Association in French Colonial Theory, 1890-1914 (Lincoln, NE, 1960); Alice L.
Conklin, *A Mission to Civilize: The Republican Idea of Empire in France and West Africa, 1895-
1930* (Stanford, CA, 1997). While arguing that a shift from assimilation to association took place in
French colonial theory in the two decades before World War I, Betts acknowledges that the
practical impact of such transformation was limited (particularly outside Indochina and North
Africa). There is no sign of a move away from assimilation in the legal field.
24. See also Coates, *Convict Labor in the Portuguese Empire*.
25. Anderson, "Transnational Histories of Penal Transportation".
26. Josep M. Fradera, *Colonias para después de un imperio* (Barcelona, 2005).
27. Fitzpatrick, *Purging the Empire*, especially ch. 1 (pp. 19–38).

it resonates with the insistent arguments of contemporary criminologists, penal reformers, and policymakers in various empires that the global powers could best use convict labour to expand internal frontiers, rather than getting involved in penal colonization overseas.[28]

Renouncing the use of the criminal justice system to remove individuals from Europe to overseas possessions did not amount to the suspension of metropole-to-colony punitive relocations. Indeed, even when penal transportation was discontinued or fell out of use, administrative and military relocations continued. For example, though Germany avoided penal transportation, it did not exclude what Matthew Fitzpatrick has described as "more inventive legal means" of forced removal. Special laws legitimated the administrative expulsion of groups of Jesuits in 1872, socialists and Poles in the 1880s and 1890s, and Roma in the early 1900s.[29] In this regard, De Vito shows how administrative and military deportations in the Spanish Empire became tools for the creation of connections between the metropole and the overseas provinces. Such punitive practices, based on the declaration of states of exception, were grounded in constitutional and legislative codes. As such, as De Vito shows, they were neither arbitrary nor contrary to the legal regime, but stemmed from, and were entirely legitimated by, constitutional legality.[30]

Meanwhile, those imperial states that practised penal transportation extensively used both administrative and military deportation too. France is a case in point. In addition to overseeing the shipment of *transportés*, sentenced under ordinary criminal law, between 1887 and 1949 the French authorities deported over 22,000 repeat offenders (including approximately 1,000 women) to French Guiana and New Caledonia under the administrative regime of *relégation*. At the same time, an even larger number of "unruly" soldiers were relocated to the North African military institutions informally known as "Biribi". These included disciplinary battalions, military prisons, the African Corps (*Bat' d'Af'*), and the *sections* for men who were otherwise excluded from joining the army due to previous criminal convictions. Parts of

---

28. Benjamin Weber, "America's Carceral Empire: Confinement, Punishment, and Work at Home and Abroad, 1865–1946" (Ph.D., Harvard University, 2017). On internal penal colonization, see, for example, Mario Da Passano (ed.), *Le colonie penali nell'Europa dell'Ottocento* (Rome, 2004); Fernando José Burillo Albacete, *La cuestión penitenciaria. Del Sexenio a la Restauración (1868–1913)* (Zaragoza, 2011), pp. 191–208; Mary Gibson and Ilaria Poerio, "Modern Europe, 1750–1950", in Anderson, *A Global History of Convicts and Penal Colonies*, pp. 337–370.
29. Fitzpatrick, *Purging the Empire*, p. 38.
30. For a similar argument, see Nasser Hussain, *The Jurisprudence of Emergency: Colonialism and the Rule of Law* (Ann Arbor, MI, 2003); Francesco Benigno and Luca Scuccimarra (eds), *Il governo dell'emergenza. Poteri straordinari e di guerra in Europa tra XVI e XX secolo* (Rome, 2007); Julie Evans, "Colonialism and the Rule of Law: The Case of South Australia", in Barry Godfrey and Graeme Dunstall (eds), *Crime and Empire 1840–1940: Criminal Justice in Local and Global Context* (Routledge, 2012), pp. 57–75; Fitzpatrick, *Purging the Empire*.

that complex punitive system remained operational until decolonization in the 1970s.[31]

So far in this section we have discussed the experience of punitive relocations to and among overseas colonial possessions. Russia and Japan are slightly different cases as their expansion was contiguous from the centre. This configuration implied a tendency to legal assimilation, as new territories were progressively annexed to the core regions. In these cases, the distinction between "metropoles" and "colonies" was blurred, and often absent altogether. Indeed, Minako Sakata notes that, in Japan in the late nineteenth and early twentieth centuries, elites altogether rejected the concept of "empire", possibly due to its association with Western colonization. Both Sakata and Popova, however, caution us against stretching this linear interpretation of legal assimilation too far, not least because simultaneous with Japan's legal incorporation of Hokkaido was its 1895 occupation of Taiwan and 1910 annexation of Korea. In the former case, Japan refused to receive Taiwanese inmates.[32] Indeed, constructed and real distinctions between core regions and borderlands mattered where penal transportation was concerned. As Popova shows, penal reforms designed at the centre of Russia's empire did not correspond to the situation at its peripheries, especially in newly colonized territories such as late nineteenth-century Western Siberia. Local officials there heavily influenced the implementation of punitive policies.

The relationship between core regions and borderlands was even more complex in the islands of Japan, because territorial contiguity was mediated by the sea. The policy of "extending homeland ideology", as Sakata tells us, de facto acknowledged the need for a transitional period before the new territories could be fully assimilated. This produced a fascinating situation in the island of Hokkaido. The relocation of sentenced convicts from "mainland" to "island" was labelled "penal transportation" during the transitional period, and was called "incarceration" after Hokkaido became part of Japan. That shift was prompted also by a switch in the Western model of penal reform initially followed by the Japanese authorities. Indeed, the French influence that had originally supported the introduction of penal transportation was replaced by the German model, which rejected the practice of convict transportation. This reminds us that nineteenth-century non-Western empires cannot be studied in isolation from their Western counterparts, given the intense global circulation of legal ideas and practices that existed during this period. In fact, while the Japanese case is not an example of mutual influence, ideological reciprocity certainly existed in the case of Russia. Western ideas of penal reform impacted on the ideas of

31. Dominique Kalifa, *Biribi. Les bagnes coloniaux de l'armée française* (Paris, 2009).
32. Daniel V. Botsman, *Punishment and Power in the Making of Modern Japan* (Princeton, NJ, 2005), p. 207.

Tsarist officials, while penal transportation in the Russian Empire was also constantly mentioned by criminologists and policymakers in other nations, in the context of their desire to introduce or reintroduce that punitive practice into Western penal codes.

PUNITIVE RELOCATIONS AND INCARCERATION

Between 1872 and 1910, the meetings of the International Prison Congress provided a key forum for the exchange of information about penal reform. Their published reports represent important sources in order to understand the level of global circulation of ideas around crime and punishment. Especially relevant are the proceedings of the congresses held in Stockholm in 1878 and in Paris in 1895, where the question of transportation was addressed extensively.[33] However, the parallel analysis of those documents with the scholarship on penal transportation reveals several ways in which the International Prison Congress provided a myopic view on the historical reality of penal transportation and incarceration. Highlighting those shortcomings gives us the scope to expose some of the analytical flaws of contemporary representations of the history of the prison, which closely resemble those of the Congresses' participants. On this basis, we can also point to some of the contributions of this special issue to a new understanding of the character of nineteenth- and twentieth-century punishment.

The impact of the International Prison Congress on penal policy and practice is hard to measure. Indeed, many of the participants' perspectives reflected their interest in penal systems and institutions rather than the daily life of punitive sites. These experts occupied themselves with theoretical blueprints rather than with the organization of punishment on the spot. And they interpreted the contradictory information and statistics gathered on specific experiences of imprisonment and transportation for the sake of strengthening their own theoretical positions. The endless debates on the success or failure of British transportation to Australia, which reproduced similar discussions at national level, are a case in point, as those experiences provided arguments for both supporters and critics of penal transportation.[34]

Moreover, the allegedly "international" nature of the Congress contrasts with its largely Western focus and deeply Eurocentric approach. Nir Shafir has shown that the Western organizers' perception of the countries' drive towards (Western-like) "civilization" played a primary role in the composition of the guest lists. Furthermore, the danger that a colony or

33. Briony Neilson, "The Paradox of Penal Colonization: Debates on Convict Transportation at the International Prison Congresses 1872–1895", *French History and Civilization*, 6 (2015), pp. 198–211.

34. See, for example, Burillo Albacete, *La cuestión penitenciaria*, pp. 62–67; Neilson, "The Paradox of Penal Colonization".

non-Western country might take part in the Congress on the same footing as a Western colonial power led to their gradual exclusion after the 1870s, including in the case of British India, then the site of some of the world's biggest prisons and a key laboratory of penal theories and practices. The remaining non-Western actors were expected to act as "silent spectators", the passive recipients of Western ideas.[35]

Unsurprisingly, this Eurocentric perspective resulted in a focus on penal transportation outwards to colonies, to the exclusion of intra- and inter-colonial punitive relocations. The practices of colonial incarceration were silenced too. However, as a relatively broad scholarship has foregrounded in the last two decades, the history of the colonial prison is key to a critical reconsideration of the nature of incarceration during the nineteenth and early twentieth centuries, and especially its coexistence with punitive violence and forced labour.[36] This special issue takes this argument further, by revealing genealogies of the prison – both in the colonies and in imperial centres – that go back to military practices, rather than to, as is often claimed, enlightened penal theories and what Norbert Elias famously called "the civilizing process".[37] Moreover, it shows the persistent connection between imprisonment and forced labour in the colonies, in the form of both direct exploitation of convict labour outside the walls of the prison and the use of incarceration to manage the coerced workforce of enslaved people, *corvée* labourers, and indentured servants. Further, it reveals the nature and scale of punitive relocations between and across colonies, which in some cases was unrelated to the institution of the prison.

The dominant discourse emerging from the International Prison Congresses was one that contrasted penal transportation and imprisonment with the aim of establishing the most appropriate and "modern" form of punishment. Indeed, as Briony Neilson has observed and the name of the Congress betrayed, even the organizers of the gatherings were partisans in that confrontation, showing a tendency to "implicit resistance" or "suspicion" towards penal transportation.[38] More detached readers of the

---

35. Nir Shafir, "The International Congress as Scientific and Diplomatic Technology: Global Intellectual Exchange in the International Prison Congress, 1860–90", *Journal of Global History*, 9:1 (2014), pp. 72–93. On the prison system in British India, see, especially, David Arnold, "India: The Contested Prison", in Dikötter and Brown, *Cultures of Confinement*, pp. 147–184; Clare Anderson, *The Indian Uprising of 1857–8. Prisons, Prisoners and Rebellion* (London, 2007), especially pp. 26–54.

36. See especially Ricardo D. Salvatore and Carlos Aguirre (eds), *The Birth of the Penitentiary in Latin America: Essays on Criminology, Prison Reform, and Social Control, 1830–1940* (Austin, TX, 1996); Bernault, *Enfermement, prison et châtiments en Afrique*; Dikötter and Brown, *Cultures of Confinement*; Gibson, "Global Perspectives on the Birth of the Prison".

37. Norbert Elias, *The Civilizing Process* (London, 1939); Garland, *Punishment and Modern Society*, ch. 10.

38. Neilson, "The Paradox of Penal Colonization", p. 11.

proceedings might note that the symmetrical nature of the arguments used by the supporters of the two systems implied that they shared at least two characteristics: they were both designed to have deterrent as well as rehabilitative functions, yet they systematically failed to meet their own goals, and therefore attracted constant and often sound critiques. Neither of the two, therefore, appeared an ideal solution to contemporaries, which possibly explains why the debate among experts continued for several decades.

By looking at the situation from the vantage point of punitive sites in the colonies, collectively the chapters add an extra dimension to this discussion. Namely, they foreground the fluidity that existed between penal transportation and incarceration, which were overlapping and co-existent at various levels. Indeed, it was not only in Hokkaido that the practices of transportation and imprisonment were overlaid. Weber shows here that this was the case in the Philippines under US rule, due to the simultaneous need to prevent prison revolts and split up and secure the insurgents. The outcome of that double process was a complex network of punitive sites called prisons and penal colonies, which presented striking similarities with the map of penal transportation under nineteenth-century Spanish rule. Moreover, De Vito describes how, within the Spanish metropolitan legal space, the incarceration of hardened criminals in Ceuta and the other North African *presidios* amounted to their transportation from peninsular Spain to the other side of the Mediterranean. More broadly, these examples are reminders of the importance that spatial mobility played (and arguably still plays) within prison systems, and of the role of immobilization within regimes of penal transportation.

More specific practices implied significant levels of connection between incarceration and penal transportation. Discussing punitive relocations from mainland British India to the Andaman Islands, for example, Anderson mentions the transfer of European and Eurasian prisoners on licence and, later, of "volunteer" Indian prisoners, and supposedly hereditary criminals belonging to groups labelled by the British as "criminal tribes". Similarly, according to De Vito, convicts held in the Spanish prisons and the North African *presidios* "volunteered" to join the imperial army at the time of the colonial wars in Santo Domingo, Puerto Rico, and Cuba. With respect to the latter, the authorities de facto extended penal transportation to the overseas provinces without creating a unified legal space including both the metropole and the colonies. Penal transportation could also complement imprisonment as a phase of the enforcement of sentences, with transportation to internal and overseas penal colonies standing between a period of imprisonment and release. In other cases, relocation to penal colonies was introduced as an "eliminative" punishment for recidivists and "professional delinquents" who had allegedly proven incompatible with the prison regime or who were seen as "incorrigibles".

The practice of *relégation* across the French Empire and the newly established penal colonies in Latin America were connected to this trend, as were the deportations of Cuban *incorregibles* to the Isle of Pines, Fernando Poo, and the Philippines.

Finally, this special issue shows that the connectivity of punitive regimes was not limited to the linkage of different kinds of convicts and prisoners, or to the relationships between prisons and penal transportation. Rather, punitive regimes incorporated a whole range of practices that stemmed from military and administrative relocations from, among, and to the colonies. It is perhaps unsurprising that these were not addressed in the International Prison Congresses, which by definition restricted their focus to the issue of penal reform. However, the marginalization or outright removal of those practices from the scholarship on punishment is problematic. By widening the lens beyond the criminal justice system, the contributions presented here show that only by taking those punitive relocations into account can we reach a balanced assessment of punishment from the nineteenth to the mid-twentieth centuries. This moves us away from the untenable but still strong narrative of the irresistible rise of the penitentiary, and towards a recognition of the ongoing significance of punitive relocation, or punitive mobility, within the more expansive and transnational history of punishment that we propose here. Indeed, when administrative and military deportation are considered alongside punishments that stemmed from the criminal justice system, the role of incarceration appears less prominent, and certainly not exclusive, not only in the colonies but also in Europe.

Our acknowledgement of the importance of administrative and military deportations in a number of contexts requires further exploration, because it has the potential to integrate the history of nineteenth- and early twentieth-century punitive relocations with studies of mass deportation under Fascist and Soviet regimes later on. The timing seems appropriate for such an endeavour. Until recently, the separation of the scholarship on imprisonment from that on penal transportation and twentieth-century concentration and labour camps had produced a paradoxical vision of the twentieth century in which the age of the penitentiary *and* the century of the camps are presented as mutually exclusive.[39] A key exception is the work of Lynne Viola, who has unveiled the "unknown Gulag" of the special settlements, integrating the study of penal transportation with an analysis of administrative relocation. In so doing, she has additionally stressed the continuity between Tsarist and Stalinist practices of punitive relocation,

---

39. On the "century of the camps", see Joël Kotek and Pierre Rigoulot, *Le siècle des camps. Détention, concentration, extermination. Cent ans de mal radical* (Paris, 2000). See also Ann Laura Stoler, *Duress: Imperial Durabilities in Our Times* (Durham, NC, 2016), ch. 3.

both of which had the goal of "internal" colonization.[40] At the same time, Nikolaus Wachsmann's *Hitler's Prisons* has foregrounded the role of the criminal justice system and state prisons in the broader punitive practices of the Third Reich. A more recent edited volume has expanded this approach to a broader set of Western European countries and to a larger range of punitive regimes.[41] Finally, several scholars have searched for colonial antecedents for twentieth-century mass deportation and concentration camps, pointing to global circulations of ideas, practices, and officers.[42] By proposing a view that integrates punitive relocations with incarceration, across numerous global contexts, this special issue contributes to this conversation.

In the chapters that follow, the authors centre on a diversity of global contexts, distinguished by various configurations and reconfigurations of spatial hierarchies, different ideas about the geopolitical borders of colonies, and diverse and distinctive relationships between centres and peripheries. They take different approaches to the perspective from the colonies, but each is committed to the elaboration of a history of convicts and penal colonies that begins in what are often considered the peripheries of empires. This enables the collection to forge new connections between histories of governmentality, punishment, and labour, and the new imperial histories of race, class, and gender. This included, as Clare Anderson shows, the employment of Anglo-Indian intermediaries in the Indian penal colony of the Andaman Islands, where crime was forgotten in lieu of the privilege of class. When the number of Anglo-Indians proved inadequate, and the drive to encourage free settlement in the Islands failed, the government of India

---

40. Lynne Viola, *The Unknown Gulag: The Lost World of Stalin's Special Settlements* (Oxford, 2007).

41. Nikolaus Wachsmann, *Hitler's Prisons: Legal Terror in Nazi Germany* (New Haven, CT, 2004); Christian G. De Vito, Ralf Futselaar, and Helen Grevers (eds), *Incarceration and Regime Change: European Prisons During and After the Second World War* (New York, 2016). See also Aidan Forth, *Barbed-Wire Imperialism: Britain's Empire of Camps, 1876–1903* (Berkeley, CA, 2017).

42. Benjamin Madley, "From Africa to Auschwitz: How German South West Africa Incubated Ideas and Methods Adopted and Developed by the Nazis in Eastern Europe", *European History Quarterly*, 35:3 (2005), pp. 429–464; Klaus Mühlhahn, "The Concentration Camp in Global Historical Perspective", *History Compass*, 8:6 (2010), pp. 543–561; Jonathan Hyslop, "The Invention of the Concentration Camp: Cuba, Southern Africa and the Philippines, 1896–1907", *South African Historical Journal*, 63:2 (2002), pp. 251–276; Jonas Kreienbaum, "Deadly Learning? Concentration Camps in Colonial Wars Around 1900", in Volker Barth and Roland Cvetkovski (eds), *Imperial Co-Operation and Transfer, 1870–1930: Empires and Encounters* (London, 2015), pp. 219–235. For different perspectives, see also Karsten Linne, "The 'New Labour Policy' in Nazi Colonial Planning for Africa", *International Review of Social History*, 49:2 (2004), pp. 197–224; Patrick Bernhard, "Hitler's Africa in the East: Italian Colonialism as a Model for German Planning in Eastern Europe", *Journal of Contemporary History*, 51:1 (2016), pp. 61–90.

targeted other marginalized populations in programmes of carceral mobility, including volunteer prisoners, anti-imperial rebels, and so-called criminal tribe families. This imperial space was managed by an Indian metropole, and its social formations resembled more those of another such periphery, Burma, than those of mainland India itself.

Islands and island archipelagos like the Andamans were attractive as sites of penal transportation for two reasons: they had natural features that enhanced convict containment, and they were often situated along trade routes or near mainland nodes of colonization and trade, making occupation desirable. The relationship between continents and islands is the focus of Katherine Roscoe's analysis of the carceral islands of Britain's Australian penal colonies. She illuminates their multi-faceted character and connections: as harsh locales for the additional punishment of transportation convicts already transported to the Australian colonies, as culturally feared places for the punishment of indigenous people, and as centres of production and in which convicts and prisoners built the maritime infrastructure necessary to encourage and enhance networks of imperial trade. Understanding the racial stratifications within and between islands as carceral spaces enables a deconstruction of imperial ideologies of labour capacity, as well as an appreciation of the deep paradox of carcerality-producing connectivity.

Labour coercion and worker management is also central to Matthias van Rossum's analysis of punitive relocations across the Dutch East Indies. Not only do these reveal the relationship between one European metropole and its Asian colonies in the accumulation and globalization of capital, they also show the connected character of punishment and labour exploitation. As in the nineteenth-century Australian colonies, convicts were the consequence of particular kinds of imperial governmentality; they were not entirely separated from other forms of coerced labour, but worked alongside them in a networked system. This was also the case in Indochina, which as Lorraine M. Paterson reveals produced staggering numbers of convicts during the period of French occupation. However, the inability of the colonial authorities to prevent convict flight, coupled with the extent of Chinese labour mobility during this vital period of global migration, opened up racialized spaces in which Indochinese convicts could "pass" as free. This enabled remarkable forms of self-reinvention, including through family formation in new locations. Not only does this analysis of inter-colonial constraint and mobility radically alter perspectives on the character of the penal colony of French Guiana, we see something of the extent of connections between empires, as convict agency and mobility straddled French and British possessions in the littorals and islands where the Atlantic Ocean meets the Caribbean Sea.

Minako Sakata shifts the focus to the Pacific, writing of the penal colonies of the Japanese possession of Ezochi (Hokkaido) at the turn of the twentieth century, and arguing that the island's eventual incorporation into Japan's empire created legal tangles around what constituted a colony and thus the possibility of penal transportation. In this way, the article traces a key point in the emergence of a terminology of Japanese imperialism, later used with respect to Taiwan and Korea: "extending homeland ideology". It shows how penal colonization had the dual function of displacing the island's indigenous peoples, and supplying a vital labour force for the building of roads into the interior. Like Japan, Russia is often absent from comparative histories of empire. Zhanna Popova's article focuses on the Siberian peripheries to appreciate the centripetal and spatially complex character of exile, its entanglements with other imperial practices, and debates about transformations in the geopolitics of "the colony". It hazards against generalizations about punitive relocation, for it presents an image of exiles abandoned rather than controlled by the state. Moreover, depending on the specific context, exile was sometimes connected or separated from the punishment of penal labour.

In Timothy J. Coates' investigation, the Depot for Transported Convicts in Angola is a lens through which we can see the changing configurations of punishment, development, urbanization, emigration, and settlement played out in imperial Portugal. Drawing on a rare glimpse of convict experience, Coates employs two published accounts of the pro-republican journalist João Pinheiro Chagas to connect together international circulations of penal knowledge, European rivalry in the continent of Africa, and the economic consequences of the abolition of slavery. Again, punitive relocation opens out for interrogation some of the key questions of imperial and global history, as well as their relationship to the distinction and management of crime, race, and gender on the ground. As in the British, French, Russian, and Portuguese empires, Spanish punitive locations received convicts from imperial centres and peripheries. Christian G. De Vito gives a rich account of the directionality of these flows, and the connections between judicial, administrative, and military transportation, and between transportation and incarceration. He foregrounds the impact of the militarist tradition in the Spanish Empire and the related extensive use of the state of exception, both in the overseas provinces and in the Spanish Peninsula. Furthermore, he notes that punitive relocations were a means of managing workers, slaves, and rebels.

The confinement of anti-imperial rebels in carceral institutions and the relationship between penal transportation and incarceration are also central themes in Benjamin Weber's contribution, on the American-occupied Philippines. The multi-directional circulation and mobility that characterized American practices were, in his analysis, legacies of the Spanish Empire. It was premised on the production of spaces organized along particular combinations of criminality, race, ethnicity, and gender. Moreover, the history of punishment in the archipelago was connected to the history of revolt, not solely because it was deployed to counter insurgents, but because it provided a space for the emergence of new kinds of political consciousness. Finally, Francesca Di Pasquale's examination of deportation from the African colonies to Italy returns to the theme of extrajudicial forms of punishment and their relationship to imperial governmentality. Convicts tended to flow outwards to borderlands, frontiers, or colonies, or between imperial possessions, and the directionality of the Italian flows generated out of imperial repression is remarkable. They can be explained through an appreciation of the relatively short distance between Italy and its North African possessions, the comparatively limited extent of the Italian Empire, and racialized representations of Italy's south, in which the empire's carceral institutions were located.

The articles in this special issue bring together expertise from different contexts, united by the common purpose of beginning their respective analysis outside of Europe, and in the colonies. They address a set of common problems. These include the way in which penal transportation, deportation, and exile created and recreated spatial hierarchies, according to particular intersections with race, class, labour, and punitive regimes. The breadth and variability of the spaces that concern us, from huge labour camps to tiny convict outposts, situated in every populated continent of the world, enable us to view the multiple functions served by punitive mobility, and in particular the way in which it lubricated the expansion, reshaping, and management of empires. Our focus on a specific moment in time, the nineteenth and twentieth centuries, reveals the importance of punitive relocation during a period most usually associated with the rise of the prison. We contend that the history of punishment cannot be separated from changes in the structure and conceptualization of empires during this period. When punishment and the geopolitics of empires are viewed in the same global frame of analysis, transportation, exile, and deportation are revealed as pervasive, enduring, and highly significant in terms of governmentality, punishment, and labour extraction. Moreover, the idea of the penal colony explodes the distinction between the accepted concepts of "cores" and of "colonies". Not only did the routes, circuits, and networks of convict mobility create new spatial hierarchies among the global powers, they enabled agency and resistance by transported, exiled, and deported people. In this respect, the perspective from the colonies reveals a new picture of empire- and nation-building in the nineteenth and twentieth centuries, and of the ambivalence of subaltern engagement with and resistance to them.

IRSH 63 (2018), Special Issue, pp. 25–43 doi:10.1017/S0020859018000202

The Andaman Islands Penal Colony: Race, Class, Criminality, and the British Empire*

CLARE ANDERSON

School of History, Politics and International Relations
University of Leicester
University Road, Leicester LE1 7RH, UK

E-mail: ca26@le.ac.uk

ABSTRACT: This article explores the British Empire's configuration of imprisonment and transportation in the Andaman Islands penal colony. It shows that British governance in the Islands produced new modes of carcerality and coerced migration in which the relocation of convicts, prisoners, and criminal tribes underpinned imperial attempts at political dominance and economic development. The article focuses on the penal transportation of Eurasian convicts, the employment of free Eurasians and Anglo-Indians as convict overseers and administrators, the migration of "volunteer" Indian prisoners from the mainland, the free settlement of Anglo-Indians, and the forced resettlement of the Bhantu "criminal tribe". It examines the issue from the periphery of British India, thus showing that class, race, and criminality combined to produce penal and social outcomes that were different from those of the imperial mainland. These were related to ideologies of imperial governmentality, including social discipline and penal practice, and the exigencies of political economy.

INTRODUCTION

Between 1858 and 1939, the British government of India transported around 83,000 Indian and Burmese convicts to the penal colony of the Andamans, an island archipelago situated in the Bay of Bengal (Figure 1). In terms of the total number of convicts received, this renders the

* The research leading to these results received funding from the European Research Council under the European Union's Seventh Framework Programme (FP/2007–2013)/ERC Grant Agreement 312542. It also received support from the Economic and Social Research Council (award no. RES-000-22-3484). I thank Shabnum Tejani for inviting me to share an early version of this work at the history research seminar at SOAS, University of London, and the participants at that gathering for their insightful comments. I also thank Keith Wilson for allowing me access to his private papers on the Deakes family, and especially Eileen Arnell for her support for this research.

Andamans the largest penal colony in the entire British Empire. A rich historiography has elucidated aspects of the Islands' history with respect to penal colonization, indigenous marginalization, convict work, and resistance, as well as Britain's use of the Islands as a place for the incarceration of Indian nationalists.[1] Missing from these accounts of British dominance, Andamanese destruction, and Indian subjugation is an appreciation of the racial and cultural spaces in between them. Attention to this reveals the presence of various non-convict populations in the Andamans, each sent to the Islands under peculiarly colonial conditions. Here, the British reconfigured imprisonment and transportation in mainland India into new modes of carcerality and coerced migration, in which relocation to the imperial peripheries underpinned attempts at political dominance and economic development.

First, the British shipped dozens of Eurasian convicts (i.e. convicts of European *and* Indian parentage) to the Andamans from the first years of occupation, and, into the twentieth century, routinely employed free Eurasians in the running of the penal colony. They became intermediaries between British officials and the Indian and Burmese convict classes, and the social, cultural, and economic artificiality of the penal colony rendered government extraordinarily reliant on them.[2] Second, after the Indian jails committee recommended the abolition of penal transportation in its scathing report on the Andamans in 1919–1920, the British looked to other forms of coerced migration and settlement. They looked again to Anglo-Indians (as Eurasians were called after 1911), this time as free settlers, and offered mainland prisoners the opportunity to go to the Islands as "voluntary" settlers, under favourable penal terms.[3] They also deported nearly 2,000 Mapalah rebels, with their families, to the Andamans, in the aftermath of the 1921 Malabar Rebellion. Finally, the British sponsored the Salvation Army to resettle in the Islands several hundred men, women, and

---

1. Clare Anderson, Madhumita Mazumdar, and Vishvajit Pandya, *New Histories of the Andaman Islands: Landscape, Place, and Identity in the Bay of Bengal, 1790–2012* (Cambridge, 2016); S.N. Aggarwal, *The Heroes of Cellular Jail* (Patiala, 1995); L.P. Mathur, *Kala Pani: History of Andaman and Nicobar Islands with a Study of India's Freedom Struggle* (New Delhi, 1985); Satadru Sen, *Disciplining Punishment: Colonialism and Convict Society in the Andaman Islands* (New Delhi, 2000); Taylor C. Sherman, "From Hell to Paradise? Voluntary Transfer of Convicts to the Andaman Islands, 1921–1940", *Modern Asian Studies*, 43:2 (2009), pp. 367–388; Pramod Kumar Srivastava, "Resistance and Repression in India: The Hunger Strike at the Andaman Cellular Jail in 1933", *Crime, History and Societies*, 7:2 (2003), pp. 81–102; Aparna Vaidik, *Imperial Andamans: Colonial Encounter and Island History* (Basingstoke, 2010).

2. Until the 1911 Census, "Anglo-Indian" described British people living in India. The words "Eurasian" and occasionally "Indo-European" signalled mixed heritage, with European descent always measured through the patrilineal line. After the 1911 Census, the term "Anglo-Indian" replaced "Eurasian". Note that people of Anglo-Burmese heritage were a significant element of the census category, though they were not usually distinguished from each other.

3. *Report of the Indian Jails Committee, 1919–20* (London, 1921), ch. 11. See also Sherman, "From Hell to Paradise?".

children from the north Indian Bhantu "criminal tribe". The presence of Eurasians/Anglo-Indians, "volunteer" prisoner settlers, Mapalah rebels, and resettled "criminal tribe" families in the Andamans raises key questions about the social and economic dynamics of the British Empire in India. This article explores the importance of class, race, and criminality to ideologies of imperial governmentality, including social discipline and penal practice, and political economy.

A vital context for understanding the history of the Andamans is that governance in the Islands was fundamentally different to that in the mainland Indian Empire. From the first year of permanent occupation in 1858, the British wavered between a policy of containing, assimilating, and destroying the Islands' indigenous populations.[4] Equally, in contrast to the rest of the subcontinent, the British had responsibility for almost every area of cultural and social life. As for the economy, Kiran Dhingra noted recently: "the arrangement of work proceeded at the behest and under the control of the government, commanded not by the economic forces of demand and supply, but organized and directed by the government to serve its needs, where the workers were all convicts, receiving wages as decreed, and selling their produce at fixed rates to the government".[5] Concerns about security worked against the employment of free Indians in government service. In the aftermath of the Great Revolt of 1857 (the catalyst for the occupation of the Islands) the British feared that their presence would stimulate anti-colonial conspiracies. It is important to stress, also, that, until the 1920s, there were no entrepreneurs or free settlers in the Andamans; the government of India considered the commercial development of the Islands as entirely secondary to their primary penal function. It prohibited free settlement, arguing that it would lead to an inevitable relaxation in penal discipline.[6]

This article begins with a discussion of the important role that Eurasian convicts played in Britain's occupation of the Andamans in 1858. It moves on to explore the transfer of Eurasian prisoners from mainland Indian jails to the Islands, and their work as convict overseers under probationary licences in the 1860s. It argues that Eurasian convicts and prisoners occupied the racial interstices of a British penal colony for Indian subjects. By the early decades of the twentieth century, the boundaries of race in the

---

4. Clare Anderson, "Colonization, Kidnap and Confinement in the Andamans Penal Colony, 1771–1864", *Journal of Historical Geography*, 37:1 (2011), pp. 68–81; Satadru Sen, *Savagery and Colonialism in the Indian Ocean: Power, Pleasure and the Andaman Islanders* (New York, 2010).
5. Kiran Dhingra, *The Andaman and Nicobar Islands in the Twentieth Century: A Gazetteer* (New Delhi, 2005), p. 227.
6. National Archives of India (NAI) Home (Port Blair) A proceedings January 1883, nos 36–9: J. H. Roberts to Secretary to Government of India, 25 August 1882; M. Protheroe to Secretary to Government of India, 31 October 1882; note of D[onald] M[artin] S[tewart] (former Chief Commissioner and member of council for the Secretary of State for India), 27 December 1882.

Andamans were more fluid than those of the mainland, and though they never occupied the highest office, Anglo-Indians were routinely employed in key government positions. Moreover, it was quite common for newly arrived British and country-born[7] men and women to marry into Anglo-Indian families in the Islands. This blurred the boundaries around the meaning of "Anglo-Indian", which in the Andamans came to stand not necessarily for people of European and Indian heritage, but for free people generally of the non-elite or subordinate official classes. The article moves on to examine the relocation of "volunteer" prisoners and Mapalahs, and then focuses in particular on the Salvation Army's Bhantu migration scheme. By placing these different categories of coerced migrants in the same frame of analysis, it argues for a multi-sited perspective from the colonies, in which officials sought to balance the demands emanating from different points of empire with those coming from different ideological vantage points.

EURASIAN AND EUROPEAN CONVICTS AND OVERSEERS

Eurasians were present in the Andamans at the first moment of permanent colonial occupation. After the British decided to establish a penal colony in the Islands in late 1857, executive engineer and superintendent of convicts in the nearby Burmese penal settlement in Moulmein, Henry Man, spent two months on Chatham Island. There, he raised the Union flag and, with a party of more than a dozen Eurasian men, and under the pretence that the Islands were *terra nullius* (nobody's land), prepared for the arrival of Indian convicts. Previously, the East India Company had routinely sent Eurasian convicts from India to penal settlements scattered along the Burmese coast. The British treated them quite differently to Indians, ensuring that they travelled in different compartments on transportation ships, lived in separate accommodation, wore distinct clothing, ate different rations, and were employed not at hard labour, but as clerks or servants. Their literacy, numeracy, and familiarity with South Asia and native languages made them very useful to the British penal establishment, and its efforts to communicate effectively with Indian transportation convicts.[8] The British arrived in the Andamans with the first batch of Indian convicts in March 1858, and soon afterwards transferred some of the Eurasian convicts in Burma to the Islands, to work as convict overseers. One such man was James David, described as a "Portuguese Eurasian" and originally transported to the Tenasserim Provinces in 1857 for murder. He went on to play a significant

---

7. White people born in India.
8. Clare Anderson, *Subaltern Lives: Biographies of Colonialism in the Indian Ocean World, 1790–1920* (Cambridge, 2012), pp. 69–72. More generally, and for the earlier period, see C.J. Hawes, *Poor Relations: The Making of a Eurasian Community in British India 1773–1833* (London, 1996).

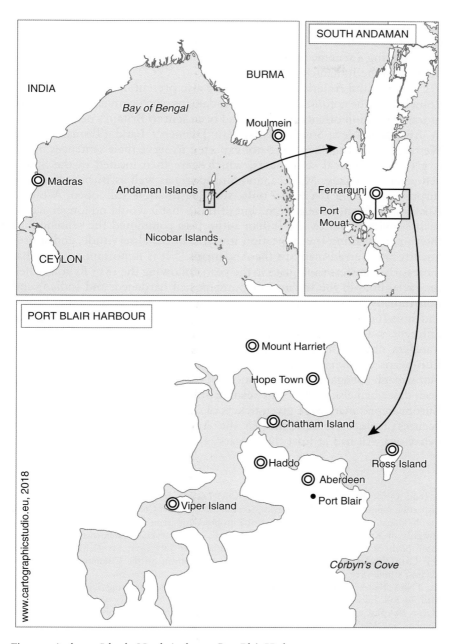

Figure 1. Andaman Islands, North Andaman, Port Blair Harbour.

role in the first contact missions between the colony and indigenous islanders, as well as working as a bookbinder in the superintendent's office. After serving a sentence of twenty years, ultimately he returned to a life of poverty in the Indian city of Madras.[9]

European and American convicts were also present in the Islands. In the years before the colonization of the Andamans, such convicts found guilty of transportation offences in India had been sent to Britain's penal colonies in Australia: New South Wales, Van Diemen's Land (Tasmania), and Western Australia. They were not expected to serve their sentences in the largely Indian penal settlements, which were then located in the Straits Settlements (Penang, Malacca, and Singapore) as well as Burma. But, in a surprise move in 1857, the only such destination still open, Western Australia, informed the government of India that it would no longer accept such convicts. And so the Indian authorities commuted the sentences of those men awaiting transportation to terms of penal servitude, and subsequently transferred many to the Andamans.[10] It is important to note that these early transfers took place in the years following the 1857 Revolt, when the racial lines in the Indian subcontinent had hardened, and Indians and non-Indians became increasingly separate. However, at this time, Indian and non-Indian prisoners were incarcerated in the same jails (though in different wards). The British administration instigated the Andaman transfers during the period before it opened entirely separate jails for Europeans in India: in Ootacamund (Madras Presidency) in 1862 and Hazaribagh (Bengal Presidency) in 1865. Meanwhile, drawing on what has been described elsewhere as the relative privilege of "the racial dividend",[11] European prisoners were given tickets of conditional release (probationary licences), subject to residence in the Andamans with continuing good behaviour. All had at least three years of their sentence to serve, and had

---

9. India Office Records, British Library (IOR) P/434/8 India (Public) 11 December 1867: Inspection report by Major H.N. Davies, Secretary to the Chief Commissioner of British Burma, enc. Nominal roll showing the number of European, Eurasian, and Native convicts receiving upwards of Rs. 8 a month, on the 23rd April, at the several settlements of Port Blair; Tamil Nadu State Archives (TNSA) Madras (Judicial) 27 July 1877, 151–6: Memorandum of D.F. Carmichael, Chief Secretary to the Madras government, to the Commissioner of Police Madras, 8 June 1877.

10. TNSA Madras (Judicial) 5 April 1869, nos 66–7: H. Man, officiating Superintendent Port Blair, to R.S. Ellis, Chief Secretary to Madras government, 9 February 1869, enc. petition of Martin Murphy, 23 January 1869. Fragmentary evidence from judicial proceedings in Bengal, Bombay, and Madras Presidency suggest that a handful of ticket-of-leave Europeans (i.e. prisoners on probation) were sent to Western Australia, until at least 1859.

11. Harald Fischer-Tiné, "Hierarchies of Punishment in Colonial India: European Convicts and the Racial Dividend, c.1860–1890", in *idem* and Susanne Gehrmann (eds), *Empires and Boundaries: Rethinking Race, Class, and Gender in Colonial Settings* (London, 2008), pp. 41–65.

skills of immediate use in the new colony. Included among them were carpenters, bricklayers, blacksmiths, sailors, and clerks.[12]

For the first two or three years after Britain's occupation of the Andamans, the Indian convicts were grouped into broad penal classes, their employment determined by a combination of their skills and behaviour. The first class were clerks and overseers of other convicts; the second were allowed to become self-supporting tradesmen (including tailors, bakers, shoemakers, and fishermen); and the third were put to work as ordinary labourers. At this time, there was a great shortage of what Superintendent J.C. Haughton called "steady and intelligent" overseers, particularly Europeans.[13] Following the success of the European transportation convict scheme, the mainland administration decided to offer European prisoners in India generally the opportunity of release conditional on taking service in the Islands. News of the possibility of transfer spread fast, and dozens of prisoners made enquiries about their prospects in Port Blair. "I am well acquainted with the Hindoostanee language and the people and will be of better service to government than if I remain here for 4 years and break stones", wrote one man, Thomas Burk, in 1861.[14] Conditions in Indian jails in the nineteenth century were so grim that there was no shortage of applications and petitions. European prisoners, it would seem, were keenly aware of the relative openness of the Andamans penal colony, and the fifty rupees per month that they would receive as wages.[15] Meanwhile, as these European overseer prisoners arrived and took up their post, the new officiating Superintendent of the Andamans, R.C. Tytler, expressed delight about the effect that their presence had on penal discipline. He wrote to the governor of Calcutta jail in 1862 that the Indian convicts did more work under their supervision than had been the case previously.[16]

Though the majority of the Indian transfer prisoners were European, included among them were several Eurasians and at least two

---

12. IOR P/146/29 Bengal (Jails) 17 July 1860, nos 48–55: proposal to transfer European prisoners to Port Blair. S. Wauchope, Commissioner of Police Calcutta to Rivers Thompson, Junior Secretary to the government of Bengal, 2 June 1860; J.C. Haughton, Superintendent Port Blair, to W. Grey, Secretary to the government of India, 13 June 1860.

13. IOR P/206/62 India (Judicial) 6 January 1860: Superintendent J.C. Haughton to W. Grey, Secretary to the government of India, 13 November 1859.

14. IOR P/145/38 Bengal (Jails) March 1861: S. Wauchope, Commissioner of Police Calcutta, to Rivers Thompson, Junior Secretary to the government of Bengal, 22 February 1861, enc. petition of M.R. Crawford, 18 February 1861, petition of Thomas Burk, 16 February 1861; TNSA Madras (Judicial) 4 March 1863: J. Rohde, Inspector-General of jails Madras, to A.J. Arbuthnot, Chief Secretary to the government of Madras, 21 November 1862.

15. TNSA Madras (Judicial) 4 March 1863, nos 6–11: Rohde to Arbuthnot, 21 November 1862.

16. IOR P/146/53 Bengal (Jails) November 1862: J. King, Governor Calcutta Jail, to David Cowie, Sheriff of Calcutta, 14 August 1862.

African-Americans. The government selected them for tickets of conditional release on the basis of their literacy and skills, in precisely the same way as for white convicts. Eurasian Santiago Gregory had been employed previously on the railways, could fell and hew timber, and make sails. He also spoke Bengali and Hindustani.[17] A thirty-two-year-old "coloured" American convict, John Peterson, was a ship's cook and steward by trade, and had also worked as a butcher. He was said to understand farming and tobacco planting, which perhaps hints at his previous enslavement.[18] Another prisoner, William Hawkins, said to be "of African descent", was described by J. Rohde, the Inspector-General of jails in Madras, as "a good cook, and a man of intelligence". Rohde expressed anxiety that the fact of his African birth "might not allow of his exercising the same control as others". The Madras government disagreed, and shipped Hawkins to Port Blair.[19] The British were as unconcerned about race as they were about crime in the selection of prisoners for transfer; any non-Indian prisoner could petition and be chosen. The Eurasian and black prisoners had been convicted of burglary, stealing, robbery, manslaughter, and murder; and two had even previously attempted to escape from jail. Just as for Europeans, it was fitness, "character", and prisoner skills that decided their transfer. Almost all had previously been to sea, and they knew sail, rope, mat, brick, and shoemaking, as well as carpentry and weaving.[20] These transfers continued after separate European jails opened during 1862–1865. However, both before and afterwards, the British did not send either mainland prisoners with poor disciplinary records, or soldiers, who were ineligible for transfer.[21]

17. IOR P/146/53 Bengal (Jails) October 1862: A. Payne, officiating Inspector-General of jails, to J. Geoghegan, Under-Secretary to the government of Bengal, 9 September 1862; memorandum of A. Payne, 29 September 1862.

18. IOR P/146/50 Bengal (Jails) May 1862: J. King, Governor of Calcutta Jail, to David Cowie, Sheriff of Calcutta, 1 May 1862, enc. petition of John Peterson, an American under sentence of penal servitude for six years, at present detained in Calcutta Jail, 2 May 1862; roll of an American (coloured) convict, 1 May 1862.

19. TNSA Madras (Judicial) 24 June 1863: J. Rohde, Inspector-General of jails Madras, to A.J. Arbuthnot, Chief Secretary to the government of Madras, 25 May 1863; Arbuthnot to E.C. Bayley, Secretary to the government of India, 8 October 1863.

20. TNSA Madras (Judicial) 24 June 1863: W.S. Nesbitt, in charge of European prison Ootacamund, to Rohde, 25 April 1863, enc. List of prisoners undergoing penal servitude in the Ootacamund European prison who are considered eligible for employment in Port Blair; TNSA Madras (Judicial) 15 July 1864, nos 185–6: E.C. Bayley, Chief Secretary to the government of India, to A.J. Arbuthnot, Chief Secretary to the government of Madras; TNSA Madras (Judicial) 8 December 1864, 119–21: J. Rohde, Inspector-General of jails, to A.J. Arbuthnot, Chief Secretary to the government of Madras, 24 November and 2 December 1864, enc. petition of Thomas Nolan, 26 October 1864; TNSA Madras (Judicial) 16 January 1866: Bayley to Superintendent Barnett Ford, 16 January 1866.

21. TNSA Madras (Judicial) 24 June 1863: J. Rohde, Inspector-General of jails, to A.J. Arbuthnot, Chief Secretary to the government of Madras, 25 May 1863; Arbuthnot to E.C. Bayley, secretary to the government of India, 8 October 1863.

By 1867, there were thirty-four European, Eurasian, and American prisoners in the Andamans, employed as clerks, painters, fishermen, and carpenters. There were 6,965 Indian convicts in the Islands at this time.[22] The majority of non-Indian prisoners – European, Eurasian, African, and American – worked as convict overseers, either in agricultural cultivation or on public works. About half lived on Ross Island, at the time the head-quarters of the penal colony. Reflecting their work in supervising the convict gangs working around the settlement, the other half was spread around the bay of Port Blair: across Aberdeen, Haddo, Chatham Island, Viper Island, and Mount Harriet, with one man at, respectively, Perseverance Point, Hope Town, Navy Point, and Port Mouat.[23] They came from many different places, including: the United States, London, Scotland, and Ireland; Calcutta, Madras, Allahabad, and Patna in India; and, even further afield, Manila, Amsterdam, Persia, and Ceylon.[24] The Andamans regime valued the presence, labour, and authority of these men, and it did not employ them differently based on racial lines.[25] The first census of the Islands, taken in December 1871, noted that there were 233 "British-born" men and women in the Islands, sixty-nine of whom had, in fact, been born in India. Most were settlement officials or soldiers. Further classifications reveal the presence of three Americans, six Africans, and sixty-four Eurasians – a rise on the 1867 figures. The total convict population in 1871 was 8,643, and the indigenous Andamanese population was estimated at 2,847.[26]

Until the 1870s, these Europeans, Eurasians, Americans, and Africans mixed freely with each other – whether they were transportation convicts or prisoners transferred on licence. All were grouped together and separated from Indians in a "Christian barrack", where they enjoyed a life of relative

22. UK Parliamentary Papers 53.269: *Statement Exhibiting the Moral and Material Progress and Condition of India During the Year 1868–69* (London, 1870), p. 65.
23. TNSA Madras (Judicial) 16 January 1866: A.J. Arbuthnot, Chief Secretary to the government of Madras, to Superintendent Barnett Ford, 31 January 1866; IOR P/434/8 India (Public) 11 December 1867: Inspection report by Major H.N. Davies, Secretary to the Chief Commissioner of British Burma, enc. Nominal roll showing the number of European, Eurasian, and Native convicts receiving upwards of Rs. 8 a month, on the 23rd April, at the several settlements of Port Blair; List of European and Eurasian prisoners on the various stations of the settlement and their employment.
24. IOR P/434/8 India (Public) 11 December 1867: Inspection report by Major H.N. Davies, Secretary to the Chief Commissioner of British Burma, enc. Nominal roll showing the number of European, Eurasian, and Native convicts receiving upwards of Rs. 8 a month, on the 23rd April, at the several settlements of Port Blair.
25. IOR P/146/52 Bengal (Jails) September 1862: Extract from a demi-official letter from the Superintendent of Port Blair to E.C. Bayley, Secretary to the government of India, 1 August 1862.
26. NAI Home (Port Blair) October 1873, nos 49–59: Census of the Andaman Islands, December 1871. The Andaman census was not included in the published Indian census "as not being strictly within Indian limits". See Henry Waterfield, *Memorandum on the Census of British India 1871–72* (London, 1875), p. 6. On indigenous people in the Islands, see Vishvajit Pandya, *In the Forest: Visual and Material Worlds of Andamanese History, 1858–2006* (Lanham MD, 2009).

luxury. They were paid wages, issued with superior rations, and appear to have had easy access to liquor. Their barracks were stone built, and each man was allotted the same space as that issued to a European soldier. Indian convicts on the other hand lived in wooden barracks, each housing 100–150 men, and divided into groups of twenty-five.[27] One transfer prisoner, J. Bluett, even had a child called James, who was enrolled in the school for Europeans and Eurasians on Ross Island.[28] However, their life of relative privilege was short-lived. One drunken night in 1871, a licenced prisoner called James Devine killed another conditional release holder (a Dutchman called Alkana) in a brawl. A murder trial followed, in which it was revealed that Devine was employed in the public works department, where another licenced prisoner Frederick Roloff worked in the commissariat, and where a third, Thomas Fernandez, was super-intendent of sail makers. Devine was found guilty and despatched to the mainland under sentence of penal servitude. The mainland government subsequently urged an enquiry into why, though of different penal status, convicts and licenced prisoners lived in the same barracks, were employed in the same positions of authority, and enjoyed various privileges so soon after their transportation or transfer. In an attempt to draw a line of criminal distinction around the prisoners, it ordered the tightening up of discipline.[29]

That the Andaman administration met with the disapprobation of its mainland counterpart for its lack of racial distinction is indicative of the social peculiarity of the Andamans as a penal colony. The government of India, which had taken control of much of the subcontinent following the 1857 Revolt, was seemingly unaware that, in a range of largely Indian penal contexts, since the 1820s, European, Eurasian, and African convicts had been important allies of the East India Company's disciplinary regime.[30] In places like Burma, the British co-opted them into convict management, and, in return, they enjoyed favourable conditions, at least compared to their fellow prisoners in Indian jails or the penal colonies of majority white settlements, including Australia. Though it may have shocked mainland free society, the Andamans penal regime was thus totally consistent with that of the earlier Indian penal settlements, where Eurasian convicts formed small proportions of the total convict population.[31] Class and race, it seems,

27. IOR P/434/8 India (Public) 11 December 1867: Inspection report by Major H.N. Davies, Secretary to the Chief Commissioner of British Burma, p. 18.
28. *Ibid.*, enc. Memorandum showing the number of scholars, names and ages, who attended the Port Blair school from January 1867, up to the present date. We know nothing about the child's mother.
29. NAI Home (Port Blair) 20 May 1871, nos 21–2: Murder by James Devine, a licenced convict.
30. The East India Company was a trading company that governed large areas of subcontinental India before 1857, including with regard to law and punishment.
31. On Eurasian convicts in South East Asia, and a biography of an African convict called George Morgan transported from India to Burma and ultimately Van Diemen's Land (Tasmania), see Anderson, *Subaltern Lives*, ch. 3.

had different meanings and produced different social formations in a penal colony such as the Andamans.

ANGLO-INDIAN SERVICE

The 1901 Andamans census recorded the presence of 280 Europeans and 71 Eurasians in the Islands.[32] This was out of a total population of 16,106, which included 11,947 convicts and 1,465 free residents, the latter including ex-convicts and their descendants.[33] In 1921, the last census for which there is data, the number of Anglo-Indians (as Eurasians were now called) had fallen to twenty-five. This dramatic reduction in numbers was likely due to the release or death of the licenced prisoners transferred during the 1860s.[34] Despite this, there were somewhere between two and four Anglo-Indians to every European living in Port Blair. This was an extraordinarily high proportion compared with that on the mainland. The relatively large number of Eurasians living in the Andamans at the start of the twentieth century reflected the extent to which the British relied on them to run the penal colony. They occupied almost all the senior positions in the management and operation of the jails, telegraph, forest, and wireless services. European men stationed in India went to the Islands to work in the wireless, telegraphs, and jail departments too. They commonly married the sisters and daughters of Anglo-Indians settled in the Islands, and then called for their female relatives to join them. They then married into Anglo-Indian families, creating tight knots of family and community that straddled hierarchies of race.[35] Race and class intertwined in the formation of the category "Anglo-Indian", for in the Andaman Islands one could be a British, Indian, or country-born European *and* Anglo-Indian. In this respect, the Andamans' bounded islandness and character as a penal colony produced an interstitial socio-racial category that distinguished the peripheries of the Indian Empire in the Bay of Bengal from the cultural formations of empire on the mainland.[36]

32. Andaman and Nicobar Administration Archives, Port Blair (A&N Archives): *Memorandum Relative to the Deputation of the Anglo-Indian and Domiciled Community of India and Burma to the Right Honourable the Secretary of State for India*, 30 July 1925.
33. R.C. Temple, *Census of India, 1901, Volume III: The Andaman and Nicobar Islands* (Calcutta, 1903), p. 289.
34. R.F. Lowis, *Census of India, 1921, Volume II: The Andaman and Nicobar Islands*, Table XVI: European and Allied Races and Anglo-Indians by Race and Age (Calcutta, 1923), p. 73.
35. N. Francis Xavier, "A House Named Blessington", *Andaman Sheekha*, 6 March 2011; author's interview with Eileen Arnell, 27 June 2011.
36. Compare the important insights of Elizabeth Buettner, "Problematic Spaces, Problematic Races: Defining 'Europeans' in Late Colonial India", *Women's History Review*, 9:2 (2000), pp. 277–278.

Figure 2. "Our Family Group with Convict Servants, 1939".
Private collection of Eileen Arnell, England. Used by permission.

Eileen Arnell's English grandfather Jack and great-uncle Patrick both worked as officers in the Andaman jails department. In 1933, Jack's daughter Mollie, Eileen's mother, travelled from England to the Islands, where she married an Anglo-Indian man called John Boomgardt. He was the great-grandson of an Englishman called James Whitby. Whitby went out to India in 1840, and by the 1860s was stationed in the Andaman Islands.[37] A few months after John and Mollie's wedding, Mollie's sister Monica travelled out and married another Anglo-Indian telegraph man. John Boomgardt's Anglo-Indian sister Coralie, meanwhile, married an Englishman stationed in the wireless department. Eileen (the little girl in the picture) was born in 1936, and a brother Peter (the baby in the photograph) a few years later. Peter died aged just fourteen months from an unknown illness.

The jail service in particular came to be almost completely staffed by Anglo-Indians. By the 1930s, eight men were in daily charge of the cellular jail and the district convict stations. The cellular jail was a large radial

---

37. It is likely that James had a brother in the Andamans; 1867 records also record the presence of one J. Whitby, a clerk in the convict record department, as well as James Whitby, who was a sergeant in the commissariat department. Two children, Thomas Whitby and Eleanor Whitby, were at Port Blair School. See IOR P/434/8 India (Public) 11 December 1867, 89–97: Inspection Report by Major H.N. Davies, B.S.C., Secretary to the Chief Commissioner of British Burma, Appendices: Nominal return of officers; Memorandum showing the number of Scholars, names and ages, who attended the Port Blair School from January 1867, up to the present date.

structure that had opened in 1906 to receive all transportation convicts for a new, initial stage of hard discipline, before their release to convict working gangs. Almost as soon as the cellular jail opened, its function changed, for it was also used to incarcerate revolutionary nationalists being transported from the mainland. They were never sent to outdoor labour. Anglo-Indian jailers and overseers were charged with monitoring all aspects of the incarceration and penal work of both ordinary and political prisoners, including taking musters, issuing rations, and keeping registers. Well known among them was John Boomgardt (see Figure 2), who was trans-ferred from the public works to the jails department in 1921.[38] They also included two brothers by the surname of Young, and a father and son named Baines.[39] The government also employed Anglo-Indians in the forest service,[40] at Chatham Island sawmill,[41] and as managers of the gov-ernment workshops that employed convicts.[42]

As noted above, following the James Devine murder trial, the Andamans administration distinguished non-Indian transportation convicts from licenced prisoners. A further layer of separation can be found in the residential patterns of Anglo-Indian government servants and the British governor and his senior officers. Indeed, socio-racial lines of distinction between them were drawn across Port Blair harbour. The British lived a lavish lifestyle in the beautiful bungalows of Ross Island, the headquarters of the penal colony. Anglo-Indians lived in more modest houses, sometimes built on stilts in a colonial South East Asian style, along a mainland urban coastline that partly faced Ross, and stretched from Corbyn's Cove to Aberdeen and Haddo. They belonged to different clubs: the British socia-lized on Ross Island, and Anglo-Indians went to the Temple Club near the Aberdeen Bazaar in Port Blair. Commissioner R.C. Temple had established the latter in 1903, as a facility for Anglo-Indians. He noted at the time that it was difficult to recruit people for service in the Islands, and he wanted to create a leisure facility to draw them.[43] Yet, despite their separate residence, the social demarcations between British and Anglo-Indian officers and staff were not as distinct as was the case in the mainland Indian Empire. In this extraordinary penal context, the British administrative classes viewed

38. IOR P/11048 Home (Port Blair) January 1921, nos 49–52 part B: A.J. Boomgardt, transfer from the public works department to the jailor establishment of Port Blair.
39. IOR Mss Eur F180: memoirs of N.K. Paterson, n.d.; Gill Chalabi's family papers: Noel Paterson, "Experiences of a District Officer 1929–1947", transcribed from audio, November 2004. I thank Selma Chalabi for sharing copies of the transcripts with me.
40. IOR Mss Eur F180: memoirs of N.K. Paterson, n.d.
41. Gill Chalabi's family papers: Noel Paterson, "Experiences of a District Officer 1929–1947".
42. IOR P/10841 Home (Port Blair) January 1920.
43. Martin Wynne (ed.), *On Honourable Terms: The Memoirs of Some Indian Police Officers, 1915–1948* (London, 1985), p. 160; IOR P/11048 Home (Port Blair) July 1921, nos 4–10 part A: Chief Commissioner H.C. Beadon to Secretary to the government of India, 30 April 1921.

Anglo-Indians as their allies, not just in running the penal colony, but in its security. They believed that in the event of a convict revolt or uprising, they would side with them, rather than with Indian and Burmese convicts. Though never explicit in colonial reports and correspondence, the fact of their Christianity was certainly relevant.

In a 1920s memoir of the Islands, Frances Stewart Robinson, daughter of the Chief Commissioner, recalled this social ambivalence. She wrote of an annual gathering, given by the British administration in honour of the jailers and their families at the Andaman Club, where majors, captains, "dusky beauties", "Anglo-Indians", and "dignified Civil Officers from Burma and India" waltzed and foxtrotted together. "Barriers of class and colour", she noted, "were temporarily down".[44] Robinson's writing anticipated that of Chief Commissioner M.L. Ferrar, who wrote in a private letter of a similarly mixed dinner party held in 1929:

> Everyone was cheery and sociable and well bred and we really had a very pleasant evening. Yet 5 of them were Indians, 5 were white country bred and 4 more with a lot of colour and several of the rest were of very ordinary English upbringing. I know of no other place in India where people have so little snobbery and artificiality among them.[45]

The Islands' remoteness from the mainland, and its peculiarly penal character, enabled such sociability.[46] Moreover, despite the "barriers of class and colour" described by Frances Robinson, Anglo-Indians lived closely with non-elite European employees of empire, and enjoyed many of the trappings of colonial privilege. As one, British-born woman who had married an Anglo-Indian in the Islands, Mollie Boomgardt, recalled in a radio interview in 2010, with their weekly dances, piano playing, and convict servants, they had lived "like kings and queens".[47]

MIGRATION IN THE 1920S: PRISONERS, REBELS, FREE ANGLO-INDIANS, AND CRIMINAL TRIBES

In 1919–1920, under the auspices of a broader review of imprisonment, the Indian jails committee recommended the abolition of penal transportation. It reported that "unnatural vice" was widespread in the Andamans, and that convicts lacked "reformatory influences". It called for the substitution of penal transportation for rigorous imprisonment, on the grounds of morality, as well as expense. Although the committee recognized that there was insufficient jail

44. IOR Mss Eur F209: Frances Stewart Robinson, "The Forgotten Islands", p. 32.
45. Centre for South Asian Studies, University of Cambridge: M.L. Ferrar papers, M.L. Ferrar to his mother, 4 June 1929.
46. See also Buettner, "Problematic Spaces, Problematic Races", pp. 277–278.
47. "Kala Pani: A Forgotten History", BBC Radio 4, 21 April 2010.

accommodation on the mainland to accomplish this goal, as criticism of the cost of the penal colony mounted, having invested so many resources in the founding of the penal colony, the British were loath to abandon it altogether, and so began to look for alternative sources of labour and settlement. To a large extent, they remained committed to coerced migration, and with the jails committee claiming that homosexual practices were widespread in the Andamans they particularly desired the migration of women. And so the British instigated a "volunteer" scheme for mainland prisoner migrants and their families, beginning in 1921. This was not successful: most prisoners were unwilling to go to the Islands, and the authorities found it difficult to balance the often conflicting demands of punishment with those of economy.[48] Second, in the wake of the mass convictions of the Malabar Rebellion of 1921–1922, the government offered favourable terms to convicted rebels willing to migrate to the Islands with their families. They would immediately assume the status of "self-supporters", in effect replacing their terms of incarceration with those of probation in the penal colony. Subsequently, the government organized the transfer of about 2,000 Mapalahs, and paid the expenses of families wanting to join them.[49]

With respect to its desire for free labourers to open up the Islands for further settlement, and compelled to foreground the Islands' economic self-sufficiency and productivity above their punitive function, in the context of its earlier policies the British again looked to Anglo-Indians. Shortly after the Mapalah transfers, in 1923, twelve agricultural "pioneers" went to the Islands under a trial scheme. Waved off from Calcutta by the Anglo-Indian Association, the British governor of Bengal even sent them a message of support.[50] However, the scheme was a disaster from start to end. The men's land allocation was fallow; they lacked agricultural skills or experience; few if any of the promised resources materialized; some of the men fell sick with malaria; and they gradually abandoned their barracks.[51]

At this time, a handful of other Anglo-Indians and country-born men and women travelled to the Islands too, and they were considerably more successful than this organized party. They included George and Dorothy Deakes who, three years after they first arrived in 1923, were granted a thirty-year licence for over fifty acres of land on Mount Harriet.[52] They built a house, made improvements to the land, cleared the jungle, planted

---

48. Sherman, "From Hell to Paradise?". For a discussion of development in the 1920s, under the stewardship of Chief Commissioner M.L. Ferrar, see Anderson *et al.*, *New Histories of the Andaman Islands*, pp. 29–61.

49. Anderson *et al.*, *New Histories of the Andaman Islands*, pp. 47–49.

50. "The Colonisation Scheme: Pioneers leave Calcutta", *The Times of India*, 27 November 1923.

51. "Anglo-Indian Colony: Possibilities in Andamans", *The Times of India*, 5 April 1924. IOR MSS Eur F531/46 Hawes papers: "Report from A.E. Young, 28 January 1926", *The Anglo-Indian*, 19:3 (1926), pp. 13–14. See also Frank Anthony, *Britain's Betrayal in India: The Story of the Anglo Indian Community* (Bombay, 1969), pp. vi, 91, 97–99, 114.

52. Personal Collection of Keith Wilson (PCKW): "Grant of Land" certificate, 15 August 1932.

fruit and vegetable orchards, kept cows and poultry, and established betel as well as coconut plantations.[53] By any measure, they seem to have made a good living; Dorothy Deakes later wrote that the couple had "gladly settled down as colonist planters".[54] Otherwise, though the government of India announced its willingness to consider applications for land grants, there were very few.[55] Most, including Deakes, already had relatives or friends working for the Andamans administration, and thus had some knowledge of the Islands.[56]

Following experiments with "volunteer" prisoners, Mapalahs, and free Anglo-Indian settlers, the British administration sponsored the Salvation Army to "rehabilitate" about 300 Bhantus in the Andamans. The three million members of this peripatetic community had been classified as hereditary criminals under the Criminal Tribes Acts (1872–1924), and were thus rounded up and forced to live on reserved land in India's Central Provinces. The Salvation Army had first petitioned the government of India regarding the prospect of settling criminal tribes in the Andamans in 1914. Special Commissioner Frederick Booth Tucker wrote: "The absence of the woman element in the present colonies is a well-known and growing evil, the seriousness of which can hardly be exaggerated". Families, he argued, would rapidly multiply and populate the Andamans, and once emigration became attractive, compulsion would no longer be necessary.[57] However, it was not until 1926–1928 that the British offered those Bhantus convicted in the criminal courts (largely for dacoity, or armed gang robbery), and incarcerated in mainland jails, the chance of paid passage to the Andamans. The conditions were as follows. First, they would be accompanied by officers of the Salvation Army, which they knew as *Mukti Fauj*. Second, they had to have been sentenced to at least ten years. Third, though they would be volunteers, they had to take their relatives with them. The convicts would be under penal restraint, but their families would have entire freedom of mobility. Despite these constraints, the British promised that, until they had acquired land and built houses, they would receive a subsistence allowance.

In 1926, Salvation Army Captain Edwin Sheard (known in India as Fauj Singh), with his wife, took around 100 convicted Bhantu dacoits with about

53. PCKW: D.M. Deakes to the Secretary to the government of India, Home Department, 25 April 1946; Board of Trade, extended Far Eastern private chattels scheme (war damage), application of Mrs Millicent Dorothy Deakes, undated (1950).

54. Mrs Milicent D. Deakes, "Isles of Peace and Happiness", *The Times of India*, 12 March 1950.

55. Home Department Resolution, 27 February 1826, reproduced in *Andaman and Nicobar Gazette: Extraordinary*, 18 March 1926; "Future of the Andamans: Conversion to a Self-Supporting Community", *The Times of India*, 1 March 1926.

56. Deakes, "Isles of Peace and Happiness".

57. IOR P/9949 Home (Port Blair) April 1914 no. 10 proposed establishment of a settlement in the Andaman and Nicobar Islands for criminal tribes from India: Frederick Booth Tucker, special commissioner for India and Ceylon, Salvation Army, Simla, to Reginald Craddock, Delhi, 2 March 1914. See also Frederick Booth-Tucker, *Criminocurology or the Indian Crim, and What to Do With Him: Being a Review of the Work of The Salvation Army Amongst the Prisoners, Habituals and Criminal Tribes of India* (Simla, 1916).

Figure 3. "Bantoo making convicts' clothing at Ferrar-Gunj".
Ferrar Collection, Centre of South Asian Studies, University of Cambridge. Used by permission.

400 members of their families to the Andamans. Salvation Army General Frederick Coutts later likened Sheard to Richard Johnson, the first Anglican priest of Britain's penal colony in New South Wales. The Bhantus settled in three villages – Ferrargunj, Cadelganj, and Anikhet – where Sheard took charge of building houses and other structures, planting fruit trees, establishing other agricultural enterprises, the employment of his charges in the sawmill and Western India Match Company's match factory at Chatham (the only privately owned industry on the Islands), and setting up a handloom weaving factory (see Figure 3). Salvationists later said that during the first two or three years, the Bhantus neglected their cattle and refused to engage in settled cultivation. But the community soon became self-supporting. One man even developed a weaving business that employed twenty people.[58] As Salvation Army Brigadier R.T. Hughes later put it:

> Prison systems should not be merely vindictive, but should resemble schools of discipline providing education and correction; so that by the time a convict has

58. Salvation Army International Heritage Centre, London (SAIHC): IN/2/1: Papers from India, Northern Territory, 1891–1993: "A Model Convict Settlement: Life in the Andaman Islands", n. d.; M.C.C. Bonington, *Census of India, 1931, Volume II: The Andaman and Nicobar Islands* (Calcutta, 1932), pp. 41–43; Frederick L. Coutts, *"I Had No Revolver": Edwin Sheard* (London, 1943); Edwin H. Sheard, *Sergeant-Major in the Andamans: Kanhaiya Gariba* (St Albans, 1957), pp. 11–12; Edwin H. Sheard, "Reforming Robbers in the Andamans", *The Officers' Review*

passed through the various classes or standards, he will be released and able to attain to full citizenship rights, and be able to carry on normally and naturally.[59]

Spurred on by the success of the scheme, in 1929, the British sent 170 Karwals, another so-called criminal tribe closely related to the Bhantus, to the Islands. However, the administration swiftly repatriated them, because they were found to be "totally unsuited" for settlement.[60] During this period, finally, the government shipped North Indian Ranchis and Burmese Karen to the Andamans to work in the forest department. This was directly related to the Islands' specific labour needs. Indeed, when the administration wound down the Islands' sawmill in 1931, the government sent most of them home.[61] Meanwhile, British administrators found the Bhantu of great interest, and for the 1931 census issued Captain Sheard with "a questionnaire on the cultural anthropology and ethnology of the Bhantus". With "unique" experience of daily contact with them, he assisted in the production of a detailed account of their "organization, habits and customs". This related almost entirely to their lives before resettlement in the Andamans, freezing them in time, though some reference was made to the loss of their particular dialect.[62]

Sheard and his wife left the Andamans after six years, and they were replaced by Major William Francis, who remained in the Islands for a decade, right up to the Japanese occupation in World War II (1942–1945). After ten years, with no special privileges on offer to converts, only sixty-six of the 295 Bhantu adults had become Christians. "It is better to win individually sincere souls who courageously step out to become seekers after truth", wrote Hughes, "than offer loaves and fishes and have an entire community as nominal Christians only".[63] If the Army's hopes of mass conversion were not entirely realized, nevertheless the scheme was successful in supporting what Madhumita Mazumdar has described as Chief Commissioner Ferrar's "improving vision" for the larger development of the

(November 1937), pp. 535–540. General accounts of Salvation Army rehabilitation include Rachel J. Tolen, "Colonizing and Transforming the Criminal Tribesman: The Salvation Army in British India", *American Ethnologist*, 18:1 (1991), pp. 106–125.

59. SAIHC: IN/2/1: Brigadier A.T. Hughes, officer commanding, Burma, "Life Among Lifers, Being a Short Account of the Ferrar Gunj Colony Run by the Salvation Army for the Government of the United Provinces, India, Among Life-Sentence (Murderer) Convicts and their Families in the Andaman Islands".

60. *Report on the Administration of the Andaman and Nicobar Islands and the Penal Settlement of Port Blair, 1st December 1929 to 31st March 1932* (Calcutta, 1932), p. 2. The report does not specify the reasons for their "unsuitability".

61. Bonington, *Census of India, 1931, Volume II*, pp. 29–30; *Report on the Administration of the Andaman and Nicobar Islands 1929–1932*; F.A.M. Dass, *The Andaman Islands* (Bangalore, 1937), pp. 70–71.

62. Bonington, *Census of India, 1931*, Appendix I: The Bhantus (language, pp. 39–41).

63. Hughes, "Life Among Lifers", p. 24. The Salvation Army called insincere converts "rice Christians".

Islands. This included large-scale dredging and other interventions into their landscape and environment.[64] Indeed, whilst the Salvation Army had reservations about the effectiveness of the resettlement scheme, the British declared it an unambiguous success. They described Bhantus as "colonists", who had become "hardworking members of the community".[65] Their number grew to 514 by the outbreak of World War II, after which all of those resettled under judicial sentence had served their time.[66]

CONCLUSIONS

Eurasians and Anglo-Indians occupy a central place in the history of the Andaman Islands. As convicts and licenced prisoners, they were vital social intermediaries between the British administration and Indian convicts, and following the recommendation of the abolition of transportation in 1919–1920 government viewed them as potential settlers in the Andamans' transition from penal colony to free society. Race and class combined to produce specifically Anglo-Indian island formations that resembled those of the penal settlements in South East Asia, but differed from those of the mainland. Notably, free white Europeans employed in the subordinate classes of the Islands' administration became subsumed in the category "Anglo-Indian". In this sense, "Anglo-Indian" in the Islands denoted social origin more than it delineated hierarchies of race.

The number of free Anglo-Indian settlers in the Andamans was always limited, however, and after the failure of experimental pioneer migration in the 1920s the British administration took advantage of the human outcomes of imperial repression on the mainland to further advance their colonization. Though the "volunteer" prisoner scheme largely failed to attract substantial numbers of migrants, the effects of British governance underlay more successful programmes, at least from a government perspective, for the coercive resettlement of Mapalahs and Bhantus, and their families, in the Andamans. Penal colonies such as the Andamans thus existed within the political borders of imperial colonies, and were subject to competing pressures regarding punishment and rehabilitation, and settlement and self-sufficiency. The Islands were, in this sense, a carceral periphery at the edge of empire that reveal a great deal about imperial governance in its Indian centre.

---

64. Anderson *et al.*, *New Histories of the Andaman Islands*, pp. 29–61.
65. *Report on the Administration of the Andaman and Nicobar Islands and the Penal Settlement of Port Blair, 1st April 1938 to 31st March 1939* (New Delhi, 1940), p. 4.
66. A&N Jails Department accession no. 203 Future of the Bhantu settlement: B.L. Pandey's note, 15 June 1945; N.K. Paterson's note, 15 June 1945. See also *Report on the Administration of the Andaman and Nicobar Islands and the Penal Settlement of Port Blair, 1st April 1937 to 31st March 1938* (New Delhi, 1939), pp. 2–3.

IRSH 63 (2018), Special Issue, pp. 45–63 doi:10.1017/S0020859018000214
© 2018 Internationaal Instituut voor Sociale Geschiedenis

A Natural Hulk: Australia's Carceral Islands in the Colonial Period, 1788–1901*

KATHERINE ROSCOE

Institute of Historical Research, University of London

Senate House, Malet Street, London, WC1E 7HU, UK

E-mail: katy.roscoe@sas.ac.uk

ABSTRACT: During the British colonial period, at least eleven islands off the coast of Australia were used as sites of "punitive relocation" for transported European convicts and Indigenous Australians. This article traces the networks of correspondence between the officials and the Colonial Office in London as they debated the merits of various offshore islands to incarcerate different populations. It identifies three roles that carceral islands served for colonial governance and economic expansion. First, the use of convicts as colonizers of strategic islands for territorial and commercial expansion. Second, to punish transported convicts found guilty of "misconduct" to maintain order in colonial society. Third, to expel Indigenous Australians who resisted colonization from their homeland. It explores how, as "colonial peripheries", islands were part of a colonial system of punishment based around mobility and distance, which mirrored in microcosm convict flows between the metropole and the Australian colonies.

ISLAND INCARCERATION

Today, the island continent of Australia has more than 8,000 smaller islands off its coast.[1] As temperatures rose 6,000 years ago, parts of the mainland flooded and islands separated. These events are remembered by many Indigenous communities through "Dreaming" stories. Some islands became bases for fishing, shellfish gathering, and hunting of larger marine animals; others were no longer reachable, but remained part of Indigenous communities' cultural landscape.[2] When the British colonizers arrived at

* The research leading to these results has received funding from the European Research Council under the European Union's Seventh Framework Programme (FP/2007–2013) / ERC Grant Agreement 312542. My thanks are due to the editors and contributors to this special issue and the anonymous reviewers for their feedback on previous versions of this article.
1. Elizabeth McMahon, "Australia, the Island Continent: How Contradictory Geography Shapes the National Imaginary", *Space and Culture*, 13:2 (2010), pp. 178–187, 179; Robert Clarke and Anna Johnston, "Travelling the Sequestered Isle: Tasmania as Penitentiary, Laboratory and Sanctuary", *Studies in Travel Writing*, 20:1 (2016), pp. 1–16, 2.
2. Peter Veth and Sue O'Connor, "The Past 50,000 Years: An Archaeological View", in Alison Bashford and Stuart Macintyre (eds), *The Cambridge History of Australia, vol. 1: Indigenous and Colonial Australia* (Cambridge, 2013), pp. 17–42, 40–41.

Botany Bay in 1788, they enforced European concepts of islands as sites of isolation for the first time. Just three weeks after the arrival of the First Fleet, at the first criminal court, convict Thomas Hill was sentenced to spend a week in chains on a rocky island in Sydney Harbour for the crime of stealing from the government stores. The island was named "Pinchgut Island" after the starvation rations that "pinched" Hill's stomach.[3] This was the first instance in what became a system of "punitive relocation" to islands off the coast of Australia for much of the colonial period.[4] Between 1788 and 1901, a network of islands surrounding the Australian continent acted as sites of expulsion, punishment, and labour extraction. The islands of Sydney Harbour were the sites of public works completed by convicts, including Pinchgut Island (Ma-te-wan-ye, 1841), Goat Island (Me-Mel, 1833–1839), and Cockatoo Island (Wa-rea-mah, 1839–1869); further down the eastern coast was St Helena Island (No-goon) in Moreton Bay (1867–1932). Off the northern coast, the large island of Melville Island was a penal settlement and military fortification (1824–1829). Off the eastern coast of Van Diemen's Land (later renamed Tasmania) there was a penal settlement on Maria Island (1825–1832), which later became a convict probation station (1842–1850), as well as Sarah Island in Macquarie Harbour, which was used for secondary punishment of convicts (1821–1833). On various islands in the Bass Strait, most notably at Flinders Island, Indigenous Tasmanians were confined on an involuntary basis for their "protection" from settler violence (1830–1847); off the Western Australian coast, near Fremantle, Carnac Island (Ngooloormayup) held Nyoongar resistance leaders in 1832, until a long-term penal establishment for Indigenous men was established on neighbouring Rottnest Island (Wadjemup, 1838–1931); finally, and most notoriously, the Pacific Island of Norfolk Island (administered first by New South Wales and then by Van Diemen's Land) was settled by convicts (1788–1814), and then reoccupied for punishment of re-transported convicts (1825–1853). The map below shows the distribution of these colonial-era carceral islands around Australia.

This article examines the colonial government's use of Australia's offshore islands as sites of "punitive relocation" from the late eighteenth to the late nineteenth century. The term "punitive relocation" is well-suited to describe the inter- and intra-colonial movement of prisoners to offshore islands, as the legal sentences varied. Indigenous people were removed to island penal establishments under custodial sentences, including both "transportation" and "imprisonment with hard labour". On the other

---

3. Thomas Keneally, *Australians: Origins to Eureka* (Sydney, 2009), pp. 95–97.
4. Amy Nethery, "Separate and Invisible: A Carceral History of Australian Islands", *Shima*, 6:2 (2012), pp. 85–98.

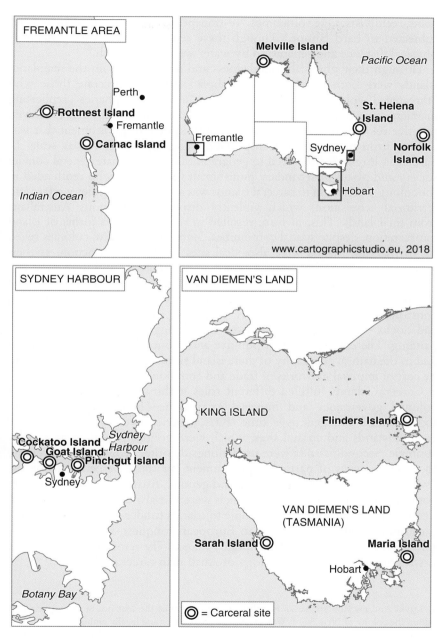

Figure 1. Australia's Carceral Islands, 1788–1901, with insets of Sydney Harbour and the Western Australian coast.

hand, recidivists were sometimes "re-transported" to penal settlements and subjected to hard labour.[5] Though these sentences were legally distinct, physical distance and separation by water were key to both.[6]

Through their physical boundedness and separation from the mainland, islands were both practical and symbolic sites to incarcerate those who "threatened" colonial society. They acted as "colonial peripheries", replicating in microcosm transportation from the metropole to the colony. However, punitive relocation to islands was a colonial system of punishment that was distinct from metropolitan transportation, in purpose as well as scale. In particular, it reflected the need to geographically differentiate general convict society and places of secondary punishment for convicts who reoffended in the colony. Relocation to carceral islands was also part of frontier warfare and territorial acquisition, which violently displaced Indigenous Australians from their lands. This, in turn, resulted in racially distinct forms of island incarceration, despite spatial continuities. Since the Australian colonies relied on free labour, islands were also ideal sites for labour extraction, as their isolation allowed limited mobility for extramural labour and they were also proximate to the sea. The convict industries on carceral islands were often maritime, with convicts logging wood and harvesting hemp to build boats, constructing maritime infrastructure – including jetties, seawalls, lighthouses, and docks – or engaging in activities like fishing, shell collecting, and salt panning. The entanglement of punitive and economic motives was directly tied to the natural geography of these island sites, and the need of colonies to be part of imperial networks of trade and communication.

Carceral islands fulfilled different roles within the colonial project for colonial governance and imperial expansion. These purposes blurred together and changed over time. First, convicts were sent to colonize remote islands and coastal sites, which were politically and commercially strategic. Second, islands were used alongside other geographically remote locations, as sites of particular punishment for those perceived to be the "worst" kind of convict. Third, Indigenous Australians were forcibly confined on island institutions, which were not always explicitly carceral; yet, by displacing Indigenous people to islands (under sentence or not) the government reduced resistance to European conquest, rendering the land one step closer to *terra nullius* (nobody's land). The remainder of the article is structured around this typology of Australian carceral islands.

---

5. David Andrew Roberts has shown that the application of the sentence of "transportation" within the colony of New South Wales was both contentious and legally ambiguous. See David Andrew Roberts, "Exile in a Land of Exiles: The Early History of Criminal Transportation Law in New South Wales, 1788–1809", *Australian Historical Studies*, 48:4 (2017), pp. 470–485.
6. Clare Anderson *et al.*, "Locating Penal Transportation: Punishment, Space and Place, c.1750–1900", in Karen M. Morin and Dominique Moran (eds), *Historical Geographies of Prisons: Unlocking the Usable Carceral Past* (London, 2015), pp. 147–167, 148–151.

TERRITORY AND TRADE

The purpose of this article is first to explore the use of distant carceral islands as strategic locations along important trading routes. In Australian historiography, there has been a long-standing debate as to whether convicts were sent to New South Wales simply to empty out Britain's overcrowded gaols after the American War of Independence (1778–1783) closed the American colonies for convicts, or whether convicts were sent to New South Wales to enhance Britain's naval power in the Pacific arena.[7] However, unlike the decision to settle Botany Bay, the Colonial Office were explicit that they decided to settle Norfolk Island to harvest flax and pine for naval use, as they were when they decided to settle Melville Island with convicts in 1824. Taking an island perspective allows us to look beyond a binary view – that Australia was settled to dump felons or to ensure British naval dominance – to show that spatial differentiation encouraged multifocal policies.

When the Crown issued Captain Phillip's instructions for settling New Holland, he was told to survey "the several ports, or harbours upon the coast, and the islands contiguous thereto" for possible settlement.[8] As well as ensuring there was no legal loophole that precluded the British from claiming territory in the region, the instructions also directed Phillip to settle Norfolk Island over 1,500 kilometres to the east of Botany Bay in the Pacific. The island was "contiguous" only in the sense that no land masses interrupted this vast stretch of ocean between Sydney and Norfolk Island. Phillip's instructions claimed Norfolk Island was "a spot which may hereafter become useful".[9] Its potential utility was two-fold. First, as a strategic site for commercial expansion. Navigating northwards past New Caledonia put vessels on the South Equatorial Current along the tip of Northern Australia and into the heart of the East India Company's trading grounds in the South East Asian archipelago. The second attraction was the cultivation of flax for ships' rigging and felling of timber for masts. The loss of the American colonies not only meant losing Britain's main convict destination, it also depleted Britain's naval supplies dramatically, and Britain's access to flax via Russia was threatened through their alliance with France. On the advice of hydrologist Alexander Dalrymple, a mixed group of twenty convict and free settlers, at a ratio of two to one, were sent to settle the island

---

7. K.M. Dallas, *Trading Posts or Penal Colonies: The Commercial Significance of Cook's New Holland Route to the Pacific* (Devonport, 1969); Alan Frost, *Botany Bay: The Real Story* (Melbourne, 2011), pp. 268–292; Geoffrey Blainey, *The Tyranny of Distance: How Distance Shaped Australia's History* (Melbourne, 1974), pp. 18–19.
8. *Historical Records of Australia* [hereafter *HRA*], ser. I, vol. I, "Instructions for our trusty and well-beloved Arthur Phillip, Esq., our Captain-General and Governor-in-Chief in and over our territory of New South Wales and its dependencies", 25 April 1787, p. 13.
9. *Ibid.*

in March 1788.[10] Among them was Joseph Lovell, who was sent to Norfolk Island "for life" as punishment for stealing from the stores (his counterpart, Joseph Hall, was, in turn, sent to Pinchgut Island). This demonstrates that even an island that was settled for economic reasons could go on to have a punitive component, reflecting the changing policies of colonial government.[11]

Governor Thomas Brisbane's decision to settle the northern coast of Australia in the mid-1820s was also explicitly motivated by commercial interests, though this time to tap into the market for *trepang* (sea cucumber) in China, and as a gateway to further trade with the southeast Asian archipelago. The British had recently relinquished territories seized from the Dutch in the Indonesian archipelago during the Napoleonic wars, so they were eager to expand their commercial reach.[12] A secondary motive was to prevent any European power claiming territory on the unsettled edges of the Australian continent.[13] In 1818, Captain Philip Parker King had surveyed the northern coast and reported back with evidence of abandoned Macassan (Sulawesi) camps for smoking *trepang*.[14] On the basis of this report, trader William Barnes wrote to the Secretary of State for the Colonies, Lord Bathurst, in July 1823 with a proposal to establish a British *trepang* fishery on the Cobourg peninsula. The chairman of the East India Trade Committee, George Larpent, urged Bathurst to approve a British settlement there for "the greatest benefit to the commerce [...] of the United Kingdom [...] [and to] place our flourishing possessions in that quarter of the Globe in greater security".[15] Despite Larpent's advice to settle on the mainland, the Colonial Office issued Captain Barlow instructions to establish a settlement in the "Apsley's Channel between Melville and Bathurst Island".[16] Looking at a map in London, the islands may have seemed to Lord Bathurst physically closer to trading routes, even though currents, winds, and reefs actually rendered them almost impossible to access.

---

10. Raymond Nobbs, *Norfolk Island's First Settlement* (North Sydney, 1988).

11. Keneally, *Australians*, pp. 95–97.

12. J.M.R. Cameron, "Traders, Government Officials and the Occupation of Melville Island in 1824", *The Great Circle*, 7:2 (1985), pp. 88–99, 88.

13. *HRA*, ser. III, vol. VI, Robert William Hay, Under-Secretary of State, to John Begbie, Secretary of the East India Trade Committee, 6 April 1826, p. 797; Mollie Gillen, "The Botany Bay Decision, 1786: Convicts, Not Empire", *English Historical Review*, 97:385 (1982), pp. 740–766; Ged Martin (ed.), *The Founding of Australia: The Argument about Australia's Origins* (Sydney, 1981).

14. Veth and O'Connor, "The Past 50,000 years", pp. 40–41.

15. *HRA*, ser. III, vol. V, George Larpent, Chairman of East India Company, to Earl Bathurst, Secretary of State for War and the Colonies, 13 December 1823, pp. 743–747.

16. *HRA*, ser. I, vol. XI, Bathurst to Thomas Brisbane, Governor of New South Wales [hereafter, NSW], 17 February 1824, London, p. 277.

In 1824, forty-five settlers – only three of them free men – were shipped aboard the *HMS Tamar* to the northern coast. The convicts were chosen by the Principal Superintendent of Convicts on the basis of their trades, with the majority skilled in construction, and their ethnicity, as thirteen of the eighty convicts selected were black as officials thought they were better able to withstand hard labour in a tropical climate than white convicts.[17] Ultimately, the difficulty of navigating the Apsley Strait – which was shallow, rocky, and subject to strong winds during the monsoon season – meant few British trading ships got through to the settlement and no Macassan vessels at all. On deciding to abandon it in 1829, Governor Ralph Darling suggested the convicts be relocated to Croker Island, a few kilometres off the Cobourg Peninsula. Instead, the convicts were transferred to the existing settlement at Port Raffles.[18] It seems that colonial governors and imperial administrators had an island bias even when local experts and East India Company officials suggested better-located mainland sites for settlement.

Underpinning these epistolary exchanges was the idea that islands were interchangeable and universally preferable for convict-built commercial hubs. This is underlined by the comparisons made by East India Company officials and colonial newspapers between the "Australian" islands – Norfolk Island and Melville Island – and Indian Ocean island penal colonies – the Straits Settlements. The Straits Settlements were East India Company penal settlements for Indian convicts at Penang, Malacca, and Singapore, and were united in 1826.[19] On 10 March 1825, *The Australian* colonial newspaper hoped that "[w]hat twenty years have accomplished at Penang, at which period it was a barren sand, it is not unreasonable to suppose that half that time will bring to pass at Melville Island".[20] In 1827, an East India Company officer (calling himself "M") suggested in the *Asiatic Journal* that Melville Island be reopened to replace "its two rivals", Penang and Singapore, as the destination for Indian convicts.[21] The anonymous officer concluded that Melville Island should not be abandoned, for "the same reasons that Norfolk Island was reoccupied" as a penal settlement in 1825, namely for "its utility to Australia, as a Northern

---

17. Heather Marshall, "Convict Pioneers and the Failure of the Management System on Melville Island, 1824-29", *The Push from the Bush*, 29 (1991), pp. 29–46, 35; Clayton Fredericksen, "Confinement by Isolation: Convict Mechanics and Labour at Fort Dundas, Melville Island", *Australasian Historical Archaeology*, 19 (2001), pp. 48–59, 50.

18. *HRA*, ser. I, vol. XII. Ralph Darling, Governor of NSW, to Hay, 18 December 1826, Sydney, p. 774.

19. C.M. Turnbull, "Convicts in the Straits Settlements, 1826–1867", *Journal of the Malaysian Branch of the Royal Asiatic Society*, 43:1 (1970), pp. 87–103.

20. *The Australian*, 10 March 1825, pp. 2–3.

21. *The Asiatic Journal and Monthly Register for British India and its Dependencies*, XXIV (1827), p. 691.

emporium and naval station".[22] Though Norfolk Island and Melville Island were administered by New South Wales, they mapped better onto Pacific and Indian Ocean maritime trading routes. These Australian islands were part of a much wider practice of sending convicts as "empire-builders" to islands that were economically and politically strategic for British imperial interests.

SECONDARY PUNISHMENT

The second purpose of transportation to carceral islands was to discipline convicts who misbehaved or reoffended, through the dual mechanism of distance and labour. In 1817, John Thomas Bigge, former deputy-judge advocate of Trinidad, was commissioned by the British parliament to report on the convict system in Van Diemen's Land and New South Wales. The two key aspects of Bigge's convict reforms were to disperse convicts across the countryside under assignment to pastoralists in order to rapidly increase the area of land under cultivation, and to introduce a multi-level system of punishment which isolated convicts undergoing secondary punishment, as well as subjecting them to hard labour. Convicts found guilty of misconduct worked either in road or chain gangs or, for more serious offences, were sent to isolated penal settlements.[23] Bigge's scheme was designed to rapidly expand agricultural and pastoral industries, situated in the coastal and interior regions of New South Wales respectively. In order to fulfil the Colonial Office's instructions to "separate the convict population from the free population", Bigge "was naturally led to inquire whether any of the islands in Bass Straits, or upon the eastern coast of New South Wales, were calculated for the reception of convicts".[24] However, upon receiving information from surveyors and locals, Bigge complained that Norfolk Island had proved too difficult to access by boat and "no other island [...] had the same advantages of soil or climate" to sustain a convict population.[25] Ultimately, Bigge recommended several sites on the coast of New South Wales as possible locations for secondary punishment stations.

However, when the Governor of New South Wales, Thomas Brisbane, and the Secretary of State for the Colonies, Lord Bathurst, came to establish

---

22. *Ibid.*
23. Hamish Maxwell-Stewart, "Convict Transportation from Britain and Ireland, 1615–1870", *History Compass*, 8:11 (2010), pp. 1221–1242.
24. BPP 1822, vol. XX, no. 448, Report of the Commissioner of Inquiry into the State of the Colony of New South Wales, p. 165; BPP 1823, vol. XIV, no. 532, NSW, "Return of an address of the Honourable the House of Commons to His Majesty, dated 3rd of July 1823 for a copy of instructions given by Earl Bathurst to Mr. Bigge on his proceeding to NSW", Lord Bathurst, Secretary of State for War and the Colonies, to John Thomas Bigge, Chairman, 6 January 1819, p. 4.
25. *Ibid.*

a new penal settlement in 1824, they rejected Bigge's suggestions and opted instead to settle Norfolk Island in the Pacific. Bathurst believed that, rather than having the "worst description of convicts [...] placed in the midst of a thriving and prosperous colony", Norfolk Island should be occupied "upon the principle of a great Hulk or Penitentiary".[26] The penal system that Bigge created relied on distance as the primary mechanism of secondary punishment within the Australian colonies, which translated into officials selecting remote islands. For Norfolk Island to act as an effective deterrent to crime for the convict population, it had to be feared, and a distant island was a powerful image in the minds of the general public. As the Lieutenant-Governor of Van Diemen's Land, George Arthur, wrote, "being sent to Norfolk Island [...] should be considered a place of ultimate limit, and a punishment short of death".[27] The fact that Norfolk Island was so distant fed into rumours and myths about the "depravity" of the convicts who were sent there.[28] Far from being the "worst" convicts, the majority of Norfolk Island's inmates had been convicted of minor property crimes and a third were serving their original sentence of transportation.[29] The imaginary of Norfolk Island was so strong in the public mind that insularity became synonymous with isolation in the Australian context, as subsequent prison islands were all understood in relation to their Pacific counterpart.

The other colony that overhauled its convict system along the lines of Bigge's report was Van Diemen's Land. Officials here were equally drawn to islands as sites of secondary punishment. At the centre of Macquarie Harbour, a body of water twice as big as Sydney Harbour, was an archipelago of carceral islands. The main settlement, with shipyard, was the vast Sarah Island (also known as Settlement Island), which stretched from the pilot station to the shores of Macquarie Harbour.[30] Next door was the "detached fort" of Grummet Island (or Small Island), which housed a hospital and penitentiary.[31] In 1826, Lieutenant-Governor George Arthur wrote to the Colonial Office recommending its closure because of the encroachment of free settlers and the high rates of escape.[32] Between 1821 and 1832, there were 150 escape attempts involving 271 individuals, or

26. *HRA*, ser. I, vol. XI, Bathurst to Thomas Brisbane, Governor of NSW, 22 July 1824, p. 321.
27. *HRA*, ser. III, vol. VI, *HRA*, ser. III, vol. VI, Document E, George Arthur, Lieutenant-Governor of Van Diemen's Land [hereafter, VDL], to Wilmot Horton, Under-Secretary, 23 March 1827, p. 676.
28. Tim Causer, "'The Worst Types of Sub-human Beings'? The Myth and Reality of the Convicts of the Norfolk Island Penal Settlement, 1825–1855", *Islands of History* (Sydney, 2011), pp. 4, 8–31.
29. *Ibid.*, pp. 5–6, 16.
30. Hamish Maxwell-Stewart, *Closing Hell's Gates: The Death of a Convict Station* (Sydney, 2008), pp. 19–21.
31. *Ibid.*, pp. 19, 117–119.
32. *HRA*, ser. III, vol. V, Arthur to Hay, 4 September 1826, Hobart, p. 345.

nearly one in four of those who had been convicted of a second crime after being transported to the colony.[33] Lieutenant-Governor George Arthur's language mimicked Bigge's when he stressed that "as the Colony becomes more and more populated, the barrier between these wretched Criminals and the rest of the Community will be decreased, and escape will constantly become more easy".[34] Even if convicts were kept on islands overnight, they worked on the mainland, which presented an opportunity for escape. On similar grounds, Arthur criticised the penal settlement on Maria Island, which had been for the punishment of less "serious" secondary offenders a year earlier, in 1825. Situated just four kilometres east of the Tasmanian mainland, Arthur complained that "it is much too near the settled districts on the Main Land to be regarded as a safe depot for very desperate offenders".[35]

For this reason, Arthur suggested King Island, to the west of the Bass Strait, as a suitable alternative, from which escape would be almost impossible. However, Arthur noted that its warm climate and natural beauty made it more akin to a paradise, than a penitentiary, rendering it in some respects undesirable as a place of punishment. In 1827, Arthur once again put forward a new island penal settlement on Phillip Island – situated off the southern coast of Australian, near modern-day Melbourne. However, Phillip Island was far from a utopia: its dry soil and swampy interior made it economically unviable for convicts to cultivate the land, though Arthur believed it could still be a "viable temporary penal establishment".[36] In the same year, Arthur formed an executive committee on the problem of educated convicts, suggesting that they should be segregated from the corrupting influence of the general convict population. Arthur seemed certain that "an island may be found much more convenient and available than any district" to keep educated convicts separate from the rabble.[37] Similarly, the Colonial Treasurer, Jocelyn Thomas, claimed that "the various islands in the Bass Strait (King, Furneaux, Cape Barren etc. etc.) all afford eligible situations for Penal Settlements".[38] Many of these islands were later used for the confinement of Indigenous Australians (as will be discussed in the third section). This demonstrates the enduring appeal of islands as "natural prisons", though officials used different arguments to explain why a certain population was best suited for confinement there. Islands offered the possibility to protect society from "dangerous" convicts, but the isolation could also protect "gentlemen" convicts from corruption from a society made up of "ex-cons".

33. Maxwell-Stewart, Closing Hell's Gates, p. 198.
34. *Ibid.*
35. *Ibid.*
36. *Ibid.*
37. *HRA*, ser. III, vol. V, Arthur to Hay, 23 March 1827, Hobart, p. 668.
38. *Ibid.*, enclosure no. 6, Minute of Jocelyn Thomas, Acting Colonial Treasurer of VDL, 20 March 1827, p. 689.

In the mid-1830s, policymakers turned away from remote islands to urban islands located in the midst of city harbours as sites that balanced surveillance, security, and labour needs. In the preceding decade, the extraction of convict labour in penal settlements had become increasingly more important than punishment through "internal relocation to the peripheries of New South Wales".[39] From the mid-1830s, islands in Sydney Harbour – including Goat Island, Cockatoo Island, and Pinchgut Island – were used as sites of secondary punishment through hard labour. From 1833 to 1839, convicts on Goat Island quarried a gunpowder magazine, soldiers' barracks, and a wharf to fortify the harbour.[40] Between 1840 and 1841, convicts levelled the top of the island to build a military fortification on the colony's first prison, Pinchgut Island (now Fort Denison).[41] On the largest island in the harbour, Cockatoo, convicts spent over a decade from 1847 quarrying a dry dock directly into the sandstone base of the island, and then built and manned the workshops to repair and outfit ships until 1869.[42] Convicts were sometimes sent to the islands under sentence by magistrates (with powers awarded under the 1830 Offenders' Punishment and Transportation Act), but more often they were simply transferred from a road gang to an island gang. The Principal Superintendent of Convicts would send convicts deemed dangerous or likely to escape to these islands, which were perceived as sites of increased security despite their proximity to Sydney. In December 1840, for example, a convict found guilty of sexual assault of an Indigenous woman, two convicts suspected of bushranging, and nine convicts who had been re-transported from South Australia were sent to Goat Island (the latter awaiting transfer to Norfolk Island).[43] When John Carroll committed burglary the convicting magistrate recommended that he be punished "at a distance from Sydney, in consequence of [...] [his] desperate character".[44] With this in mind, Governor George Gipps instructed that he be "sent either to Cockatoo or Pinchgut Island", rather than mainland stockades that were several hundred kilometres distant from the capital. Clearly, officials viewed the islands of Sydney Harbour as both extra-punitive sites and locales for extra-mural convict labour.

39. Lisa Ford and David Andrew Roberts, "New South Wales Penal Settlements and the Transformation of Secondary Punishment in the Nineteenth-Century British Empire", *Journal of Colonialism and Colonial History*, 15:3 (2014).
40. Graham Connah, *The Archaeology of Australia's History* (Cambridge, 1988), p. 57.
41. Ian Hoskins, *Sydney Harbour: A History* (Sydney, 2009), p. 132.
42. Sue Castrique, "Under the Colony's Eye: Cockatoo Island and the Fitzroy Dock, 1847–1857", *Journal of the Royal Australian Historical Society*, 98:2 (2012), pp. 51–66.
43. State Records of New South Wales, 4/3891, Thomas Cudbert Harington, Acting Colonial Secretary, to Major George Barney, Commander of Royal Engineers, 9 December 1840, 11 December 1840, 17 December 1840, Sydney, pp. 124–125, 134.
44. *Ibid.*, Harington to Barney, 15 October 1840, Sydney, pp. 100–101.

In 1837, the British parliament commissioned a Select Committee on Transportation, which was chaired by Sir Henry Molesworth and comprised anti-slavery abolitionists and evangelicals. Based on testimony by a carefully selected set of anti-transportation witnesses, the committee concluded that the Australian convict system was characterized by excessive violence (flogging and chaining) and many forms of vice (including rape, sodomy, and child molestation).[45] When it became clear that convict transportation to New South Wales would likely cease, the former Secretary of State Viscount Howick issued a memorandum with a list of possible destinations for British and Irish convicts – all of them islands. He rejected the Ionian Islands off the coast of Greece, St Helena in the Atlantic, and the Falkland Islands off the coast of Argentina before settling on Norfolk Island as the best site.[46] This indicates there was a wider British imperial consensus about islands' suitability as penal colonies, and islands were also favoured as penal colonies in other empires (as is reflected in the essays that comprise this special issue).

The Colonial Office, eager to reform convict discipline along rehabilitative lines, offered Captain Alexander Maconochie the command of Norfolk Island to trial his system of penal reform on newly arrived convict transportees. Maconochie's "mark system" incentivized convicts to work hard and behave well by allowing them to earn time off their sentence through good conduct and labour.[47] However, Maconochie contested the choice of island, complaining that it was "too remote", "inaccessible", and "tropical" for profitable industry. In Maconochie's view, successful rehabilitation relied on prison labour reflecting real world economies as much as possible, making proximity to urban settlement more desirable. Instead, Maconochie suggested dividing the convicts – according to their behaviour – between two peninsulas of Van Diemen's Land and Maria Island off the eastern coast. He also put forward a similar spatial configuration of punishment whereby King Island in the Bass Strait would house the majority of convicts working in agriculture, and recalcitrant convicts would be sent to two small islands (New Year Island and Christmas Island), which would act as "penitentiaries for separate imprisonment [...] with little expense of masonry".[48] Maconochie was so confident that his scheme could

---

45. John Ritchie, "Towards Ending an Unclean Thing: The Molesworth Committee and the Abolition of Transportation to New South Wales, 1837–40", *Australian Historical Studies*, 17:67 (1976), pp. 144–164.

46. The National Archives (London) [hereafter, TNA], CO 201/302, Viscount Howick, Secretary of State for War and the Colonies, Memorandum, 23 November 1838, p. 321.

47. Raymond Nobbs (ed.), *Norfolk Island's and its Second Settlement* (Sydney, 1991); John Moore, "Alexander Maconochie's Mark System", *Prison Service Journal*, 198 (2011), pp. 38–46.

48. TNA, CO 201/288, Captain Alexander Maconochie, Commandant of Norfolk Island, to George Gipps, Governor of NSW, 13 November 1839, pp. 130–133.

incentivize good behaviour that he was eager to trial it on mainland road gangs, but Governor Gipps knew there would be public uproar if the scheme were trialled within the vicinity of free settlers: for Maconochie's "experiment" an island laboratory was needed.[49] In his letter to the Colonial Office in 1840, Gipps commented that all the natural geographical features that made Norfolk Island a good carceral island were the features Maconochie complained about: "namely, its remote situation, its insular character, its limited extent".[50]

It was incumbent upon Gipps to find a new penal settlement for secondarily transported convicts who needed to be removed from Norfolk Island. However, since convict transportation to New South Wales had ceased, Gipps could no longer transport convicts to penal settlements within the colony, leading him to pass legislation to remove convicts from penal settlements to any "site of hard labour".[51] Thus, relocation to islands continued, under a different legal sentence, as a regional practice after transportation between the metropole and colony had ceased. In February 1840, Gipps proposed that either Tasman's Peninsula or King Island in the Bass Strait replace Norfolk Island as "a new penal colony".[52] However, Governor John Franklin refused to accept secondarily transported convicts within the limits of Van Diemen's Land. Franklin, for his part, proposed Auckland Island, off the coast of New Zealand. In 1841, Lord Russell suggested Goat Island in Sydney Harbour, but Governor Gipps adapted his instructions to send convicts to another harbour island, Cockatoo Island, because it was not safe to send convicts to a "place already occupied by a magazine of gunpowder".[53] Despite being separated from Sydney's shore by just a few kilometres, Gipps insisted it was "the place of greatest security within the colony, not actually a prison".[54] Indeed, Gipps asserted that proximity was preferable to isolation when it came to secondary punishment, claiming that "stations for doubly convicted men, seem to me to have been erroneously placed at great distances from the seat of Government [...] [so they] have rarely, if ever, been visited by the Governor of the Colony, or by any person high in authority".[55] Cockatoo

49. TNA, CO 201/296, Gipps to Lord Russell, Secretary of State for the Colonies, 25 February 1840, p. 149.

50. *Ibid.*, p. 151.

51. An Act for the conditional remission of sentences of convicts transported to Norfolk Island and Moreton Bay, and to enforce the conditions thereof, 2 Vic. 1, 1838.

52. TNA, CO 201/296, Gipps to Russell, 27 February 1840, Sydney, pp. 173–174.

53. British Parliamentary Papers [hereafter, BPP] 1843, vol. XLII, no. 158, Convict Discipline: Copies of Extracts of any Correspondence between the Secretary of State and the Governor of Van Diemen's Land, on the subject of Convict Discipline, Part I, Gipps to Russell, 13 October 1841, pp. 11–13.

54. *Ibid.*

55. TNA, CO 201/286, Gipps to Lord Glenelg, Secretary of State for War and the Colonies, 8 July 1839, pp. 249–250.

Island, in the midst of Sydney Harbour, was both secure and easy to survey; or, as Gipps put it, Cockatoo Island was "surrounded [...] by deep water, and yet under the very eye of authority".[56]

Over the next five years, secondarily transported convicts were transferred from Norfolk Island to Cockatoo Island under a scheme that more than halved the terms of their remaining sentences. They were joined by the Superintendent of Agriculture, Charles Ormsby, who became Superintendent of Cockatoo Island from 1841.[57] The movement of both the Superintendent and a large body of convicts from one to the other led convict James Laurence to remark that Cockatoo Island was the same as Norfolk Island in every respect, except for the fact that Cockatoo was a "small island".[58] This marks a decisive shift away from isolation as punishment, which was replaced with hard labour for the public benefit, but with the added value of the security offered by water and walls to keep the felons in. Despite Cockatoo Island's proximity to Sydney, Godfrey Charles Munday described it as a "natural hulk", using the same descriptor as Lord Bathurst had for Norfolk Island.[59] Long after the majority of secondarily transported convicts had left, and Cockatoo Island effectively operated as a local gaol, it retained its associations with the convict system through its Pacific predecessor. In an 1857 inquiry, Cockatoo Island was dubbed a "worse hell-on-earth even than Norfolk Island", and Henry Parkes claimed that the superintendent "Mr. Ormsby is so isolated, as much indeed as if he were a thousand miles off in the Pacific".[60] Despite their clearly opposite geographies in relation to the mainland – the former just one-and-a half kilometres and the other 1,500 kilometres away from Sydney – they were considered comparable due to their insularity. Though from the mid-1830s a clear shift had taken place in favour of proximate urban islands, in the public mind islands were by definition "isolated" – an idea dating back to Robinson Crusoe's "desert island" (1719), which was further entrenched in the Australian colonies through Norfolk Island's

---

56. *Ibid.*
57. TNA, CO 201/310, Maconochiem Judgement in Ormsby's Case, 16 June 1841; TNA, CO 201/296, Gipps to Russell, 24 February 1840, Sydney, no. 27, p. 137; "The Board of Inquiry into the Management of Cockatoo Island", *Votes and Proceedings of the Legislative Assembly*, vol. II, no. 17 (Sydney, 1858), p. 298.
58. BPP 1847, vol. VII, no. 534, Second Report from the Select Committee of the House of Lords appointed to inquire into the execution of the criminal law, especially respecting juvenile offenders and transportation, together with the minutes of evidence taken before the said committee and an appendix, testimony of "A.B." (James Laurence), 26 April 1847, pp. 448–449; Rob Wills, *Alias Blind Larry: The Mostly True Memoir of James Laurence the Singing Convict* (Melbourne, 2015), pp. 272–280.
59. Godfrey Charles Munday, *Our Antipodes: Or, Residence and Rambles in the Australasian Colonies, with a Glimpse of the Gold Fields* (London, 1852), p. 111.
60. "The Board of Inquiry into the Management of Cockatoo Island", p. 298.

mythology. This led officials to believe that Australian islands were a better deterrent and were more suitable for the "worst" offenders.

CONFINEMENT OF INDIGENOUS AUSTRALIANS

The third purpose that the colonial government used carceral islands for was to confine Indigenous people. In the 1830s, the colonial government established "Aboriginal Settlements" on a series of islands off the coast of Van Diemen's Land. During the Black War, Lieutenant-Governor George Augustus Robinson convinced Indigenous Tasmanians fleeing from settler violence to voluntarily go to islands for their own "protection". These temporary measures became permanent establishments that Indigenous inhabitants were not allowed to leave, and where they were subjected to poor living conditions, restrictive routines, and punishment. Thus, they operated like carceral institutions, despite the evasive language of the archive. According to N.J.B. Plomley, for the colonial administration it was always a question of which "island [was] suitable for aboriginal settlement".[61] The "Aborigines Committee" was charged with finding the best site for the reserve and considered Maria Island, King Island, Bruny Island, and the Hunter Islands in the Bass Strait as possible locations.[62] The committee were looking for an island large enough for the Indigenous inhabitants to roam freely and with an abundance of game for them to hunt.[63] This showed the government's intention for Indigenous people to live as "hunter-gatherers", though they ignored both the ecological and cultural connection between the many different communities represented on the island and their particular homelands. This was only partially recognized by the committee's fear that if the island were in sight of the mainland then the Indigenous Tasmanians would "pine away", meaning that homesickness would cause their health to deteriorate. The coercive nature of these island reserves is clear as the committee repeatedly insists that the island could not be too close to the mainland, otherwise the Indigenous Tasmanians would swim across and escape. In 1831, the committee noted that a benefit of choosing Maria Island, formerly a penal establishment for European convicts, would be re-using the prisoners' barracks and having the police crew on Lacklan's Island sweep the water for escapees.[64] The overlapping of carceral spaces for European convicts undergoing punishment and Indigenous Australians under government

---

61. N.J.B. Plomley, *Weep in Silence: A History of the Flinders Island Aboriginal Settlement with the Flinders Island Journal of George Augustus Robinson, 1835–1839* (Hobart, 1987), p. 13.
62. *Ibid.*, pp. 13–43.
63. BPP 1834, Papers Relative to the Aboriginal Tribes in British Possessions, Minute of Aborigines Committee, 28 September 1831, p. 161.
64. *Ibid.*

"protection" suggests how malleable and persistent islands were as sites of incarceration and coercion, though ideas of "race" shaped how these policies were presented and understood.

It was George Augustus Robinson who actually surveyed these islands for their suitability as a settlement. After convincing the first party of Indigenous Tasmanians to join him on Swan Island in November 1830, they were transferred to different islands – including to Clarke Island and Preservation Island – as he inspected them before settling on Gun Carriage Island in May 1831.[65] A lack of fresh water and poor access for ships led to the abandonment of Gun Carriage Island and a move to Flinders Island in 1833 due to its good anchorage, warm weather, abundant game, and access to fresh water.[66] In reality, extremely poor conditions prevailed on the island, leading to the death of half of the Indigenous population of the island due to neglect, malnourishment, trauma, and disease.[67] These conditions were resisted by the community on the island. In March 1847, eight inhabitants petitioned Queen Victoria, complaining about being treated as prisoners on Flinders. They wrote that they "freely gave up our country to Colonal [sic] Arthur […] after defending ourself" and that they were "a quiet and free people and not put in gaol".[68]

These failures were explained away by Robinson in his 1837 report to the Colonial Office through the idea that Indigenous people were "weak" and would inevitably become extinct after their encounter with the superior white race. On these islands, they were at least not victim to settler violence, and they were "civilized" by being taught both farming techniques and Christian principles. The Colonial Office readily accepted this fiction because Robinson's island settlements seemed to align with the 1835–1837 British Parliamentary Select Committee on Aboriginal Tribes, which recommended appointing "protectors" to prevent settler violence and encourage "civilization" through Christian teachings.[69] Islands epitomized the Colonial Office's justification for imperial conquest of Indigenous lands through "humanitarian" governance. Sending Indigenous people to islands effectively cleared the way for European settlement, but without visibly imprisoning them, offering instead limited mobility in a natural environment.

65. Plomley, *Weep in Silence*, p. 15.
66. *Ibid.*, p. 21.
67. James Boyce, "Appendix: Towards Genocide: Government Policy on the Aborigines, 1827–38", in *idem, Van Diemen's Land* (Melbourne, 2010), pp. 261–313.
68. "Petition to Her Majesty Queen Victoria", 17 February 1847, in Bain Attwood and Andrew Markus (eds), *The Struggle for Aboriginal Rights: A Documentary History* (Sydney, 1999), pp. 38–39; Henry Reynolds, *Fate of a Free People* (Ringwood, 1995), p. 15.
69. Alan Lester and Fae Dussart, *Colonization and the Origins of Humanitarian Governance: Protecting Aborigines across the Nineteenth-Century British Empire* (Cambridge, 2014).

In Western Australia, Governor Hutt pursued a policy based on the Committee's suggestions by appointing Protectors of Aborigines who would administer British law on behalf of, and more often against, Indigenous peoples to "protect" them from settler violence.[70] In this view, punishment was actually protection. So even when the failure of Flinders Island was known, the Colonial Office still "aggressively pursued a policy [...] that attempted to replicate Robinson's fantasy island", including in the newly settled colony of Western Australia.[71] As early as 1830, barrister and Western Australian colonist George Fletcher Moore said he feared violent conflict unless members of the Indigenous Nyoongar community were "removed wholesale to some island".[72] In 1832, Carnac Island, off the coast of Fremantle, was used to detain a group of Nyoongar resistance leaders, including Yagan and Midigoroo. They were treated as prisoners of war and had their capital sentences commuted to confinement on Carnac Island at the recommendation of surveyor John Septimus Roe. After just a month, the prisoners escaped to the mainland on an unattended dinghy and were eventually shot and killed by the authorities.[73] In July 1838, the government established a permanent and "humanitarian" prison for Indigenous men on neighbouring Rottnest Island. It believed that the eighteen kilometres that separated the island from the mainland made escape so difficult for the Indigenous convicts that they could be worked without chains and be allowed to hunt and roam regularly without compromising security. This was necessary because, as was stated in the 1840 Act to Constitute Rottnest a Legal Prison, "the close confinement of a gaol [...] [had] been found to operate most prejudicially to their health".[74] In the early years, the policy pursued on the island reflected those on missions, as prisoners were taught agriculture and allowed to roam and hunt on the island on Sundays.[75]

Yet, underlying these official humanitarian reasons was deterrence: as Rottnest was "winnaitch" (or forbidden) for Nyoongar Whadiuk as a realm for bad spirits.[76] Thus, the colonial administration argued that

70. Amanda Nettelbeck, "'A Halo of Protection': Colonial Protectors and the Principle of Aboriginal Protection through Punishment", *Australian Historical Studies*, 43:3 (2012), pp. 396–411.

71. Tom Lawson, *The Last Man: A British Genocide in Tasmania* (London, 2014), p. 108.

72. George Fletcher Moore, *Diary of Ten Years Eventful Life of an Early Settler in Western Australia* (London, 1884), p. 215.

73. Neville Green, *Broken Spears: Aborigines and Europeans in the Southwest of Australia* (Perth, 1984), pp. 82–84.

74. BPP 1844, vol. XXXIV, no. 627, Aborigines (Australian colonies), "An Act to Constitute Rottnest a Legal Prison", 2 July 1840, p. 375.

75. TNA, CO 18/31, John Hutt, Governor of Western Australia, to Russell, 1 March 1843, Perth, pp. 82–83; Neville Green and Susan Moon, *Far From Home: Aboriginal Prisoners of Rottnest Island, 1838–1931* (Nedlands, 1998), p. 16.

76. Glen Stasiuk, "Wadjemup: Rottnest Island as Black Prison and White Playground" (Ph.D., Murdoch University, 2015), pp. 27–28.

transportation to Rottnest elicited a particular kind of dread that could not be replicated by local imprisonment or even capital punishment.[77] In the Tasmanian context, the island was seen by the Colonial Office as a sliver of land to replace what had been conquered. On Rottnest Island, in contrast, the cultural meaning of the island was used as a deterrence. As late as 1884, a Nyoongar prisoner named Bob Thomas told a commission that "Natives do not like the sea voyage [...] Rottnest is dreaded by the natives".[78]

In 1847, George Augustus Robinson described Rottnest Island in a way that showed clear parallels with its predecessor Flinders Island, though he made no explicit comparison.

> At Western Australia an island is appropriated exclusively to their [Indigenous peoples'] use and judging from the reports of the Rottnest establishment the best results have been realized, could a similar boon be conceded to the aborigines convicted of a crime in these colonies, banishment instead of a curse would be a blessing and expatriation an advantage.[79]

This shows that the colonial administration was intent on presenting islands as "boons" and "blessings" to the Indigenous populations who were (in Robinson's own words) "banished" from their country. This encapsulates the ambiguity of colonial governance that justified territorial acquisition and economic gain through their presumed superiority. Studying islands is an important part of recognizing the spatial trajectories of the criminal justice system as applied to Indigenous Australians. In particular, the political and social imperative to eliminate Indigenous communities – conceptually, physically, or politically – in order to clear "space" for colonizers. Since the majority of prisoners were serving sentences for theft (mostly of livestock), and were often prosecuted as a group, transportation to Rottnest effectively dispossessed Indigenous communities, just as the Tasmanian reserves had.[80] A key difference between the two was that no women were incarcerated on Rottnest, though by removing so many men it still effectively disrupted Indigenous

---

77. BPP 1844, vol. XXXIV, no. 627, Aborigines (Australian colonies), Hutt to Russell, Perth, 15 May 1841, p. 380.

78. *Ibid.*

79. Ian Clark (ed.), *The Journals of George Augustus Robinson, Chief Protector, Port Phillip Aboriginal Protectorate, Vol. 4: 1 January 1844–24 October 1845* (Melbourne, 1998); George Augustus Robinson, "Annual Report for 1845", p. 101, quoted in Kristyn Harman, "Aboriginal Convicts: Race, Law and Transportation (Ph.D., University of Tasmania, 2008), p. 293.

80. 956 of 1,682 Indigenous prisoners whose offence was listed in the Rottnest Island prison register (1855–1881) were sentenced for theft, and of these twenty-three per cent was for "stealing", with no item specified, and eighteen per cent for livestock theft. This is the author's analysis of State Records of Western Australia [hereafter, SROWA], cons. 130, Commitment Book [Rottnest Island]. According to Neville Green, Rottnest prisoners sentenced between 1841 and 1849 were convicted "mostly [for] theft, sheep spearing, threats to settlers and tribal disputes". See Green and Moon, *Far From Home*, p. 18.

communities and weakened resistance to European conquest of "country". The colonial government briefly considered a scheme for incarcerating Indigenous women, making a deal with James Reid on Garden Island to confine short-sentenced Indigenous women at a cost to the Treasury of nine pence per person per day.[81] No more mention of this scheme appears in the Colonial Secretary's correspondence and it did not become an institutionalized practice. Thus, we see Flinders Island was the model for a constellation of island sites in Western Australia, which by virtue of being "natural prison hulks" satisfied a contradictory logic of "punishment" and "protection" in the colonial context.

CONCLUSION

This article has shown that "punitive relocation" to offshore islands was an important part of the colonial system of punishment that emerged in Australia between 1788 and 1901. It operated as a system because colonial officials in Australia and London compared islands to one another, explicitly modelling future establishments on the perceived successes or failures of the past. Islands were flexible spaces, and sending convicts to them fulfilled various aspects of colonial governmentality, including territorial acquisition, commercial expansion, and the governance of both European convicts and Indigenous populations. Colonial officials viewed the same islands differently, depending on whether they would incarcerate Indigenous or European convicts, showing how "race" inflected criminal-justice policies. Colonial penal regimes were also distinct from metropolitan ones in the emphasis on labour extraction, which hinged on convicts' mobility outside prison walls. Islands were no exception, because though they may have been relatively isolated from the mainland, making them ideal for punishment, they were often relatively connected to sea routes. This series of punitive relocations made offshore islands into "enclaves" of (often fragile) empire-building, whilst serving an important purpose for colonial governance. Rather than viewing the colonies as homogenous spaces, defined in relation to the metropole, this article has focused on islands as peripheral spaces *within* the Australia colonies. The use of distance as punishment, even across "micro-geographies", is usually side-lined in favour of convict flows between metropole and colony, or between two distant colonies. The importance of taking a "view from the colonies" is underlined by the fact that inter- and intra-colonial punitive relocation to islands, though small, transcended the cessation of transportation from the metropole to Australian colonies, and persisted under different guises into the twentieth century.

---

81. SROWA, acc. 36, vol. 212, Colonial Secretary Inward Correspondence, Aborigines, 2 January–3 December 1851, Charles Symmons, Guardian of Aborigines, to Thomas Yule, Acting Colonial Secretary, 22 October 1851, Perth, p. 475.

IRSH 63 (2018), Special Issue, pp. 65–88 doi:10.1017/S0020859018000226
© 2018 Internationaal Instituut voor Sociale Geschiedenis

The Carceral Colony: Colonial Exploitation, Coercion, and Control in the Dutch East Indies, 1810s–1940s

M ATTHIAS VAN ROSSUM

International Institute of Social History
Cruquiusweg 31, 1019 AT Amsterdam, The Netherlands

E-mail: mvr@iisg.nl

ABSTRACT: This article studies the strategic disciplinary and productive function of the colonial penal system of the Dutch East Indies (1816–1942). Developing convict labour as the main punishment for minor public and labour offences, the Dutch colonial regime created an increasingly effective system of exploitation that weaved together colonial discipline, control, and coercion. This system was based on two major *carceral connections*: firstly, the interrelated development and employment of different coerced labour regimes, and, secondly, the disciplinary role of the legal-carceral regime within the wider colonial project, supporting not only the management of public order and labour control, but also colonial production systems. Punishment of colonial subjects through "administrative justice" (police law) accelerated in the second half of the nineteenth century, leading to an explosion in the number of convictions. The convict labour force produced by this carceral regime was vital for colonial production, supporting colonial goals such as expansion, infrastructure, extraction, and production. The Dutch colonial system was a very early, but quite advanced, case of a colonial carceral state.

INTRODUCTION: CARCERAL CONNECTIONS

Although the course of history is often portrayed as one in which modernization and, more recently, globalization have propelled the world forward on a path of increasing freedom, the impact of historical lines of coercive, incarcerating, and disciplining strategies cannot be ignored. It can even be argued that coercion and incarceration are not diminishing, but are one of the trends affecting labour relations in a globalizing world, alongside those of increasing wage labour, growing precariousness, and the declining power of labour organizations.[1] In any attempt to understand these "long"

---

1. As argued in M. van Rossum, "Redirecting Global Labor History?", in C. Antunes and K. Fatah-Black (eds), *Explorations in History and Globalization* (London, 2016), pp. 47–62. For the general trends in the world of work, see J. Lucassen, *Een geschiedenis van de arbeid in grote lijnen*,

lines, or "deep" histories, of practices of coercion and incarceration, the colonial links are key. In the crucial and transformative colonial era, European imperial projects deeply impacted societies in South and South East Asia, changing them from often developed and sometimes market-oriented societies into colonial societies marked by state-directed bonded and tributary labour regimes. This not only brings together the histories of Europe and Asia – which are all too often studied in a disconnected fashion – but also brings to light the interconnections between histories of coercion, incarceration, and exploitation. Shifting the perspective to that of the colonies, therefore, means more than shifting the centre of attention in an attempt to chart lesser studied terrain, or to provincialize Europe. It is a crucial step in understanding some of the major global linkages and processes behind the transformation of the modern world.

This article aims to contribute to shifting this perspective by studying the operation of the carceral system in the Dutch East Indies. It indicates, firstly, that the development of different labour relations that were coerced (convict and slave labour) or marked by strong coercive elements (*corvée* and contract labour) was interrelated. Secondly, it argues that there were deep links between the penal system and wider regimes of colonial-administrative and labour control. Combined, these two different *carceral connections* underpinned the colonial system and were crucial for accelerating the mobilization of coerced convict labour in the second half of the nineteenth century. This was no coincidence, as the second half of this article shows. The system was geared towards the employment of convict labour in vital parts of the colonial economy. We go on to emphasize the pivotal function of the penal system in the wider colonial project, but also the entanglement of colonial regimes of production and control.

The historiography of convict labour and convict transportation is well developed. Convict transportations from Britain to North America and to Australia have received the most attention among scholars, although interest has now shifted to the Indian Ocean and other parts of the British Empire.[2] In the case of the Dutch Empire in the nineteenth and twentieth centuries, the historiography is much less rich. Whereas we now have an extensive literature on the history of colonial labour systems, the penal

---

valedictory lecture (Amsterdam, 2012); for an English translation, see https://socialhistory.org/en/publications/outlines-history-labour.

2. See the introduction to this special issue for a more detailed elaboration of the historiography. See also C.G. De Vito and A. Lichtenstein, *Global Convict Labour* (Leiden, 2015). For the Indian Ocean World, see, for example, A. Yang, "Indian Convict Workers in Southeast Asia in the Late Eighteenth and Early Nineteenth Centuries", *Journal of World History*, 14:2 (2003), pp. 179–208; Clare Anderson, *Subaltern Lives: Biographies of Colonials in the Indian Ocean World, 1790–1920* (Cambridge, 2012).

system has mainly been studied through specific elements, such as the police system, punishment, and prisons.[3]

The wider functioning of the Dutch colonial penal system remains understudied. In her study of the notorious Ombilin coal mines, Erwiza Erman touched on some of the local dynamics of convict labour.[4] In an overview dealing with the decline of slavery, Anthony Reid observed both the persistent character of the *corvée* labour system and the increasing importance of convict labour. Contrasting the use of convicts with that of *corvée* workers and slaves, who "could not be sent far from home", he argued that "the Netherlands Indian government made use of convicts" "to open up the frontiers of the colony". In the process, convicts "became overwhelmingly dominant as a form of punishment for every type of crime".[5] Reid's observations aptly capture the importance and strategic use of convict labour but leave under-examined the vital link between the penal system and the wider colonial disciplinary and coercive labour regimes.

FROM SLAVERY TO *CORVÉE* AND CONVICT LABOUR

It is crucial to note two characteristics of the Dutch colonial penal system. First, the Dutch colonial penal system was not based on the export of convicts from the metropole to the colony. The flows from the Netherlands to the colonies, and vice versa, were minimal. Most convicts were from the colonies, and remained there. Within the colony, long distance and local circuits existed side by side. Second, the Dutch colonial case does not indicate a clear or linear development towards the imprisonment of convicts in rehabilitative prisons. Although the worksites where convicts were placed were increasingly labelled "prisons" (*gevangenissen*), most convicts were employed at "extramural" convict labour sites, especially in mines, and on infrastructural or military projects.

This system evolved from largely pre-existing patterns developed in the seventeenth and eighteenth centuries by the Dutch East India Company

---

3. Jan Breman, *Mobilizing Labour for the Global Coffee Market: Profits From an Unfree Work Regime in Colonial Java* (Amsterdam, 2015), available at: http://www.oapen.org/search?identifier=597440; last accessed 17 May 2018; M. Bloembergen, *De geschiedenis van de politie in Nederlands-Indië. Uit zorg en angst* (Amsterdam, 2009); A.M.C. Bruinink-Darlang, *Het penitentiair stelsel in Nederlands-Indië van 1905 tot 1940* (Alblasserdam, 1986); P. Consten, "Geweld in dienst van de koloniale discipline. Een onderzoek naar de afschaffing van de straf van rottingslagen op Java", *Tijdschrift voor Sociale Geschiedenis*, 24:2 (1998), pp. 138–158.
4. Erman Erwiza, *Miners, Managers and the State: A Socio-political History of the Ombilin Coalmines, West Sumatra, 1892–1996* (Amsterdam, 1996).
5. A. Reid, "The Decline of Slavery in Nineteenth-Century Indonesia", in Martin Klein (ed.), *Breaking the Chains: Slavery, Bondage, and Emancipation in Modern Africa and Asia* (London, 1993), pp. 64–82.

Figure 1. Forced labourers at work repairing a railway line for the Aceh tram at Meureudu on the stretch from Sigli to Samalanga. 1905.
KITLV 90437. Creative Commons CC-BY License.

(VOC). The VOC employed convicts for hard labour in various urban public works and on five convict islands: Onrust and Edam (near Batavia), Rosingain (Banda), Robben Island (Cape of Good Hope), and Allelande (Tuticorin). On the islands, convicts were employed at the wharf, the rope factory, or in collecting limestone, shells, or wood. The urban public works (*gemeene werken*) consisted of convict quarters (*kettinggangerskwartier*) from where convicts were sent out mainly to work on infrastructure (roads, canals) and fortifications.[6] This system remained in place after the VOC's possessions had been assumed by the Dutch state (1815) following an intermediate period of British rule. Power was only effectively transferred after April 1816.

Patterns of incarceration and use of convict labour changed only gradually, corresponding to the evolving strategies of colonial exploitation in the nineteen and twentieth centuries. In the first few decades of its existence, the

6. For a complete overview, see M. van Rossum, "The Dutch East India Company in Asia, 1595–1811", in C. Anderson (ed.), *A Global History of Convicts and Penal Colonies* (Bloomsbury, 2018), pp. 157–182; K. Ward, *Networks of Empire: Forced Migration in the Dutch East India Company* (Cambridge, 2008).

Figure 2. Accommodation in the Bengkulu residence at Seluma for *herendienst* conscripts from Aer Priokan. 1920.
KITLV 32353. Creative Commons CC-BY License.

new colonial state further developed a refined system of mobilization of labour through compulsory labour services (*herendiensten*) in combination with the compulsory cultivation of market crops (*cultuurstelsel*). This entailed large-scale *corvée* by local populations, employed for plantation work, infrastructure, and public services. The simultaneous increase in *corvée* and convict labour was not coincidental. These forms of coerced labour were deeply connected, and their rise was related to the changing landscape of possibilities available to the colonial state in employing labour.

Here we encounter our first carceral connection. The abolition of the slave trade stimulated the search for alternative forms of cheap and controllable labour. The expansion and intensification of *corvée* labour systems was a response to the rising labour demands brought about by the colonial aim of maximizing the commercial exploitation of the colony. The growing use of convict labour in places such as Banda and Banka was linked to this combination of exploitative aims and the limited scope to employ slave labour in a similar fashion. Throughout the seventeenth and eighteenth centuries, slaves had been an important part of the workforce in the same places in which convicts were later employed. Convicts were sent to replace slaves, but also to replace other labourers in mines (Banka; Padang), on urban *public works* (Batavia; Semarang), and on plantations (Banda; Java).

As early as 1819, the Resident of Banka "proposed to send 300 to 400 *kettinggangers* from Java to here, in order to be able to discharge the Chinese workers". He suggested that "if such a number of convicts were not readily available", "the convicts who are destined for Banda" should be sent to Banka.[7] As late as 1837, reports from colonial administrators were still considering "the possibility to transfer 400 Balinese [enslaved] women for the *landsperken* on Banda", but such plans were abandoned as being incompatible with the ban on the trade in slaves.[8] Contract workers and convicts took their place. By the mid-nineteenth century, it was reported that "the number of banished, who are placed in the gardens as well as on other works, present at Banda-Neira, is replenished yearly through the supply from Java. This number should normally be 1,500 to 1,600 heads, but in 1845 it was merely 1,387 men, with 400 women and children".[9]

COLONIAL LAW AND COERCIVE LABOUR REGIMES

The second carceral connection lies hidden in the mechanisms developed to secure public order and control labour through the local administration of justice. To explain this, it is important to first highlight the colonial legal system in relation to the control of colonial labour. The colonial judicial system in the Dutch East Indies consisted of a range of courts, varying from the Raad van Justitie (High Court of Justice) in Batavia to local courts of justice (for Europeans), and *landraden*, police judges, and local courts (for colonial subjects).[10] Only the most serious criminal cases, such as murder or major theft, punishable by longer sentences, were dealt with by the criminal courts. All "minor" offences and other crimes were dealt with under the *politierol*. This police or magistrate law was executed by local colonial officials without extensive legal procedures, and dealt especially with labour, mobility, and public order offences.

Administrative (or police) law became pivotal in expanding colonial control and coercive colonial labour mobilization. On Java, the foundations for these dynamics were established in the eighteenth century when greater VOC interference, especially in Preanger (West Java), led to increasing demands for the local population to supply market crops, especially coffee and indigo. The local population performed *herendiensten* for their own leaders, but were now frequently deployed by the VOC to work on plantations, infrastructure, and transportation. The VOC claimed that these

---

7. Nationaal Archief, The Hague [hereafter, NA], Archief Koloniën, 1814–1849, archive number 2.10.01, inventory number 2452, n16.
8. NA, 2.10.01, 3088.
9. J.B.J. van Doren, *Herinneringen der laatste oogenblikken van mijn verblijf in de Molukko's* (The Hague, 1852), pp. 43–45.
10. Bruinink-Darlang, *Het penitentiair stelsel*, pp. 24–28.

were a continuation of pre-VOC traditions, but duties seem to have intensified. In response to the increasing number of "desertions" – people evading *corvée* obligations by fleeing to other areas – new regulations were implemented to bind local populations more directly to local heads of districts (1728) and to criminalize refusal to comply with the compulsory delivery of produce and goods. The VOC was unable to completely effectuate these regulations and increased the severity of the punishment meted out to "deserters" in the second half of the eighteenth century (1778) to include physical punishment and, for a repeat offence, convict labour "in chains" for six months.[11]

This mechanism accelerated under Dutch state colonialism. *Herendiensten* were further intensified from the early nineteenth century onwards and extended to entire districts. *Corvée* labourers were employed in constructing infrastructure (roads, canals, bridges, buildings), in transport (goods, post, and personnel), in maintenance and service activities (demanded by local colonial officials), but also in local community services (cleaning, policing, watching over plantations).[12] Similar rules existed for the owners of "private land", although the state explicitly preserved its rights over the *corvée* obligations of local populations as well.[13] Despite increasing anti-colonial criticism and the abolition of the *cultuurstelsel* in the second half of the nineteenth century, these *herendiensten* would remain an important phenomenon throughout the nineteenth century and well into the twentieth century. They were slowly abolished for Java and Madura in the early twentieth century, but were continued in the Outer Districts right until the end of the colonial period. In the 1880s and 1890s, a large proportion of the population of Java and Madura, roughly some three million people, were still obliged to perform these services, sometimes even up to fifty-two days a year. The total number of days' compulsory service slowly declined, but it was still some twenty million on Java and Madura in 1895.[14] It was not until the 1920s that it became possible to substitute monetary taxation for *corvée* labour.[15]

Simultaneously, the nineteenth century witnessed increasing labour mobilization through the use of contracts. The restrictive elements of labour contracts were obvious in the special "penal laws on coolie contracts", issued for Sumatra from the 1870s onwards to safeguard the fulfilment of labour contracts, criminalizing the labour offences committed by "coolies". However, in the "regular" labour contracts that were in use,

---

11. Breman, *Mobilizing Labour*, pp. 75–85.
12. *Ibid.*; Bloembergen, *De geschiedenis van de politie in Nederlands-Indië*.
13. "Reglement voor de partikuliere landerijen, gelegen ten Westen de rivier Tjimanok, op Java", 28 February 1836, *Staatsblad*.
14. Centrale Commissie voor de Statistiek, *Jaarcijfers Koloniën 1895* (The Hague, 1897).
15. Reid, "The Decline of Slavery", pp. 74–75.

especially on Java and much earlier on Madura, similar criminalizing restrictions bound workers to their contracts and turned mobility (or "exit") into a punishable offence. The regulations relating to "private land" in West Java drafted in the early nineteenth century provided a means to ensure that "hirelings", who were employed for more than three months, were registered by the landowner with the local authorities. Their contracts were limited to three years, but renewal was possible after registration. The regulations intended to ensure that contract workers signed "freely", but also dictated that "local authorities were to closely inspect" whether

> workers or hirelings, in turn, perform all to which they have committed them-selves, making sure that when they are in breach of this, desert or evade their duties, either due to excessive laziness or unwillingness, they will be punished in accordance with the nature of the matter and in accordance with existing laws and regulations.[16]

This was exactly what created a connection between *corvée* labour, contract labour, and the practice of magistrate (or police) law. *Corvée* duties were performed partly through compulsory participation in local policing, watch and patrol tasks, and through taking care of security and order in the villages and on the lands.[17] In addition to a whole range of social (and increasingly political) issues for which the local police were employed, this explicitly included inspecting and enforcing compliance with the *herendiensten* as well as with labour contracts, both the general contracts (often referred to as "free") as well as the "coolie" contracts (non-com-pliance with which could lead to penal sanctions).[18] In 1836, the regulations stated that the local authorities in West Java, to which police matters were reported, were authorized to

> inspect and decide without any higher authority all matters of crime or offence, and breach of the rules decided in the present regulation [for private lands], and, whenever there are no special sanctions, to sanction Europeans, their descendants, or equals with a fine of up to fifty guilders, or imprisonment of up to eight days; and a native or equal with a) a fine of up twenty-five guilders; b) imprisonment of up to fourteen days; c) punishment by being beaten with a rattan stick, up to a maximum of twenty-five strokes; d) employment on public works, for up to three months, without chains, for one's livelihood, but without a wage.[19]

---

16. "Reglement voor de partikuliere landerijen".
17. Bloembergen, *De geschiedenis van de politie in Nederlands-Indië*; "Reglement voor de par-tikuliere landerijen", articles 50–59.
18. Bloembergen, *De geschiedenis van de politie in Nederlands-Indië*, p. 299. Even as late as 1934, people were arrested in the Moluccas for not performing *corvée* labour.
19. "Reglement voor de partikuliere landerijen", article 60.

THE CARCERAL COLONY

The arrangements could vary from region to region, and they changed over time. However, in general, "minor" offences and crimes were dealt with at the local level under the *politierol* –police law.[20] These "minor" offences and crimes included those relating to labour regulations (and restrictions) for contract workers, workers subject to coolie laws, and *corvée* workers. In the second half of the nineteenth century, the cases trialled under the *politierol* were recorded in the colonial judicial statistics as *magistraatsrecht* (magistrate law). Governors, assistant governors, and district heads were empowered to judge minor crimes and offences under the *politierol*.[21] These locally administered sentences led to ever growing numbers of convicts serving short-term sentences for minor, more often labour-related offences. The form of convict labour referred to as *tenarbeidstelling* (being put to work) was the most frequently used sentence for these short-term convictions, ranging from a few days to three months.

At the level of the criminal courts, such as the *landraden* and Raad van Justitie, sentences were of longer duration. Here, the main type of punishment was mid- to long-term convict labour, which could be either in or outside the district, and with or without chains. Convicts sentenced to forced labour for more than three months were not registered under *tenarbeidstelling* (short-term convict labour), but under *dwangarbeid* (long-term convict labour). Their numbers were included in the prison population, while the short-term convicts seem not to have been included in these statistics.

The distinction between short-term local or regional punishment and long-term punishment with the possibility of long-distance displacement would remain until the end of the colonial period. In 1946, Jonkers' handbook on Dutch East Indies criminal law explained that "the prime difference between a prison sentence [*gevangenisstraf*] and detention [*hechtenis*] was that the prisoner could be sent everywhere to serve his punishment, while the detained does not have to serve *against* his will *outside* the district in which he resided at the time the punishment is executed". In this context, the detained included individuals convicted under police law – for "culpable crimes and offences" – but also those detained while awaiting trial.[22] The essence of all forms of colonial punishment, however, remained convict labour. The handbook further noted that everyone "sentenced to prison or to detention could be *compelled* to perform labour both inside and outside the walls". The number of hours to be worked was nine hours per day for prisoners and eight hours for those detained. The "nature of the labour" was

20. Bruinink-Darlang, *Het penitentiair stelsel*.
21. Bloembergen, *De geschiedenis van de politie in Nederlands-Indië*; Breman, *Mobilizing Labour*; Bruinink-Darlang, *Het penitentiair stelsel*.
22. J.E. Jonkers, *Handboek van het Nederlandsch-Indische Strafrecht* (Leiden, 1946), pp. 182–185.

to be organized by the Director of Justice. Convicts would "receive monetary reward only for the work performed *in excess of the number of hours per day they were required to work*".[23]

The nineteenth and twentieth centuries witnessed a remarkable rise in the number of long-term convicts in the Dutch East Indies, with the average population "in prison" growing from 10,000 in 1870 to 57,000 in 1920.[24] This was preceded by a much larger growth in the number of sentences for short-term convict labour (*tenarbeidstelling*) under the *politierol*. The final decades of the nineteenth century witnessed a rapid rise in the number of such sentences – from 69,500 per annum in 1870 to 275,000 per annum in 1900.[25]

In part, this can be explained as an effect of the abolition in 1866 of the *rotanstraf* – a punishment that involved being whipped with a rattan or bamboo stick.[26] The relationship between the sharp rise in short-term convict labour and the abolition of whipping as a formal punishment was also noted in the colonial press, and it effects were debated.[27] On Java and Madura, however, another important factor may have been the slowly diminishing labour output provided by *herendiensten*. Although the size of the population on Java and Madura tied to such obligations grew from 9.6 million in 1886 to 11.1 million in 1895, the total number of days deployed in *corvée* services declined from 26.4 million per annum in 1886 to 20.6 million in 1895. These statistics provide only a limited perspective on the effects of centralized colonial attempts to restore the role of *corvée* labour. They should also be used with care as they exclude compulsory local municipal labour services.[28] As the formal supply of *corvée* labour slowly declined, and whipping simultaneously disappeared as a means to ensure the mobilization and discipline of *corvée* workers, "administrative" punishments gained importance (Table 1).

The relationship between the two coercive labour regimes – *corvée* and *convict* labour – was explicitly noted in the early twentieth-century colonial press, for example by the writer of a critique in the *Java-bode*, who remarked that "the number detained in prisons usually comprises roughly

23. *Ibid*. See also "Preventieve hechtenis in Indië", *De locomotief. Samarangsch handels- en advertentie-blad*, 31 July 1900, p. 9.

24. "De rottingstraf", *De locomotief*, 14 January 1875, p. 1; Bruinink-Darlang, *Het penitentiair stelsel*.

25. "De rottingstraf", *De locomotief*, p. 1; "Preventieve hechtenis in Indië", *De locomotief*, p. 9.

26. Consten, "Geweld in dienst van de koloniale discipline".

27. "Dwangarbeid", *Java-bode*, 31 May 1876, p. 3; "Verspreide Indische berichten. Indische gevangenissen", *Algemeen Handelsblad*, 6 August 1894, p. 2. See also Consten, "Geweld in dienst van de koloniale discipline".

28. *Jaarcijfers Koloniën 1895 en vorige jaren, uitgegeven door de Centrale Commissie voor de Statistiek*.

Table 1. *Convict labour sentences and prison population, 1870–1930.*

		No. sentenced to convict labour (total per year)				Prison population (daily average)	
Year	Population of Dutch East Indies (total)	Short-term (*Tenarbeid-stelling*)	Long-term (*Dwang-arbeid*)	Total	Rate (per 100,000)	Total	Rate (per 100,000)
1870	24,800,000	69,498	10,648	80,146	323	10,045	41
1880	29,200,000	82,334	22,269	104,603	358		
1885		100,015	11,773	111,788	356		
1890	33,600,000	175,561	9,725	185,286	551		
1900	38,000,000	275,000			[>724]		
1903				319,313	811	33,180	84
1910	45,800,000						
1920	53,600,000					57,006	106
1930	61,400,000					40,735	66

Figures based on ClioInfra (www.clio-infra.eu); *Verslag van de statistiek der rechtsbe-deeling in Nederlandsch-Indië over de jaren 1881 en 1882* (Batavia, 1885); *Koloniaal verslag* 1875, 1886, 1889 (The Hague, 1875/1886/1889); "De rottingstraf", *De locomo-tief*, p. 1; "Verspreide Indische berichten. Indische gevangenissen", *Algemeen Handels-blad*, p. 2; "Preventieve hechtenis in Indië", *De locomotief*, p. 9; *Soerabaijasch handelsblad*, 22 March 1906, p. 17.

half to three-quarters of punished conscripted *corvée* workers".[29] The observation was part of a complaint that, in many cases, evasion of *corvée* labour was not punished severely enough by local colonial officials, "the dereliction of twenty days of *corvée* labour being punished with two or three days of convict labour". This left private landowners, who claimed the local population for their *corvée* labour, without sufficient means to enforce the *corvée* and led to conflicts between private landowners and colonial officials.[30]

EMPLOYING CONVICT LABOUR

The Dutch colonial-carceral system had not only a disciplinary role in relation to other coercive or coerced colonial labour regimes, it also had a pivotal function in the wider colonial project and in the regime of production itself. Convicts were employed with the intention to maximize the use of their labour and minimize their costs. As early as 1828, it had been proclaimed as "the express will of the king that forced labour should as far as possible replace all other punishments, so that the state could make use of the labour of the

29. As referred to in "Tegenwerking", *Het nieuws van den dag voor Nederlandsch-Indië*, 2 March 1903, p. 5.
30. *Ibid.*

Table 2. *Overview of places of employment of convicts, Dutch East Indies, 1816–1942.*

	Expansion	Infrastructure		Extraction			Production	
	Military expeditions*	Road, rail and water	Irrigation works	Geological expeditions	Tin mines	Coal mines	Agricultural	Prison production
1810s		X			Banka		Banda	
1820s		X			Banka		Banda	
1830s	Bonjol	X			Banka		Banda	
1840s		X		***	**	Martapoera	Banda	
1850s	Lampong	X		Moluccas	**	Pengaron	Banda	
1860s		X		Kalimantan	**	Pengaron Pelarang	***	
1870s	Aceh	X		***	**	Pengaron Pelarang		
1880s	Aceh	X			**	Pengaron		
1890s	Aceh Lombok	X			**	Ombilin		X
1900s	Aceh Korintji New Guinea	X			**	Ombilin	Noesa Kambangan	X
1910s		X	X			Ombilin Poeloe Laoet	Noesa Kambangan	X
1920s		X	X			Ombilin Poeloe Laoet Boekit-Asam	Noesa Kambangan	X
1930s		X	X			Ombilin Poeloe Laoet	Noesa Kambangan	X

*Not all expeditions are listed.
**In later periods, convicts on the island of Banka might have been employed to work on infrastructure and general services instead of mining.
***Uncertain.

criminals".[31] And as late as 1905, the Director of Justice was still instructing colonial officials that "it was of the utmost importance to choose work that leads to the highest possible monetary benefit in order to compensate for the costs of housing, control, and food of the prisoners as much as possible".[32] From this perspective, it was not surprising that convicts were employed in vital sectors of the colonial project (Table 2 and Figure 3).

The placement of convict workers to some extent followed the division between convicts subject to *tenarbeidstelling* with short sentences, and convicts subject to *dwangarbeid* with longer sentences. There was, however, much flexibility in employing convicts on sentences of medium duration (ranging roughly from several weeks to eighteen months). As districts were large, the limitation that convicts serving short-term sentences were to be placed on worksites within the district did not exclude the possibility of movement over significant

31. L.S. Louwes, "Strafrecht", in *Encyclopaedie van Nederlandsch-Indië*, 7 vols (The Hague and Leiden, 1917–1939), IV p. 133. Quoted in Reid, "The Decline of Slavery", p. 75.
32. "Dwangarbeiders", *De Sumatra Post*, 22 August 1905.

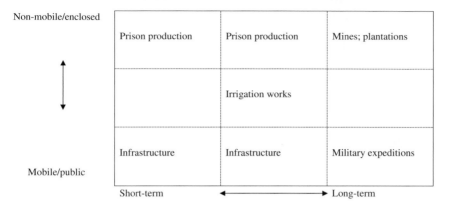

Non-mobile/enclosed			
Prison production	Prison production	Mines; plantations
	Irrigation works	
Infrastructure	Infrastructure	Military expeditions

Mobile/public

Short-term ←——————————————→ Long-term

Figure 3. Role and characteristics of convict labour sites, Dutch East Indies.

distances. The different groups of convicts were employed in a range of activities related to colonial expansion, infrastructure, extraction, and production.

Extractive activities were performed mainly by long-term convicts at more isolated sites, such as mines and agricultural colonies. Activities related to colonial expansion, especially military and geological expeditions, were often highly mobile and public. These, too, however, were mainly the domain of hardened long-term convicts. Convicts serving short- or mid-term sentences were used for other purposes. Some activities were also highly mobile and public, such as work on road and railway construction. Other activities, for example road and waterway maintenance in and near urban regions, could be marked by less mobility, but they were outdoors and sometimes public. The labour on irrigation works was often performed in more outlying agricultural or developing regions. The rise of productive prison environments from the late nineteenth century onwards supplemented this landscape with productive activities in more or less isolated or enclosed environments, performed mainly by convicts serving short- or mid-term sentences.

Most local, short-term convicts were housed in so-called *kettinggangerskwartieren*. These were quarters where convicts were kept while not at work. Such convict quarters existed throughout the Dutch East Indies, often located in the middle of urban settlements, and sometimes dating back to the *kettinggangerskwartieren* of the VOC period (in Batavia and Semarang, for example). These quarters could also be located in more remote areas. Some were built later in the nineteenth and twentieth century. In Ujung Kulon, the most easterly part of Java, for example, the lighthouse had quarters for convicts and an overseer's house.[33] In 1882, four building

33. "Het schiereiland Djoengkoelon", *Tijdschrift voor het binnenlandsch bestuur*, 1:39 (1910), p. 136.

contractors signed up for the open competition for the construction of a *kettinggangerskwartier* in Probolinggo with a capacity to house 600 convicts.[34] While in 1929, a *dwangarbeiderskwartier* (forced labourers' quarters) for 400 convicts was built near Sangiang (Bali) for their work on the Negara-Tjandi Kasoema-Gilimanoek road.[35]

Convicts were employed on a range of tasks. One of the most well-known and visible was road maintenance, famously referred to as *krakallen*, but convicts also performed other kinds of public work. On the island Onrust, convicts were used at the wharf and the military station. In 1912, some 600 convicts were employed on the island for constructing a quarantine station for *hadj* travellers.[36] Sometimes, the boundaries between public and private employment were vague. In 1844, for example, the Resident of the Preanger district (Java) wanted to employ 300 *kettingjongens* (convicts) at the two factories of an emerging tea plantation. Later, some fifty-five convicts were employed at Wonosobo (Java), sawing planks for some 3,000 chests that were needed for the transport of tea.[37] Over time, the department of civic public works (Burgerlijke Openbare Werken, BOW) gained increasing control over the work undertaken by convicts on infrastructural projects. In the early 1920s, for example, the BOW employed some one hundred convicts on the small island of Pulau Pandan, just off Padang (Sumatra), collecting granite under the supervision of a European overseer and a number of policemen.[38] In 1919, the Director of the BOW declared that he aimed to employ some 4,000 convicts per day on the construction of the road to Korintji (southwest Sumatra) in order to finish it in two years' time.[39]

As *corvée* labour declined, large-scale projects came to rely increasingly on convict labour. In the early nineteenth century, irrigation projects were undertaken mainly using contract labour (coolies), with local populations providing *corvée* labour. In the 1880s, it was suggested employing convict labour on irrigation works.[40] And, in 1891, the colonial press discussed the

---

34. *De Indische opmerker. Orgaan voor nijverheid en landbouw in Nederlandsch-Indië*, 1:5 (February 1882), p. 7.

35. "Bali", *Soerabaijasch handelsblad*, 3 January 1929, p. 2.

36. *Bataviaasch nieuwsblad*, 6 April 1912, p. 18.

37. J.A. van der Chijs, *Geschiedenis van de gouvernements thee-cultuur op Java. Samengesteld voornamelijk uit officiëele bronnen* (Batavia and The Hague, 1903), pp. 227, 374.

38. M. Hamerster, *Bijdrage tot de kennis van de afdeeling Asahan* (Amsterdam, 1926), p. 21.

39. *Het nieuws van den dag voor Nederlandsch-Indië*, 14 July 1919, p. 5.

40. The former Governor of Aceh, A. Pruys van der Hoeven, published an essay in the *Economist* in September 1885, providing ideas on how to improve the colonial government, including a suggestion to diminish *corvée* labour by making it possible to replace labour by monetary compensation. The suggestion on the use of convict workers for irrigation projects resonated in the colonial press. *Soerabaijasch handelsblad*, 7 November 1885, p. 7; *Bataviaasch handelsblad*, 12 November 1885, p. 4.

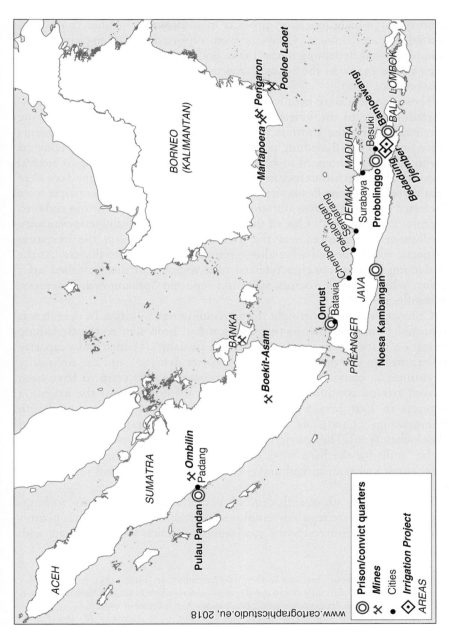

Figure 4. Location of penal institutions and sites of convict labour in the Dutch East Indies.

benefits of replacing the "3,000 free coolies" at the irrigation works of Demak (Central Java) by convict labourers.[41] From the early twentieth century, large-scale irrigation projects in southwest Djember (East Java) started to use convicts. Convicts were reported to be employed near Rambipuji and Bedadung in the 1910s, and near the Djatiroto sugar enterprise in the 1920s. In the 1930s, convicts were employed in Besuki (north coast of East Java).

These convicts were mainly serving medium-term sentences. The transportation time to the irrigation works limited the scope for employing convicts serving the shortest sentences, but the minimum requirements were low. For the Bedadung project, it was reported in 1912 that convicts "who had been sentenced to *krakallen* [in this context referring to general coerced labour on infrastructure] for a duration longer than eight days were sent there".[42] On the Besuki irrigation projects in the 1930s, convicts were "selected especially whose duration of punishment expires within eighteen months at the latest".[43] One of the main reasons for sending convicts with medium-term sentences was the unhealthy conditions at the irrigation projects, which formed a breeding ground for all kinds of disease. At the Bedadung project, convicts referred to a widespread disease called *sakit kring*, while colonial doctors at Besuki reported "pneumonia, dysentery, and influenza".[44]

Convicts were often brought from prisons in nearby cities. In 1912, it was reported from Bondowoso that convicts had been sent to the Bedadung irrigation works from a prison in "Tjoeradmalang" – which had a capacity of 720 to 840 convicts.[45] To balance project demands and the unhealthy environment, convicts employed on irrigation works seem to have been moved around continuously. In the 1930s, the convicts for the irrigation projects in East Java were reported to have been stationed in South Banjoewangi (1,500), in Pondok Lawu (500), and in Kasijam and Woeloehan (500). The convicts stationed in Woeloehan were explicitly said to be "unfit for the hard work demanded at the irrigation works". They were employed at an agricultural enterprise, growing rice and vegetables to feed the prisoners.[46]

From the early nineteenth century, convicts serving medium- to long-term sentences were regularly employed on military expeditions as porters and as general labourers. Some 300 Javanese convicts were sent along with

---

41. "Heerendiensten voor Openbare Werken", *De locomotief*, 26 January 1891, p. 1.
42. "Al te harde straf", *Het nieuws van den dag voor Nederlandsch-Indië*, 15 October 1912, p. 6.
43. "Productief maken der gevangenissen", *De Sumatra Post*, 1 October 1932, p. 14.
44. *Ibid.*; "Al te harde straf", *Het nieuws van den dag*, p. 6; *Algemeen Handelsblad*, 10 November 1919, p. 2.
45. "Al te harde straf", *Het nieuws van den dag*, p. 6.
46. "Productief maken", *De Sumatra Post*, p. 14.

Figure 5. Transport of guns by four columns of forced labourers from Aceh, during the seventh Bali expedition. 1906.
KITLV 43219. Creative Commons CC-BY License.

Colonel Bauer's regiment to join the expedition to Bonjol in 1835.[47] During the Timor expedition of 1857, the 250 "press-ganged coolies" were soon replaced by convict labourers. After the conquest of the Lampong region (South Sumatra) in 1859, it was reported that "in those and following years a great number of regiments of forced labourers and chained convicts were transported from Anjer via the Sunda Straits to Teloengbetoeng for the construction of roads and the rebuilding of this city".[48] The expeditions during the colonial wars in Aceh between 1873 and 1903 were accompanied by some 500 to 1,000 convicts yearly. Van Heutsz's 1898 expedition included more than 3,800 convicts.[49] Convicts were employed in other colonial wars simultaneously. The Lombok expedition of 1894 included some 1,000 convicts, while 250 convicts were sent with the New Guinea expedition in 1902, and some 500 convicts were sent on the expedition to Korintji (west coast of Sumatra)

47. "Culturele gegevens uit familiepapieren", *Cultureel Indië / Afdeeling volkenkunde*, January 1944, p. 41.
48. A. Hallema, "De ramp van de Krakatau-uitbarsting een halve eeuw geleden", *Tropisch Nederland. Veertiendaagsch tijdschrift ter verbreiding van kennis omtrent Nederlandsch Oost- en West-Indië*, 6:9 (21 August 1933), pp. 134–141.
49. Reid, "The Decline of Slavery".

Table 3. *Importance of convict labour in coal and rubber sector, Dutch East Indies, 1910–1923.*

| Year | Sector | Production using convicts as % of total sector | Rubber production (tons) | | Coal production (tons) | | |
			Nusa Kambangan	Dutch East Indies	Ombilin	Poeloe Laoet	Dutch East Indies
1910	Coal	96%			387,000	134,000	545,000
1920	Coal	75%			542,000	[160,000]	938,000
1925	Coal	54%			[500,000]	[100,000]	[1,100,000]
1930	Coal	59%			[582,000]	173,000	[990,000]
1919	Rubber	0.14%	127	[90,000]			
1923	Rubber	0.10%	135	[135,000]			

in 1903.[50] It is estimated that, after 1903, some 700 convicts were employed for military purposes each year.[51]

Convicts were also sent out on other types of expedition, especially exploratory geological missions under the command of mining and geology experts. In 1854, for example, forty-eight convicts were employed under the engineer Schreuder on the island of Batjan (Moluccas) in search of coal and gold.[52] The military and mining expeditions competed for the same convict workers as the mines and other operations using long-sentence convicts. In July 1861, a colonial journal of natural sciences reported that "in the course of this month twenty-one *kettinggangers* were sent to the coal mines of Koetei [Pelarang, East Kalimantan], and thirty-one *kettinggangers* departed with a military expedition to Kanangan [South Kalimantan] to provide coolie services".[53] These instances indicate the close connections between the military, the colonial bureaucracy, and specialists such as geologists. Geological exploration missions and mines were protected by military regiments, while convicts were withdrawn from mines and other projects to supply the necessary support for military expeditions.

The mines were perhaps one of the most important places where convicts were employed (Tables 2 and 3). The Banka tin mines had been a destination for convicts from as early as the early nineteenth century. The mines were

50. *De locomotief*, 11 July 1896, p. 2; *Het nieuws van den dag voor Nederlandsch-Indië*, 4 February 1902, p. 3; "Kanonen-futter", *Het nieuws van den dag voor Nederlandsch-Indië*, 6 January 1903, p. 2.
51. Reid, "The Decline of Slavery".
52. *Natuurkundig tijdschrift voor Nederlandsch-Indië*, 6:5 (1854), pp. 538–539.
53. *Natuurkundig tijdschrift voor Nederlandsch-Indië*, 23:2 (1861), p. 545.

operated mainly by Chinese contract labourers, but convicts continued to be employed there until the early twentieth century.[54] In the 1840s, the colonial government experimented with coal mining near Martapoera (South Kalimantan). The experiment at the mining site "De Hoop" was short-lived.[55] From 1849 to 1884 the "Oranje Nassau" coal mines in Pengaron (near Banjermassin, South Kalimantan) were run by the colonial government using convict labour. Convicts were reported to have been brought from Java, Madura, and Bali.[56] Between 1860 and 1873 the government coal mine at Pelarang (East Kalimantan) was also operated using convicts as miners.[57]

In 1892, the colonial government started to exploit coal mines in the Ombilin region. The railway between Ombilin and Padang needed to transport the coal was constructed by convict workers. The mines began operating with a workforce of some 300 convicts in January 1893. By the end of the year this number had grown to some 1,250. The workforce continued to grow, to over 2,400 convicts by April 1898. The next month, the workforce was reduced as large numbers were used for the military expedition to Aceh.[58] In subsequent years, the size of the workforce slowly rose again, with some 2,000 convicts being deployed around 1900. From the late 1890s onwards, increasing numbers of contract workers, too, were employed at the mines. By 1910, the workforce at the Ombilin mines consisted of 1,620 convicts and 4,761 contract workers.[59] In the 1920s, the "capacity" of Sawah Loento was 1,790 convicts.[60] Nevertheless, the convict population was more than double this figure by the early 1920s, peaking at 4,747 convicts in 1922.

The Ombilin mines provide an interesting insight in the financial organization of government undertakings that deployed convict labour. In the first few years of its operation (1893–1894) all costs related to the convict workforce were charged to the government's mining company. Only the expenses incurred for the convicts' clothing were paid from the Department of Justice's budget.[61] This changed after large numbers of convicts were withdrawn from the Ombilin mines to join the military expedition to Lombok in the autumn of 1894. The directors of the mines

54. *Natuurkundig tijdschrift voor Nederlandsch-Indië*, 19:3 (1859), p. 460; "Behandeling der mijnwerkers op Banka", *De Sumatra Post*, 27 August 1903, p. 5.
55. R.J. van Lier, *Onze koloniale mijnbouw III: De steenkolenindustrie* (Haarlem, 1917).
56. *Verslagen der vergaderingen*, 1 (12 February 1889), p. 12.
57. *Java-bode*, 3 March 1883, p. 7.
58. Erwiza, *Miners, Managers and the State*, p. 38.
59. "Sawahloento", *Indië: geïllustreerd weekblad voor Nederland en koloniën*, 5:25 (1921), p. 407.
60. *Indisch Verslag*, 1931, Part 1, p. 359. Taken from Bruinink-Darlang, *Het penitentiair stelsel*, p. 30.
61. *De locomotief*, 17 August 1895, p. 1.

complained that the "able-bodied forced workers" were taken to Lombok, while "the majority of the remaining [convicts] consisted of the less useful and ill". The several hundred hired workers – mostly Chinese and some from Nias – cost the mines forty to fifty cents per day. This led to a new arrangement from 1895 onwards in which the Department of Justice agreed to pay all costs relating to convicts sent to the Ombilin mines, while the mining company was charged a fixed amount for every day the convicts worked for the company, regardless of whether it was inside or outside the mines.[62]

Convicts were also deployed in the coal mines on Poeloe Laoet (southeast Kalimantan). The mine was started by a private company, but was taken over by the colonial government in 1913. In 1924, some 980 convicts were employed out of a total workforce of over 2,000. By 1929, the total workforce had grown to almost 3,300, while the number of convicts had decreased to somewhat over 700.[63] In 1919, the colonial government started to operate another coal mine in Boekit-Asam (Sumatra). For most of its existence the mine was operated using Chinese contract workers, but for a brief period in the early 1920s large numbers of convicts were brought in. The much criticized first director of the mine, Tromp, would later recall that problems with Chinese contract workers were the reason for this. He complained that it was difficult to get Chinese workers to work, and it did not help "to send the coolie to the magistrate for punishment".

> These lazy workers did not mind taking a holiday from the mines and being required to carry out easy work (cleaning the roads, etc.). At the request of the manager of the prisons department, a temporary measure permitted putting the *politioneel gestraften* (convicts sentenced under police law) to work in the mine. A group of convicts would be put to work under the supervision of armed police, but these workers performed just as little.[64]

In the Ombilin mines, convicts worked around the clock in eight-hour shifts. European overseers were assisted by *mandoers*, selected from among the most hardworking and loyal convicts. In their quarters, convicts were monitored by a European prison warder and several *mandoers*.[65] In the mines, convicts were employed on work deep in the shafts; contract workers were employed on less risky tasks. The death tolls following explosions in mineshafts indicate that this was the case elsewhere too.

---

62. "Ombilien-steenkolen", *Algemeen Handelsblad*, 16 April 1896, p. 1.
63. *Het nieuws van den dag voor Nederlandsch-Indië*, 10 September 1924, p. 2; "Dwangarbeiders in het Gouvernements Mijnbedrijf", *Bataviaasch nieuwsblad*, 2 December 1925, p. 1; *Het nieuws van den dag voor Nederlandsch-Indië*, 14 October 1930, p. 13.
64. H. van Hettinga Tromp, "Schetsen uit den Indischen Mijnbouw", *Het Vaderland. Staat- en letterkundig nieuwsblad*, 18 September 1926, p. 9.
65. "Ombilien-steenkolen", *Algemeen Handelsblad*, p. 1.

An explosion in the Poeloe Laoet mine in 1924, for example, killed sixty-three workers, of whom fifty-seven were convicts and only five were contract workers.[66]

Conditions in the mines were tough and the disciplinary regime was brutal. The records indicate that thousands of beatings using rattan sticks were carried out every year at the Ombilin mines alone. The period 1922–1924 was marked by a severe crisis in the disciplinary regime. Perhaps due to overpopulation, the number of registered rattan beatings inflicted on the mines' convict population more than doubled in these years. This was followed by a sharp rise in the number of cases of solitary confinement and attempts to desert.[67] Desertion was a common phenomenon. As early as 1894, it was noted that 176 convicts had attempted to run away in the first eleven months – given an average convict population this meant a desertion rate of nineteen per cent. Most convicts were recaptured (146), bringing the real annual rate of desertion to some three per cent.[68] At times, the rate of successful desertion increased to six per cent, not only at Ombilin but also at the Djember irrigation works. Noesa Kambangan seems to have had lower desertion rates, perhaps because it is an island.[69] Similar arguments were used in favour of deploying convicts at the mines on the island of Poeloe Laoet instead of at the Ombilin mines.[70] In most places, a range of disciplinary measures were employed, varying from severe punishments (rattan-stick beatings) to monitoring the quarters and workplaces of the convicts, and from policing nearby public locations (the *passar* – market) to rewarding local residents for returning runaway convicts.[71]

From the late nineteenth century, the landscape of penal institutions was broadened to include institutions that seem to have aimed at combining the profitability of convict production with more rehabilitative elements (Table 2).[72] In 1881, a budget of 100,000 guilders was approved for the construction of new quarters for convict workers in Semarang and a central prison for men in Surabaya.[73] The Semarang prison, *Mlaten*, was still being referred to as a *dwangarbeiderskwartier* (forced workers' quarters) in the

66. *Het nieuws van den dag voor Nederlandsch-Indië*, 10 September 1924, p. 2.

67. Bruinink-Darlang, *Het penitentiair stelsel*, Tables 3 and 4.

68. "Ombilien-steenkolen", *Algemeen Handelsblad*, p. 1.

69. Bruinink-Darlang, *Het penitentiair stelsel*.

70. "Dwangarbeiders in het Gouvernements Mijnbedrijf", *Bataviaasch nieuwsblad*, p. 1.

71. *Ibid.*; M. van Rossum, "From Contracts to Labour Camps? Desertion and Control in South Asia", in *idem* and J. Kamp (eds), *Desertion in the Early Modern World: A Comparative History* (London, 2016), pp. 187–202, 199.

72. Bruinink-Darlang, *Het penitentiair stelsel*, pp. 113–140.

73. "De Indische Begrooting voor 1881", *Het nieuws van den dag. Kleine courant*, 6 November 1880, p. 2.

1910s,[74] but it was used as a *kleermakerij*, a workshop for the production of clothing.[75] Other convict quarters were renewed or replaced by new prison buildings. The main aim seems to have been to make prisons into more effective production sites. The Yogyakarta prison housed over 1,000 convicts in the mid-1920s and functioned as a leather workshop. The central prison in Cheribon was a textile factory. Production capacity there was increased from 100 looms in 1921 to 212 looms in 1926. Half of the looms were driven by a steam engine, the other half by an electric motor. The prison housed 900 convicts, with a daily convict workforce of 600, producing 1.4 million metres, mostly dyed, per annum. Convicts were incentivized to increase production. Unwilling convicts were isolated and forced to work on "the old Dutch handloom".[76] In the Tjipinang prison in Batavia in 1930, the 2,400 convicts produced clothing, sheets, uniforms, furniture, and other goods needed by the various departments of the colonial government or army. The 550 communist prisoners were separated in an enclosed department, to work on administrative tasks or make bamboo heads.[77] The Pekalongan prison functioned first as a printing press and bookbinding workshop (1925) and later also produced carpets and kitchen goods (1929). In the 1930s, it was referred to as *kokosbedrijf* – a workshop processing coconuts.[78]

Alongside these prison factories, the colonial government created an agricultural colony on the island of Noesa Kambangan.[79] Soon after its creation in 1903, the colony was used as a rubber plantation, deploying convict labourers. The role of this project within the wider carceral system should be scrutinized further, especially since the prison-based production of rubber could hardly compete with the market (mainly "native") production of rubber (Table 3). In 1922, Noesa Kambangan housed more than 3,200 convicts, mainly employed on collecting rubber and other work related to the plantation. Nearby prisons housed smaller groups of convicts – the most important being the prisons in Karang-Anjar (425) and Gliger (350).[80] The convicts came from different parts of the Dutch East Indies (especially Java and Aceh). In 1926, roughly 700 convicted communists were sent to Noesa Kambangan and remained there until they were transferred to prisons in Pamekasan (East Java) and Ambarawa (Central Java)

74. [Notification concerning the new director of the Mlaten convict quarters Lempereur], *Het nieuws van den dag voor Nederlandsch-Indië*, 15 January 1913, p. 2.
75. "Gevraagd", *Bataviaasch Nieuwsblad*, 26 November 1914, p. 8.
76. "De Textiel-fabriek te Cheribon in de Centrale Gevangenis", *Het nieuws van den dag voor Nederlandsch-Indië*, 9 July 1930, p. 5.
77. "Een kijkje in Tjipinang", *Bataviaasch nieuwsblad*, 27 September 1930, p. 2.
78. *Soerabaijasch handelsblad*, 5 October 1929, p. 17. *Leeuwarder courant*, 20 April 1931, p. 3.
79. "Genezing van lepra. Leprozenkoloniën", *Vragen van den dag; Populair wetenschappelijk bijblad van het tijdschrift vragen van de dag*, 18 (1903), p. 147.
80. "In tropisch Siberië", *De Indische Courant. Oost-Java Editie*, 18 October 1922, p. 1.

in 1932.[81] Meanwhile, the population of the agricultural colony increased to over 4,000 convicts by the end of the 1920s.[82] The conditions on Noesa Kambangan, especially the unhealthy living conditions there and the scope for desertion, were a recurrent theme in the colonial press.[83]

The impact of convict labour varied by sector. As the extraction of coal was vital for most of the operations forming the backbone of the colonial project – from transport to warfare – the colonial government held a tight grip on the coal-mining sector and operated its mines to a large extent using the cheap labour extracted from long-term convicts. The proportion of coal mines in the Dutch East Indies using convict labour declined only slowly, as more mines opened and production doubled in the course of the first half of the twentieth century. In the field of rubber production, the reverse was the case. Although rubber was a vital commodity, the proportion of total government production that involved the use of convicts was fairly small, and generally took the form of private production throughout the Dutch East Indies. However, the Noesa Kambangan was a large and, initially, very profitable undertaking. It was also argued that teaching convicts the skills required to produce rubber during their time in prison would have beneficial effects. Similar arguments were made to justify the large-scale and growing production of commodities in colonial prisons from the 1910s and 1920s onwards.

CONCLUSION: CARCERAL REGIME AND COLONIAL EXPLOITATION

Thinking in terms of "prisons" can be misleading if we want to understand the Dutch colonial carceral system. At the height of the colonial penal industry, convicts were deployed in a broad range of colonial activities, including military expansion (warfare), creating and maintaining colonial infrastructure (roads, railways, waterways), extracting crucial resources (tin, coal), and producing for world markets (rubber) and to meet colonial-bureaucratic needs (varying from uniforms to furniture). Convict labour was strategic in supporting the colonial project. The function of the penal system was twofold. Firstly, convict labour as a form of punishment had a *disciplinary function*. Over the course of the nineteenth century, the use of administrative measures to sentence colonial subjects to convict labour were strongly expanded, strengthening the carceral connection between the different colonial coercive labour regimes. These convicts were sentenced under the *politierol*, or police law, to short-term convict labour

---

81. "Van communisten gezuiverd!", *Bataviaasch Nieuwsblad*, 16 June 1932, p. 6.
82. "De strafkolonie Noeskambangan", *De Sumatra Post*, 5 August 1929, p. 5.
83. "Het Caoutchoucbedrijf op Noesa Kambangan in 1923", *Bataviaasch Nieuwsblad*, 20 October 1924, p. 2; "Malariabestrijding op Noesa-Kembangan", *Bataviaasch Nieuwsblad*, 1 March 1926, p. 1; "Noesa Kembangan. Verbeteringen", *De Sumatra Post*, 3 September 1926, p. 2.

(*tenarbeidstelling*). This route was adopted increasingly in the final decades of the nineteenth century, with the government administration of these sentences disappearing from the records after 1900, by which time the number of convictions had peaked at 275,000 per annum. The number of convicts sentenced to medium- or long-term convict labour by the criminal courts (*landraad* and Raad van Justitie) was much smaller. The average size of this population "in prison" nevertheless grew over time. Overall, the Dutch East Indies witnessed a carceral boom, with both the colonial sentencing rate and the prison population increasing greatly between 1870 and 1920 (Table 1).

Secondly, the carceral system had a *productive function* in the colonial production regime, supporting the various colonial aims with regard to expansion, infrastructure, extraction, and actual production. All convicts in the Dutch East Indies were employed as forced labourers, and most them worked at extramural convict sites. Convicts were initially concentrated in activities related more to the infrastructural and expansionist aims of the colonial government. Responding to the abolition of the slave trade, however, the authorities started to send convicts to Bandanese and Javanese plantations. Increasingly, convicts were also deployed in the Banka tin mines, and later in the coal mines of Sumatra and Kalimantan. It was only towards the end of the nineteenth century that we see something of a shift towards the deployment of convicts in more enclosed production sites, both "outdoor" (the Noesa Kambangan rubber colony) and "indoor" (the expanding prison factories). The colonial government continued to employ convicts, however, in large-scale extramural and expansionist projects. The first half of the twentieth century especially witnessed ever larger numbers of convicts being sent to work on irrigation projects in East (and Central) Java, paving the way for the growing colonial plantation economy.

What should we make of this understudied aspect of Dutch colonial history? The convict system was not merely about mobilizing labour through the coercive means of convict labour relations. The nature of the system was more strategic. The productive and disciplinary functions of the penal system were key elements of a colonial regime effectively weaving together control, coercion, and exploitation. This was not just an early exercise in something that we nowadays try to understand as the "carceral state"; it must be understood, too, as a matured form of a phenomenon that actually seems to have been one of the roots of present-day carceral regimes, the "carceral colony".

IRSH 63 (2018), Special Issue, pp. 89–107 doi:10.1017/S0020859018000238
© 2018 Internationaal Instituut voor Sociale Geschiedenis

Ethnoscapes of Exile: Political Prisoners from Indochina in a Colonial Asian World*

LORRAINE M. PATERSON

School of History, Politics and International Relations
University of Leicester
University Road, Leicester LE1 7RH, UK

E-mail: lp283@leicester.ac.uk

ABSTRACT: During the French colonization of Indochina (1863–1954), approximately 8,000 prisoners – many of them convicted of political crimes – were exiled to twelve different geographical locations throughout the French empire. Many of these prisoners came from a Chinese background or a culturally Chinese world, and the sites to which they were exiled (even the penal colonies themselves) contained diasporic Chinese communities. Knowing Chinese might be their greatest asset, or being able to "pass" as Chinese the most valuable tool to facilitate escape. This article explores a group of political prisoners sent from French Indochina to French Guiana in 1913 and their subsequent escape, with the aid of Chinese residents. If exile is, in one sense, the ultimate exercise of colonial power – capable of moving bodies to distant locales – examining these lives through a Vietnamese lens reveals a very different story than the colonial archival record reflects.

In 1923, in the British colony of Trinidad, a young English woman returned from visiting her family in a suburb of the capital, Port of Spain, to find that her Chinese husband of six years, Lý Liễu, had packed up his possessions and left her and their two small children.[1] A Chinese trader, originally from Hong Kong, Lý had been working at a Chinese import/export company when this woman met and married him.[2] Now, without warning or

---

* The research leading to these results has received funding from the European Research Council under the European Union's Seventh Framework Programme (FP/2007–2013) / ERC Grant Agreement 312542.

1. The figure of six years is cited by Nguyễn Văn Hầu, *Chí sĩ Nguyễn Quang Diệu. Một lãnh tụ trọng yếu trong phong trào Đông Du miền Nam* [Strong-willed Scholar Nguyễn Quang Diệu: A Key Leader in the Đông Du Movement in Cochinchina], Tựa của Nguyễn Hiến Lê [Preface by Nguyễn-Hiển Lê] (Saigon, 1964), p. 59.
2. As is customary in Vietnamese names, the family name comes first. For citations containing the family name Nguyễn, the usual historical convention of citing the given name will be used (due to the overwhelming number of individuals with the surname Nguyễn).

explanation, he had vanished, presumably to return to Hong Kong. Indeed, he never returned to Trinidad or saw her, or their children, again. In his later reminiscences, Lý did not refer to his wife or children by name, but conveyed his terrible guilt at having abandoned them. In a less predictable regret, Lý expressed sadness that his wife would forever assume he was racially Chinese and would never know his real race and identity.³ For, despite his appearance, his fluency in Cantonese, his position at a Chinese company, and his years spent in Hong Kong, he was not the overseas Chinese businessman he pretended to be. In fact, he was an escaped Vietnamese political prisoner from the notoriously harsh penal colony of French Guiana, about seventeen days away from Port of Spain by boat.

Such a story goes against the stereotype of the penal colony of French Guiana, usually positioned as a hellish prison from which escape was nigh on impossible. Its horrific reputation was encapsulated by its name among prisoners, and eventually the general public: the *guillotine sèche*, the "dry guillotine", as it killed slowly, but just as surely, as a guillotine.⁴ Films like *Papillon* (1973) depict the extraordinary lengths to which prisoners had to go to escape; impersonating a Chinese businessman was not one of them.⁵ The apparent ease with which Lý and his compatriots escaped from the supposedly secure penal colony of French Guiana to sail to Trinidad is striking. And they were not alone; their stories trace threads of "punitive mobility" that are not reflected at all in the colonial archival record.⁶

To understand how these exiles and subsequent groups of Vietnamese prisoners engineered their escapes, and reclaimed agency in their transportation, it is necessary to explore the skills they learned while circulating within a cosmopolitan East Asian world. A world they inhabited at the beginning of the twentieth century as they sought expertise, which they strategically applied to the predicament of exile and imprisonment. Narrating their histories is undoubtedly a perspective from the colonies, one that is about the unique world – and resources – of East Asian convicts in the colonial French empire. However, it also shows the societal and penal layers of French Guiana refracted through a different lens, which is not just from the colonial perspective or using the sources of the archival apparatus of the colonial power to mould the historical narrative. Examining the lives of these exiles reveals that the ability of the colonial state to act as a

---

3. Nguyễn Văn Hầu, "Lý Liễu và phong trào đại đông du" ["Lý Liễu and the Study East Movement"] *Bách Khoa*, CXXXXV (1963), pp. 39–49.

4. This phrase inspired the title of René Belbenoit's memoir, *Dry Guillotine: Fifteen Years among the Living Dead* (New York, 1938), one of the most famous memoirs of French Guiana. Such was its popularity that it went through fourteen printings the year it was published.

5. The film *Papillon* was based on a 1970 book of the same title by escaped convict Henri Charrière.

6. Introduction to this special issue, p.2.

surveillance apparatus was often far more limited than imagined. French authorities were often unable to police boundaries between prisoners from Indochina and the resident Chinese communities in the penal sites. Many Vietnamese prisoners came from an ethnically Chinese background, or a culturally Chinese world, and the sites to which they were exiled (even the penal colonies themselves) contained diasporic Chinese communities. For many prisoners, knowing Chinese was their greatest asset or being able to "pass" as Chinese the most valuable tool to facilitate escape. Arguably, for many of these prisoners, the ethnoscapes of their exile were not as unfamiliar a world as the French authorities had intended. As well as being within a penal context, they were within the cultural and linguistic milieu of the Chinese diaspora – a diaspora that traversed both French and British colonial boundaries.

Colonial scholarship concerned with colonial projects has largely focused on connections between the metropole and the colonies as opposed to intercolony exchange. This article seeks to make connections from Indochina within a wider world of transcolonial constraint and mobility. Some connections were new, while others have historical roots. In this case, the historic flows and circulations between southern China and Vietnam were transposed to a new – Caribbean – context. Therefore, this article moves beyond notions of imperial centre and colonial penal periphery by examining South–South connections and by examining these prisoners' lives beyond the stream of scholarship on colonial institutions of incarceration. Exploring their exilic trajectory from their perspective, and not through a colonial lens, tells an entirely different historical story; one that does not end in French Guiana with one-page prisoner dossiers, but instead with a historical narrative that indicates "expressing choice and identity in the most unpromising of penal circumstances".[7]

A caveat: undeniably, these prisoners' stories are not the stories of all prisoners within the often brutal penal colony of French Guiana. Many prisoners – Indochinese or other – experienced aspects of the violence and despair of the "dry guillotine" just as the memoirs described. As the Introduction to this special issue indicates, "to speak of punitive sites as 'contact zones' is not to downplay the brutality of convict labour regimes".[8] However, the penal colony was not monolithic. Different sites of imprisonment, different racial backgrounds, and different temporal periods of confinement all reveal the diversity of punishment, captivity, and agency within one penal colony and its various penal sites. To be able to trace these threads, it is necessary to look at this historical narrative from the Vietnamese perspective.

7. *Ibid.*, p. 7.
8. *Ibid.*, p. 10.

THE SOCIETY FOR THE ENCOURAGEMENT OF LEARNING

The leafy campus of St Joseph's College, an elite Catholic secondary school in Hong Kong, founded in 1875 and still enrolling students today, seems an unlikely place for a meeting that ultimately led to Lý Liễu's double life in Trinidad. Lý was sent there in 1905 at the age of twelve, his forward-looking father determined that Lý should benefit from a cosmopolitan education. Vietnam's colonized status was greatly resented by many Vietnamese, who sought wider East Asian milieus – especially Hong Kong and Yokohama in Japan – in which to organize anti-colonial activities. For Vietnam, a shared intellectual history with China meant that locations in southern China were the logical sites of such interactions. Indeed, it was at St Joseph's College that Lý met anti-French activists, and by the time he was fifteen he had joined a group with the innocuous name of "Khuyến Du Học Hội" ("The Society for the Encouragement of Learning"), hereafter KDHH.[9] After leaving St Joseph's College, Lý studied at a Centre for English Studies in Hong Kong, while helping students clandestinely arriving from Vietnam and assisting with the broader anti-colonial effort directed by Vietnamese nationalists in various South East- and East Asian countries.

Another key member of the KDHH was Nguyễn Quang Diêu, who was born, in 1880, in a small village in Sa Đéc province, southern Vietnam, into a family of Confucian scholars.[10] As was customary, Diêu began his studies of the Confucian classics at the age of six, and by ten he was known locally as a skilled writer.[11] A glorious future in the Vietnamese civil service beckoned throughout his teenage years. However, Diêu eventually decided to break off studying the texts of the Vietnamese examination system, "apparently having concluded that clandestine fund-raising, recruitment, and distribution of propaganda held more possibility of saving his country than the most conscientious, sophisticated interpretation of the [Chinese] classics".[12]

Members of the KDHH spent their time travelling between Indochina and southern China (including Hong Kong) to circulate money and publications. However, these East Asian activities came to an end on 16 June 1913, when British authorities in Hong Kong received a tip-off and Diêu and his colleagues were arrested at a supporter's house. The Consul of Hong Kong, Gaston Liebert, briefly mentioned their arrest in his private papers: "[S]ix Annamites have been arrested by the English police in Hong Kong where they went to make bombs. Ba Liễu, or Lý Liễu, a former

---

9. A so-called new learning group, the Society was dedicated to exploring philosophies and ideologies that would assist Vietnam in fighting against French colonialism.

10. Nguyễn, *Chí sĩ Nguyễn Quang Diêu*.

11. *Ibid.*, p. 12.

12. David Marr, *Vietnamese Anticolonialism, 1885–1925* (Berkeley, CA, 1981) p. 27. Study of the Confucian classics was a prerequisite to passing the Vietnamese examination system and becoming part of the Vietnamese civil service.

student at St Joseph's school in Hong Kong, was one of them".[13] Some reports indicated that bomb-making equipment was discovered in the house, which may be factual given British reticence to arrest Vietnamese without material evidence of criminal involvement.[14]

Deportation to French Indochina followed and a criminal tribunal in Hanoi subsequently sentenced four of the group on 5 September 1913.[15] Only one deportation dossier still exists in the French colonial archives, for a member of the Society called Đinh Hữu Thật, citing his crime as "criminal association".[16] Such lack of documentation makes it difficult to determine why the length of their sentences varied dramatically: all were deported to French Guiana, but the sentences ranged from perpetual labour to five years (which was Lý's short sentence, perhaps on account of his youth?). However, they were all sentenced to *relégation*, i.e. following the completion of their sentences, under the law of *relégation*, they had to remain in French Guiana for the rest of their lives. Issuance of the sentences in 1913 meant the group was exiled just before the advent of World War I disrupted overseas deportation.[17]

TRANSPORTATION, RACE, AND LABOUR

Nguyễn Quang Diêu and Lý Liễu joined the stream of prisoners – both common-law and political – who travelled from French Indochina to various points throughout the French empire. Throughout the ninety-year French colonization of Indochina (1863–1954), approximately 8,000 prisoners – many of them convicted of political crimes – were exiled to twelve different geographical locations. From Gabon to Guiana, there was hardly a corner of the French empire to which they were not sent. However, the exile location mostly depended on the category (and context) of the prisoner in question. Some prisoners required special surveillance (or, more rarely, special privilege). Different locales accepted different kinds of prisoners at different times. Sometimes, French territories submitted

---

13. Cornell University Libraries, Gaston Liebert Papers, Box 2: Dossier 7. Consul of France in Hong Kong to Governor-General of Indochina, 23 June 1913. This is the only reference to Lý Liễu by the name Ba Liễu. There is one other reference to the arrest of the group in Centre des Archives d'Outre Mer [hereafter, CAOM], GGI Indo/NF28, but no names are mentioned.

14. French authorities were angered by British recalcitrance to arrest and deport without due evidence and process.

15. A criminal tribunal was the exception rather than the rule.

16. CAOM, Đinh HữuThật's dossier. Đinh Hữu Thật's name is misspelled as Dang Hun Thanh (with no diacritics), but the date, sentence, and exile locale all match, so I am assuming it is him.

17. Indeed, one of the reasons given for a formidable prison uprising in Thái Nguyên, northern Vietnam, in 1917 was that prisoners could not be deported to the penal colonies. See Peter Zinoman, *The Colonial Bastille: A History of Imprisonment in Colonial Vietnam 1862–1940* (Berkeley, CA, 2001), p. 188.

Lorraine M. Paterson

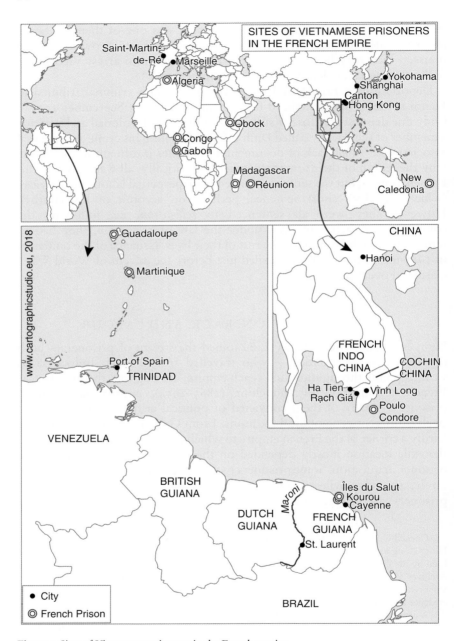

Figure 1. Sites of Vietnamese prisoners in the French empire.

requests for hard labour convicts for specific colonial projects and their requests may or may not have been granted. At different periods, prisoners from Indochina could be sent to the following exilic locales: Gabon, Congo (both incorporated into French Equatorial Africa in 1910), Obock (later part of French Somaliland), French Guiana, New Caledonia, Madagascar, Réunion, Martinique, Guadeloupe, Algeria, and French Oceania (both Tahiti and the Marquesas). Some locations – Algeria, Tahiti, and the Marquesas – were used only for elite political prisoners. Indeed, there were three key categories of prisoner: exiles, deported prisoners (political motivation), and transported prisoners (common-law prisoners). However, the categories blurred and overlapped in many ways. Prisoners were sent from Indochina for a variety of reasons, from serious criminal crimes like murder to suspected sedition against the colonial authorities. Confusion applied to the world of deportation and exile; those accused of political crimes and common criminals, *forçats*, were often placed in the same convoys and had similar fates. In that sense, being transported and being exiled were often synonymous, even if the terminology used was slightly different. Exiles required an exile decree, which had to stipulate the grounds for exile; additionally, a tribunal or trial might take place, but the decree was sufficient. Deportation came through the established French court or, as in September 1913, a specially convened criminal commission.

French Guiana was the most common destination for prisoners from Indochina as they were considered constitutionally better equipped to withstand tropical diseases.[18] Although exposure to malaria in the climates of Indochina could certainly assist in building up immunity, yellow fever was initially the most virulent (and often fatal) disease in French Guiana.

Situated on the northern coast of South America, French Guiana was established as a French settler colony in 1852.[19] One reason for its selection as a site for penal settlements was the hope that this new role would stimulate its development after a disastrous French settlement had been attempted at Kourou. Prisoners seemed the next logical step. There was a desire to punish and a desire to reform and to re-socialize criminals so as to reinsert them into civil society. Out of this unresolved dichotomy evolved provisions for the transportation of certain categories of criminal to French

18. It is difficult to estimate the overall number of deportees sent to French Guiana from Indochina given the inconclusive nature of the archive. French historian Danielle Donet-Vincent suggests that just under 1,000 deportees were sent from Indochina to French Guiana from 1885 to 1922: Danielle Donet-Vincent, "Les Bagnes des Indochinois en Guyane (1931–1963)", *Outre-Mer. Revue d'Histoire*, 88:330–331 (2001), pp. 209–221, available at http://www.persee.fr/doc/outre_1631-0438_2001_num_88_330_3849; last accessed 12 January 2018. Donet-Vincent admits that it is impossible to know the breakdown between common-law prisoners and political prisoners.
19. Louis Lacroix, *Les Derniers Voyages de Forçats et de Voiliers en Guyane, les Derniers Antillais* (Paris, 1970).

Guiana in 1852 (two years before an 1854 law officially created the *bagne* there) and then to New Caledonia. Although the intention was to punish the criminals, it was also assumed that they would be regenerated by life and work in a far-off rural environment, that their work would contribute strongly to the colony, and that the recidivist would be an agent in the service of France's larger colonial project.[20]

However, yellow fever meant French Guiana was an extremely difficult place in which to thrive, although the reason for the fever's prevalence was not understood until the end of the nineteenth century.[21] Malaria also posed a big problem. Mortality rates were high, and in the first years of the penal colony between 1852 and 1866 close to forty per cent of all the convicts died.[22] In 1867, the government prohibited the transportation of French citizens to French Guiana. Only "African and Arab prisoners whose constitutions are resistant to the climate of the colony should be sent".[23] New Caledonia was used instead for French prisoners until 1897, when there was some metropolitan debate that it had become too comfortable an exilic locale and French prisoners were again sent to French Guiana. Overall, 70,000 prisoners were sent to French Guiana and it operated as a penal colony until 1952, with the last convicts arriving from France in 1937.

JOURNEY TO THE JUNGLE

Whether classified as political or common-law, prisoners from French Indochina were transported to French Guiana under similar conditions. The Society for the Encouragement of Learning group did not go directly to Cayenne, French Guiana's main town, but via Marseille and St Martin de Ré.[24] From his two-week stay in a prison in Marseille, Diêu described the French city as an attractive port, organized in a very "civilized" way, rendering French treatment of colonized people even more perplexing. A poem Diêu claimed to have composed in Marseille refers to the fact that he found the justifications for his imprisonment opaque:

> Heaven and earth give birth to us to have will
> Not knowing at all what crime I have committed
> Resign oneself without understanding
> How is this the law of civilization?[25]

20. See Stephen A. Toth, "Colonisation or Incarceration? The Changing Role of the French Penal Colony in Fin-de-Siècle New Caledonia", *The Journal of Pacific History*, 34:1 (1999), pp. 59–74, 61.
21. *Idem, Beyond Papillon: The French Overseas Penal Colonies, 1854–1952* (Lincoln, 2006).
22. Colin Forster, "Convicts: Unwilling Migrants from Britain and France", in David Eltis (ed.), *Coerced and Free Migration: Global Perspectives* (Stanford, CA, 2002), p. 284. Peter Redfield, *Space in the Tropics: From Convicts to Rockets in French Guiana* (Berkeley, CA, 2000), also quotes this statistic, p. 70.
23. CAOM, H/ Notice sur la transportation en Guyane et en Nouvelle Calédonie (1866–1867).
24. Nguyễn, *Chí sĩ Nguyễn Quang Diệu*, p. 51.
25. *Ibid.*

From Marseille, the prisoners were sent to St Martin de Ré off La Rochelle in northern France, to await a biannual sailing. On the boat, they were locked into cages holding sixty to eighty people each, and made the journey in fifteen to twenty days, depending on whether the ship, the transportation vessel the *Martinière*, stopped in Algeria. In a later account, Lương Duyên Hồi, a Vietnamese prisoner, described the conditions on the *Martinière*. "The ocean waves were very high and many Vietnamese people on the boat were seasick".[26] Unaccustomed to such rough seas, it was vital to remain vigilant for people falling unconscious from seasickness.[27] Tensions on board could be exacerbated by the length of the exiles' sentences. For example, in 1890, a convoy of 133 deportees from Indochina contained eighty prisoners sentenced to perpetual exile, which added to their "anxiety and tendency to disrupt".[28] The *Martinère* deposited the prisoners on the Maroni River near Dutch Guiana. The largest prison camps in French Guiana, St Laurent and St Jean, were located near the Maroni River.

The convict population of French Guiana ranged between 3,000 and 7,000 prisoners; despite the arrival of some 700 new arrivals per year, deaths and attempted escapes kept the number of prisoners relatively constant.[29] Following their arrival, French convicts were sorted by sentence category and then given work assignments accordingly. The convicts were almost all male; the high mortality among French women meant that their transportation ended in 1906.[30] Few women from Indochina were transported. Only ten Vietnamese women are recorded out of the 3,185 female dossiers extant in the archive, with no female Cambodians or Laotians listed.[31]

Those designated as "recalcitrant" were assigned to cut down trees in the rainforest or sent to the Iles du Salut. Even here, a hierarchy emerged among the islands – on the Ile Royale, convicts were left relatively alone; those who attempted escape were sent to solitary confinement on the Ile du Diable [Devil's Island] was reserved primarily for European convicts – however, conditions there were generally better than on the Ile du Diable.[32] In addition to these were the main camp at St Laurent, the notorious disciplinary camp of Charvin, and Camp Hatte, to which disabled prisoners were sent. Only the best-behaved convicts were allowed in Cayenne.

---

26. Lương Duyên Hồi, unpublished manuscript, in the possession of his grandson, Đỗ Thái Bình.
27. *Ibid.*
28. CAOM, Indo/NF76 1890. The report also mentions that one convict had leprosy.
29. Redfield, *Space in the Tropics*, p.70. The number of prisoners varied subject to the time period examined.
30. Colin Forster, *France and Botany Bay* (Melbourne, 1992), p. 287. As mentioned before, mortality rates were also high for men, but did not cause as much consternation.
31. CAOM, Catalogue of Female Exiles to French Guiana.
32. Redfield, *Space in the Tropics*, pp. 79–80. Despite the islands being only fifteen kilometres from the shore, the voyage could take up to eighteen hours.

In 1890, the Governor-General of French Guiana assured the Minister of Colonies that political prisoners from Indochina were immediately separated and given tasks commensurate with their sentences, but this assertion does not reflect other archival and anecdotal sources.[33] Prisoners from Indochina almost always occupied one of three roles: domestic servant, agricultural worker, or fisherman. Indeed, the stereotype that Indochinese (especially Vietnamese) were diligent workers sometimes assisted them in getting lighter, less guarded, tasks. For example, Cambodians were often put into domestic agricultural work, including attempts at rice cultivation, considered less arduous than clearing forests.[34] Throughout the 1890s, Vietnamese convicts were allowed to build "Vietnamese-style" houses and had a virtual monopoly over fishing; catches were presumably used to supplement the meagre fare of the guards.[35] On the Laussant Canal, which ran through Cayenne, it was reported that "the Vietnamese have formed a veritable village, where they help people with illnesses which are dealt with within the community".[36]

THE HARBOUR OF CAYENNE

> For so long I've waited to see Cai Danh
> As I glance upon the scenery, I am emotionally stirred.
> The broad, vast sea courses with azure,
> While green forests mist over the land.[37]

The landscape Diêu described in this poem – the scenery of "Cai Danh" – was not a port on the waterways of the Mekong Delta in southern Vietnam where he grew up, but rather the harbour of Cayenne. The emotions roused come at the end of an arduous voyage during which many of his fellow prisoners suffered terrible seasickness and "crossing the ocean for those unaccustomed to sea travel made them feel ill, especially at his advanced age".[38]

Diêu wrote the poem in a traditional Vietnamese poetic form: the *luật thi*, consisting of eight even syllable lines. As historian George Dutton points out: "The best-known poems in this [poetic] form were those produced by court officials who travelled to China on embassies to the Chinese court, poems that commented most frequently on the scenery but also on events of

33. This was the case at least until 1910, when legal distinctions in Indochina became more defined. Prior to 1910, there was no clear division between political and common-law prisoners.
34. CAOM, Indo/NF76, Letter from Governor-General of Guiana informing the Minister of Colonies that as soon as Cambodians arrived, they were instantly assigned an agricultural task.
35. From the archival record it is unclear what "Vietnamese-style" house means exactly.
36. The Laussant Canal was a dyke built in 1777. CAOM, Indo/NF75.
37. A copy of the poem, titled "Cảm Tác Khi Đi Đày Đến Cai Danh", can be found in various locations, including Nguyễn, *Chí sĩ Nguyễn Quang Diệu*, p. 51.
38. Nguyễn, *Chí sĩ Nguyễn Quang Diệu*, p. 18.

the journey".[39] By rendering the unfamiliar into this familiar poetic scheme, Diêu laid claim to the landscape of French Guiana. He made legible to his (eventual) audience back in Vietnam this foreign topography.[40] By creating a literary connection from exilic locale to homeland, Diêu was creating a punitive cultural circuit along which his eventual readers could travel.

Although the opening of the poem is framed by traditional Vietnamese poetic tropes, as it progresses it betrays more modern anxieties about the position of the Vietnamese in a world where countries have ceased to exist. After the opening lines, Diêu continues:

> But barbaric catastrophes befall these people;
> How much misery shall my own stock endure?
> Extinction is mirrored glaringly before my eyes,
> Witnessing the race, I shudder to think![41]

The indigenous inhabitants of French Guiana are evoked in the penultimate lines as facing extinction. The use of the word *chủng*, "race", suggests Diêu was referring to the race inhabiting this "catastrophic" place: the Amerindians, indigenous inhabitants of French Guiana, rather than the annihilation of the penal colony detainees.[42] The intricacies of a racially mixed Caribbean society were almost certainly lost on him. That Diêu refracted this landscape through a lens of Social Darwinism and fears of racial extinction is not surprising.[43]

Although Diêu later claimed to have penned this poem when he first saw the harbour of French Guiana, this is poetic licence. Supposedly moved to write by the scenery itself, he creates an allusion of the emotional moment of arrival and of horror. However, as mentioned above, convict ships arriving from St Martin de Ré did not dock at the harbour of Cayenne; they sailed to St Laurent du Maroni in western French Guiana, which was the main processing centre for prisoners arriving at the penal colony. It is also unlikely that Diêu saw any Amerindians at the harbour of St Laurent du Maroni; the arrival of the French had pushed them further and further inland.

---

39. George Dutton, "Crossing Oceans, Crossing Boundaries: The Remarkable Life of Philiphê Binh (1759–1832)", in Tran Nhung Tuyet and Anthony Reid (eds), *Việt Nam: Borderless Histories* (Madison, WI, 2006), pp. 219–255, 248. The poem was written in the Vietnamese character-based system.

40. It is unclear when this poem first circulated in Vietnam.

41. "Tuyệt-chủng" is the phrase used here, indicating that the race suffered complete annihilation. Nguyễn, *Chí sĩ* Nguyễn *Quang Diệu*, p. 51.

42. The indigenous inhabitants of French Guiana included the Arawak, Carib, Teko, Kalina, Palikur, Wayampi, and Wayana. As well as the Amerindians, there was a population of maroons (descendants of runaway slaves).

43. Ideas of Social Darwinism were popular among Chinese and Vietnamese intellectuals at the time.

DENSE JUNGLE TOIL

When they arrived in French Guiana, the group of four was assigned to a work unit to cut wood in an inland region, and Lý was placed as a guard in charge of his fellow prisoners. Putting Vietnamese prisoners in charge of other Vietnamese prisoners was also a feature of the prison system in Indochina, where so-called *caplans*, who were half-prisoner and half-guard, occupied this role.[44] Convicts at work were not accompanied by guards. What is striking here is borne out in other writings on the *bagne*, which is simply that the penal colony of French Guiana was understaffed. In *Beyond Papillon*, historian Stephen Toth argues that "physical violence and punishment of the body was ever present" in French Guiana.[45] He also argues that the penal colony was severely lacking in personnel.[46] Contradictions abound. Physical punishment was undoubtedly part of the regime of the penal colony, but its omission from the recollections of the KDHH is striking. As is the absence of the guards, and their sadism, which figured so predominantly in French memoirs.[47] There are two ways to think about this: firstly, that Diêu and Lý wanted to represent themselves as more autonomous and with greater agency than was actually the case. Secondly, that they were essentially left unguarded on the premise that escape was impossible and, as mentioned before, the number of guards was insufficient.[48] The idea of spreading out convicts to labour in small work crews also meant it was difficult to guard them.[49]

Due to his *caplan* position, Lý could slip away from the camp and was able to go to Cayenne at night to mix with the Chinese community. His many years of education in Hong Kong meant that, even though he was the youngest member of the four, Lý spoke English, Cantonese, and French fluently. His Cantonese came in especially useful; he was able to get medicine, non-prison clothing, and send and receive letters clandestinely.[50] Convicts were dressed in distinctive grey clothing that made escape harder; medicine was also vitally important because of the rampant diseases of the penal colony.

44. Zinoman, *Colonial Bastille*, pp. 111–112. A similar system was also used in British penal sites in South Asia and also for Javanese exiles to Cape Town. There, convicts could wield power as "company police". See Kerry Ward, *Networks of Empire: Forced Migration in the Dutch East India Company* (Cambridge, 2009).
45. Toth, *Beyond Papillon*, p. 153.
46. *Ibid*. See ch. 4, "The Lords of Discipline: The French Penal Colony Service", pp. 59–82.
47. Michel Le Clère, *La Vie Quotidienne dans Les Bagnes* (Paris, 1973), p. 94, discusses the sadism of the guards.
48. The situation of the guards before and after an 1867 decree formed them into a kind of corps of overseas prison guards, recruited predominantly from former non-commissioned army and navy personnel. See Toth, *Beyond Papillon*, p. 76.
49. Toth discusses the small work crew policy. See *ibid.*, p. 78.
50. Nguyễn, *Chí sĩ Nguyễn Quang Diệu*, p. 56.

These affinities with the Chinese world meant that the landscape of the penal colony had a different cultural legibility to him than to most of the inmates. In colonial Cayenne, indeed throughout French Guiana, Chinese trading communities (many Cantonese-speaking) were intimately woven into the fabric of penal colony society. Most had migrated from Shanghai and Canton, and as "commercial possibilities such as running a small store failed to attract many Creoles, it opened the way for Chinese domination of the small-scale retail market".[51] Indeed, the term "Le Chinois" came to mean "corner market" in Guyanese French. Chinese were renowned for selling everything from "champagne to sun-helmets".[52] Anecdotal accounts from both prisoners and visitors to the penal colony indicate that Chinese traders throughout French Guiana acted as conduits for the sending of (unauthorized) correspondence, and not just for Vietnamese prisoners.[53] Although an anecdotal observation, one visitor noted that "it is surprising what knowledge these Chinese possess of certain convicts, through acting as the medium by which letters are sent and received. Often they know more about the men than the authorities".[54] Lý claimed he mingled with this Chinese community on almost nightly visits.

Meeting a young Cantonese speaker, educated at the prestigious St Joseph's College of Hong Kong, must have been an unexpected encounter to these Chinese, many of whom had emigrated from areas with which Lý was very familiar. Diêu also portrayed the exiles as being connected to global events through Lý's contacts in Cayenne, who told him of the progress of World War I and the exile to Réunion of the former Vietnamese Emperor Thành Thái and his son Emperor Duy Tan. The news of these other exiles inspired them, raising hopes that the need to exile the emperor indicated France's weakened condition.[55] On the premise that France's position in Indochina was compromised due to its involvement in the war, it seemed an opportune moment to attempt escape.[56]

---

51. Redfield, *Space in the Tropics*, p. 217. In discussing the 1990s, Redfield also mentions that "[t]he Chinese, despite their relatively small numbers, occupy a position of social prominence as a result of their near-monopoly on small stores and related commerce", p. 44. Although this is a contemporary assessment, the "near-monopoly" (if not the "social prominence") would hold true for the colonial period. The observation about the breadth of their stock selection was made by William Edwin Allison-Booth, *Hell's Outpost: The True Story of Devil's Island by a Man Who Exiled Himself There* (New York, 1931), p. 13.
52. Redfield, *Space in the Tropics*, p. 292.
53. Allison-Booth, *Hell's Outpost*, p. 28. Peter Redfield discusses this memoir and some of its dubious claims, in *Space in the Tropics*, pp. 93–94.
54. Allison-Booth, *Hell's Outpost*, p. 199. This is echoed in William Willis, *Damned and Damned Again* (New York, 1959), p. 123.
55. Thành Thái had already been imprisoned from 1907–1916 for displaying signs of madness to the French. CAOM, GGI-22138, details the symptoms.
56. Nguyễn, *Chí sĩ Nguyễn Quang Diêu*, p. 72.

TAFIA DREAMS OF ESCAPE

Anecdotal accounts indicate that prisoners in French Guiana had two fixations to help them endure the penal colony: "*tafia* [cheap homebrewed rum] and the hope of escape".[57] Anthropologists, social scientists, and historians may differ in their opinions about aspects of the penal system in French Guiana; however, there is one fact on which they all agree: escape was difficult and dangerous. Anthropologist Peter Redfield estimates non-returned escapees at between two and three per cent of the prison population, but it is impossible to know how many made it to a safe locale.[58] Historian Stephen Toth simply states: "To flee was a truly remarkable feat."[59] Or, to be more precise, to flee successfully was a truly remarkable feat. Even if the guard system was understaffed there were "two constantly watching guards who are always at their post: the jungle and the sea".[60] French Guiana for the most part operated as a prison without walls in which the lack of money, travel documents, non-prison clothing, and access to a seaworthy boat or raft all precluded escape. Even if acquiring the necessities for escape was possible, trusting both your co-conspirators and a boat captain (if involved) was vital.[61] Maps of South America carried a huge premium. Lack of geographical knowledge made many prisoners dependent on prison rumour to understand the surrounding terrains.[62] Lý had access to many necessities, including maps, through his Chinese contacts in Cayenne.[63]

Several possible escape routes existed and "the most common was to head northeast into what was then Dutch Guiana, either through the jungle or floating on a raft".[64] However, escaped prisoners carried a one-hundred-franc capture award, an inducement for Amerindians living in the area.[65] To reach Brazil, British Guiana, Venezuela, or Trinidad was even harder.[66] Often, attempts to reach Trinidad ended in death – the sea could be rough

---

57. Convicts referred to Cayenne as "Tafiatown" as numerous shops there sold it. Belbenoit, *Dry Guillotine*, p. 219.

58. Redfield, *Space in the Tropics*, p. 80. The highest rate of successful escapes in one year was approximately five per cent, but that was exceptional. Redfield is drawing on the statistical analysis of French historians to make this statement.

59. Toth, *Beyond Papillon*, p. 57.

60. Belbenoit, *Dry Guillotine*, p. 54.

61. In one particularly notorious incident, a shipowner in Cayenne claimed he was taking convicts to Brazil and drowned them en route.

62. This comes up in various accounts of the penal colony. For example, Belbenoit, *Dry Guillotine*, p. 45, talks in detail about the difficulties of finding out geographical information.

63. Nguyễn, *Chí sĩ Nguyễn Quang Diệu*, p. 32.

64. Redfield, *Space in the Tropics*, p. 80.

65. Jean-Pierre Fournier, *Bonjour les Bagnes de Guyane. L'Amazonie Française. La Vie des Forçats de St-Martin-de-Ré à la Guyane* (Paris, 1999), p. 24.

66. In French Guiana and New Caledonia, the *doublage* law meant permanent exile for French convicts sentenced to over eight years.

and difficult to negotiate without skilled nautical expertise – or in extradition. In 1931, a law was passed in Trinidad to stop escapee extraditions to French Guiana because of British concern over conditions in the penal colony, but that was comparatively late for most prisoners.[67] An unsuccessful escape meant solitary confinement for a period of time, and between two and five additional years of forced labour added to the original sentence. This penalty increased over time as more prisoners attempted to escape.[68]

It could be argued that it was not altruism, a fictive sense of kinship, or racial solidarity that motivated the Chinese in Cayenne to assist Lý and his friends in their escape. Rather, there was recognition that members of the KDHH had both linguistic and business acumen, marketable commodities in the transcolonial South American/Caribbean world. The prisoners were all literate in Chinese, Lý was fluent in English, and they participated in commercial enterprises to raise funds for the KDHH. They were potentially valuable assets among overseas Chinese networks. On the other hand, the Chinese in Cayenne who facilitated their escape from French Guiana did not benefit directly from their escape in terms of either labour or skill. Instead, these Chinese residents jeopardized their permission to live and work in French Guiana. Acting as a postal service for prisoners was certainly unauthorized, but a blind eye could be turned; facilitating the flight of hard-labour political deportees was definitely a different level of assistance.

Aiding prisoners to escape would have elicited severe repercussions from the prison authorities. A sense of affinity to the group, perhaps especially to Lý due to his many years in Hong Kong, may have induced them to assist; it was rare for the Chinese communities to assist in helping so-called *bagnards* (penal colony convicts) escape. As one memoir mentions, some Chinese near the river in St Laurent du Maroni would undertake to arrange escapes in return for a suitable bribe, but such an arrangement was expensive.[69] Indeed, there were groups better known for providing this kind of assistance – e.g. Brazilian ship captains and crew.

Two differing accounts have the group leaving for Trinidad in a "native" fishing boat as well as a Chinese-owned boat. However, in both accounts they were disguised as members of the Chinese community in Cayenne, with their passage paid for by that community.[70] For the members of the KDHH, racial masquerading was a skill perfected in their years travelling between China and Vietnam. As for the British authorities in Trinidad, one

---

67. In 1876, the British consul in Trinidad reported that the Chinese labourers in French Guiana suffered "barbarous and inhuman treatment".
68. These penalties were modelled on those imposed in metropolitan French prisons.
69. See George John Seaton, *Isle of the Damned: Twenty Years in the Penal Colony of French Guiana* (New York, 1951), p. 111.
70. Nguyễn Đình Đầu, "Nguyễn Quang Diêu: Một Kiếp Thề Ghi Với Nước Non", *Nhà Lao Annam ở Guyane* (Ho Chi Minh City, 2008), p. 87, claims it was a "native" fishing boat.

Asian looked pretty much like the next. Probably because of its small
population and relative underdevelopment, Trinidad offered greater
economic opportunities to ex-indentured Chinese, and about 3,000
Chinese left French Guiana and relocated there in the 1870s and 1880s.[71]
In Trinidad itself, the Chinese had moved off the plantations and into trade
as early as the 1870s.[72] This meant there were strong connections between
Chinese communities in Trinidad and French Guiana, and may explain why
the Chinese in Cayenne were able to facilitate contacts in Port of Spain.
Many Chinese Christians had converted in the West Indies or elsewhere
prior to coming to Trinidad.[73] This impacted how they were viewed within
the colonial hierarchy as they were assessed positively in contrast to the
Indians or Africans.[74] Therefore, relations between the Chinese community
and the British authorities were generally good and the addition of a few
more Chinese members to their ranks would not have elicited comment.
Indeed, Dieu mentioned that the group knew very little about this English
tobacco island called "Tri-li-ni-dich" island, except that there was a large
Chinese community there. The Chinese contacts who facilitated their
escape gave the men letters of introduction to Chinese businesses in Port of
Spain, Trinidad. It is unclear how much these Chinese employers in Port of
Spain knew of the background of their new employees. An 1886 ordinance
meant that all those suspected of being escapees from French Guiana were
meticulously photographed, fingerprinted, and their physical appearance
documented in detail by British authorities.[75] Their details were then sent to
the French authorities in Cayenne for verification. Several of the prisoners
picked up were still in prison uniform or clearly had no travel documents,
problems that this group did not encounter.[76] It is undoubtedly true that
dishevelled white men were more identifiable as escapees from the penal
colony than "Chinese" travellers among a group of Chinese traders.

Once they arrived in Port of Spain, the men worked "undercover" of being
Chinese in different Chinese companies. Dieu worked for an Anglo-Chinese

71. Bridget Jones and Elie Stephenson, "Society, Culture and Politics in French Guiana", in
Richard D. E. Burton and Fred Reno (eds), *French and West Indian: Martinique, Guadeloupe,
and French Guiana Today* (London, 1995), p. 67.
72. Andrew R. Wilson (ed.), *The Chinese in the Caribbean* (Princeton, NJ, 2004),
Introduction, p. 18.
73. Kim Johnson, *Descendants of the Dragon: The Chinese in Trinidad 1806–2006* (Kingston,
2006), p. 62.
74. See Anne-Marie Lee-Loy, "Kissing the Cross: Nineteenth-Century Representations of
Chinese and Indian Immigrants Chinese in British Guiana and Trinidad", in Wilson, *The Chinese
in the Caribbean*, pp. 25–40.
75. CAOM, H/5354. The lists of escapees sent to the British in Trinidad from French Guiana do
not include any of the names of the group in any year between 1915 and 1919, so they did not
come to colonial attention in Trinidad.
76. CAOM, H/5354, Dossiers of the Escapees in British Custody in Trinidad.

commercial firm. Lý married the unnamed English woman he met through the Chinese business that employed him – an interracial marriage facilitated by his fluency in English. The fact that his wife never realized he was Vietnamese, or an escapee from French Guiana, may demonstrate that his true identity did not circulate within his Chinese firm in Port of Spain. Given Trinidad's extradition policies, discretion was essential and Lý took that discretion even into the matrimonial home. After Lý married, he was able to borrow money from his wife's family and set up a small store, which he and his wife ran together.[77]

In his recollections, Lý discussed how, on the day he left, when his wife and children were visiting her parents, he removed some of their joint savings to assist with his passage from Port of Spain. "He was not able to speak one sentence to say goodbye, but left and was separated from her forever."[78] The Chinese community in Port of Spain raised funds to facilitate four passages, which the group supplemented from their savings.[79] They left Trinidad in 1920 or 1921 and spent the next few years in various locations in southern China.

Little is known of Lý's precise activities over the next few years based in southern China and Hong Kong. However, in 1929, Lý decided to return to Vietnam. Ironically, this ultimately led to his rearrest in the city of Vinh Long in southern Vietnam four years later. In 1933, a colonial tribunal found him guilty of fomenting rebellion and sentenced him to fifteen years' hard labour on the prison island of Poulo Condore (off the southern coast of Vietnam). Established in 1861, prior to the consolidation of French Indochina, Poulo Condore was a notorious penal site for prisoners from all the territories of French Indochina. As historian Peter Zinoman points out, "[T]he intensity of the Vietnamese resistance [against the French] generated demands for fortified camps where anticolonial leaders and prisoners of war could be locked away".[80] That fortified place was Poulo Condore, where thousands of Vietnamese prisoners died during the colonial period. Lý died there, shortly after his sentencing, at the age of forty.

Although Diêu claimed that, in 1921, he returned to China and Vietnam via the United States and visited Washington DC, there is no evidence to corroborate that this was indeed the route taken.[81] When Diêu reached Canton he met up with many members of the exiled Vietnamese community and wrote a pamphlet, *Việt Nam cách mạng lưu vong chư*

---

77. Very little can be found out about the couple's marriage or the store that they established together. This information comes from the interviews that Nguyễn Văn Hầu conducted with people who had known him.
78. Nguyễn, "Lý Liễu và phong trào đại đông du", p. 47.
79. *Idem, Chí sĩ Nguyễn Quang Diệu*, p. 62.
80. Zinoman, *Colonial Bastille*, p. 29.
81. Nguyễn, *Chí sĩ Nguyễn Quang Diệu*, p. 58.

nhân vật [Vietnamese Revolutionary Exiles] in Chinese.[82] On his return to Vietnam, he published poetry and political treatises, which circulated widely in the Mekong Delta at the end of the 1920s.[83] Diêu was never rearrested.

Lý Liễu and his colleagues were not the only Vietnamese group to escape French Guiana through Chinese contacts. Between 1907 and 1924, another thirteen members of groups attached to "new learning" groups escaped from French Guiana to Trinidad with Chinese assistance. Ironically, the four members of the KDHH may have passed by these other Vietnamese escapees from French Guiana in the streets of Port of Spain unaware of their racial origins, or entertaining suspicions but not wanting to draw attention to themselves.[84] Not as much is known about the members of these other groups, except for information from the grandson of one of the escapees, Đỗ Văn Phong.[85] No year of escape was narrated to his family, just that in Trinidad "a number of Chinese people protected him".[86] However, it was prior to 1924 because it was then that his family got news of his escape to Port of Spain, where he pretended to be a practitioner in Chinese herbal medicine after establishing a small business.[87] Đỗ eventually returned safely to Vietnam and became a successful publisher.

Perhaps from the perspective of a Western historian, Lý Liễu's decision to return to Hong Kong, and eventually Vietnam, marked a tragic turn in his tale that ended in his untimely death in Poulo Condore. However, for the only Vietnamese historian who has written about Lý Liễu, the real tragedy is Lý's endlessly restless spirit. The fact that his half-English, half-Vietnamese children in Trinidad were unable to place a grave in his natal village means a spirit who will never be at peace and who will ceaselessly haunt the penal vestiges of Poulo Condore.[88] There is no marker of his grave, no artefact connecting him to his natal village, a different kind of "marker" than Western historians seek.

Narratives of prisoners within French penal flows can often be reconstructed from the extensive extant archives at the Centre des Archives d'Outre Mer in Aix en Provence. Lý Liễu's is not one of them. He makes only three very brief appearances in an official archive. He appears at the times

82. In this title, he uses the word *lưu vong* to mean "in exile".

83. For a translation of this exhortation see Hue-Tam Ho Tai, *Millenarianism and Peasant Politics in Vietnam* (Cambridge, MA, 1983), pp. 178–179.

84. This is speculative, because Đỗ Văn Phong and the other escapees may have arrived after the KDHH members had left.

85. The story of Đỗ Văn Phong was related by his grandson, Đỗ Thái Bình, to Huỳnh Thanh Bình, "Một Kiếp Thề Ghi Với Nước Non", in *Nhà Lao An Nam Ở Guyane*, p. 104.

86. *Ibid.*

87. *Ibid.*

88. *Bách Khoa*, CXXXXV, pp. 39–49. Poulo Condore is now known as Con Son Island and has both a national park and a luxury resort on it.

of sentencing – 1913 and 1933 – and he appears briefly in the private papers of Gaston Liebert, the French consul in Hong Kong at the time of his arrest. Although there are voluminous files in the French archives on French Guiana, Lý Liễu's story also shows the lacunae of the archives and the need to read widely in different contexts in order to piece together a multinational narrative of a very cosmopolitan prisoner. Traces of his life had to be carefully reconstructed from historical strands and in Vietnamese and Chinese texts so that his hidden life, one far from the eye of colonial surveillance, could be told. Lý Liễu's life history illustrates the necessity of going beyond the apparatus of the archive to explore penal circulations and connections not readily apparent, and the vital importance of transcending national and/or colonial textual and archival boundaries to examine both the constraints on, and mobility of the lives of, transcolonial exiles.

IRSH 63 (2018), Special Issue, pp. 109–130 doi:10.1017/S002085901800024X
© 2018 Internationaal Instituut voor Sociale Geschiedenis

The Transformation of Hokkaido from Penal Colony to Homeland Territory*

MINAKO SAKATA

Faculty of Intercultural Studies,
Tomakomai Komazawa University
521-293, Nishikioka, Tomakomai, Hokkaido
059-1292, Japan

E-mail: sakatam@r7.dion.ne.jp

ABSTRACT: This article focuses on penal transportation to Hokkaido and considers the role of convict transportation in nation-state building and empire building in Japan. In the course of its discussion, the fluidity of the status of the new Japanese territory of Hokkaido will be examined along with continuities of transportation and incarceration. Although Hokkaido was officially incorporated into Japan only in 1869, many Japanese politicians and intellectuals had believed ideologically that it had been a Japanese territory since the early modern period. Depending on the domestic and diplomatic matters confronting them, the Japanese modified the status of Hokkaido and their policy towards it. For example, to secure their borders with Russia, the Japanese introduced penal transportation on the French model in 1881, but the Japanese Ministry of Justice later shifted their legal system to the German model and articles concerning transportation were deleted from the penal code. Nonetheless, the Japanese government continued to send long-term prisoners to Hokkaido, which was reframed as incarceration in a mainland prison.

INTRODUCTION

Today Hokkaido is one of Japan's four main islands. It was called Ezochi until 1869, when it officially became Japanese territory and was renamed Hokkaido. Ezochi means the land of "the Ezo", or "the barbarian", which referred to the indigenous people, now called the Ainu. While Ezochi referred to Hokkaido in general, the term broadly included what are now known as Sakhalin, Hokkaido, and the Kuril. In this article, I have therefore used the term "Ezo Islands" to refer to the latter. While the Ezo Islands were not officially part of Japan in the early modern period (1603–1867), the Japanese believed that they were under Japanese control regardless of their

* The research leading to these results has received funding from the European Research Council under the European Union's Seventh Framework Programme (FP/2007–2013) / ERC Grant Agreement 312542.

actual relations with the Ainu and whether the Ainu recognized their claim. The ambiguous status of the Ezo Islands came to an end during border negotiations with Russia, which began in 1853. Based on the above view, Japan asserted territorial rights over all the Ezo Islands. However, Japan then lost Sakhalin under the Treaty of St Petersburg in 1875, when Hokkaido and the Kuril Islands became Japanese territory.

Many scholars of modern Japanese history have regarded Hokkaido as a frontier within the Japanese national border. Meanwhile, the status of Hokkaido after 1869 has rarely been disputed, for, as Mason points out, "Hokkaido's status as a colony is commonly denied, implicitly or explicitly [...] in colonial and postcolonial research".[1] However, in his lectures on colonial studies at Tokyo Imperial University given in the mid-1910s, Inazo Nitobe treated Hokkaido as a colony together with other Japanese colonies such as Taiwan (1895–1945), Southern Sakhalin (1905–1945), and Korea (1910–1945). More recently, Hiroyuki Shiode has argued that Hokkaido had been a dependency until 1903, when it was officially incorporated into *Naichi*, or the mainland.[2] The Japanese mainland consists of the three islands of Honshu, Shikoku, and Kyushu, which have been Japanese territory since the beginning of the early modern period.

Even many of the scholars studying Hokkaido have failed to remain free of national ideology, and there was a contradiction between what the Japanese government did and what it said. The focus of this article is Hokkaido's role as a penal colony. I shall therefore consider here the transition in Hokkaido's status within the Japanese process of building first a nation state, and then an empire. The first treaty with Russia was concluded in 1855 and drew the Japanese-Russian border between the islands of Iturup and Urup in the Kuril. Subsequently, both the Tokugawa Shogunate and its successor Meiji government (1868 onwards) considered the introduction of penal transportation as a means to facilitate the rapid settlement of Japanese people on Ezochi. Both regimes were aware that one of the strategies of Russia, as much as of Western countries, was to expand by means of colonization, and that awareness, in turn, implies that, at that time, Hokkaido was not thought of as part of the Japanese mainland.

Although it is well known that penal transportation and convict labour were implemented in Hokkaido in the late nineteenth century, it has always been regarded by historians as being less important than other forms of migration. Penal transportation has traditionally been seen as a temporary labour system used in the very early stages of the Japanese project to

---

1. Michele M. Mason, *Dominant Narratives of Colonial Hokkaido and Imperial Japan: Envisioning the Periphery and the Modern Nation-State* (New York, 2012), p. 3.
2. Hiroyuki Shiode, *Ekkyōsha no seijishi. Ajia taiheiyō niokeru nihonjin no imin to shokumin* (Nagoya, 2016).

develop Hokkaido[3] and as a measure to deal with the shortage of prison space resulting from the aftermath of anti-government movements and revolts from the 1870s to the 1880s.[4] Certain scholars mention, too, its broader context, which required revision of unequal treaties, for which it was necessary to establish a Western-style penal system.[5] The Japanese were also anxious about further Russian incursion southward,[6] and scholars have tended simply to conflate all those background considerations so that the relationships among various demands have not been well described. Moreover, previous researchers have tended to dwell on how penal transportation was introduced, rather neglecting the abolition process, which has consequently not been well studied. This article serves to clarify the relationship between the Japanese penal system and its empire building by describing Hokkaido's place in the Japanese criminal justice system, from the introduction to the abolition of penal transportation.

During the late nineteenth century, when the Japanese began to build a nation state and an empire along Western lines, within the European countries that had provided the colonial template attitudes to penal transportation were divided broadly in line with colonial policies. France and Portugal continued penal transportation, but Britain discontinued it and, for their part, Germany never introduced it,[7] for incarceration was regarded as a more civilized and suitable punishment than transportation.[8] Meanwhile, Japan's choice of mode of punishment mirrored contemporary Western debate as its nation building involved drastic reform of social and judicial systems in which the decision was made to deal with both domestic and diplomatic matters. In terms of its penal system, Japan first followed the French model in implementing penal transportation to Hokkaido and then, in the early 1890s, decided to follow the German model and so abolished it. However, Hokkaido continued to be a place of punishment for long-term prisoners. In describing how events unfolded, this article will show the fluidity between transportation and incarceration.

The history of Hokkaido's shift from having the status of a colony to becoming part of the Japanese mainland set a precedent for subsequent Japanese colonial rule. *Naichi enchō shugi*, or "extending homeland ideology", is the term usually applied to Japanese policy in colonial Taiwan and

---

3. Osamu Tanaka, *Nihon shihonshugi to Hokkaido* (Sapporo, 1986); *Masato Kuwabara, Kindai Hokkaidoshi kenkyū josetsu* (Sapporo, 1982).
4. Kazuyoshi Shigematsu, *Hokkaido gyōkeishi* (Sapporo, 1970); Daniel V. Botsman, *Punishment and Power in the Making of Modern Japan* (Princeton, NJ, 2005); Tanaka, *Nihon shihonshugi*.
5. Shigematsu, *Hokkaido gyōkeishi*; Botsman, *Punishment and Power*.
6. Shigematsu, *Hokkaido gyōkeishi*; Botsman, *Punishment and Power*.
7. Christian De Vito, Clare Anderson, and Ulbe Bosma, "Penal Transportation, Deportation, and Exile in the Nineteenth and Twentieth Centuries: Perspectives from the Colonies", in this special issue.
8. *Ibid.*

Korea, and, in general, Japanese colonies were regarded as places that, once fully assimilated, would eventually be incorporated into mainland Japan. The term first appeared sometime after 1919, applied to colonial policy relating to Taiwan, but the case of Hokkaido can be seen as the first true instance of it, indicating continuity between nation-state building and empire building in Japan. This article will show, too, how the penal system of the mainland affected that of colonial Taiwan and Korea in the sense of "extending homeland ideology".

PENAL TRANSPORTATION TO HOKKAIDO

It was in the late eighteenth century that Japan first faced foreign expansion southwards into northeast Asia when Russian territorial growth began to encroach on the Ezo Islands. Although, at that time, the islands were not formally Japanese territory, many officials of the Tokugawa Shogunate and contemporary intellectuals felt strongly that the islands were nevertheless Japanese territory. The Ainu and the Matsumae-han, the northernmost domain of early modern Japan, had long enjoyed trade relations, with Japanese merchants gaining permission from Matsumae to establish fishing grounds around Ezochi and the southern coast of Sakhalin, employing the Ainu as labour. Then, from 1799 to 1821, the shogunate took direct control of Ezochi for reasons of national defence against Russia. Garrison forces were dispatched and the Ainu were ordered to cooperate in securing the islands against the Russians.[9] However, the Japanese government did not actually enforce annexation of the Ezo Islands and the shogunate abandoned its migration policy as soon as direct control began. As a result, the policy to assimilate the Ainu was also abandoned.[10] Tributary trade, called *omemie*, was carried on between the Ainu chiefs and shogunate officials (or Matsumae-han officials) and that, at least for the Japanese, implied that the Ainu were subject to Japanese authority. That, then, was the basis for Japanese rule over the Ezo Islands, as far as the Japanese were concerned.

On the other hand, until the early nineteenth century, many Japanese intellectuals, among them Toshiaki Honda and Nobuhiro Satō, advocated a national defence policy. They made reference to Western imperialism and asserted that Japanese migration, including transportation of convicts to the Ezo Islands, was necessary to Japan's defence.[11] Indeed, they also called for

9. Azusa Matsumoto, "Kinsei kōuki Ezochi ni okeru ikokusen bōbi taisei. 'Basho' kōseiin no hensei o chūshin ni", *Shigaku zasshi*, 115:3 (2006), pp. 79–80.

10. Satoru Fujita, *Kinsei kōki seijishi to taigai kankei* (Tokyo, 2005), pp. 167–169.

11. Toshiaki Honda, "Hondashi sakuron ezo shūi", in Shirō Yokokawa (ed.), *Honda Toshiaki Shū* (1789; Tokyo, 1935); Toshiaki Honda, "Sekii dōsei", in Hajime Terasawa *et al.* (eds), *Hoppō mikōkai komonjo shūsei*, 3 (1791; Tokyo, 1978); Nobuhiro Satō, "Bōkaisaku", in Seiichi Takimoto (ed.), *Satō Nobuhiro kagaku zenshū ge* (1808; Tokyo, 1927), p. 827.

further expansion into Kamchatka and North America[12] and, still in the name of national defence, promoted the idea that Japan should occupy territory far beyond its actual borders. That, however, did not become government policy.

By the late nineteenth century, the Ezo Islands had been divided between Japan and Russia. In 1855, a border was drawn between Iturup and Urup, part of the Kuril Islands, but negotiations over Sakhalin took another twenty years to resolve. Until then, Sakhalin was left open to settlement by both nations, and the Japanese and Russians competed to settle their own people on the island with the intention of strengthening their claims to territorial rights. In the end, Russia prevailed, and in 1875 Japan and Russia concluded the Treaty of St Petersburg under which the whole island of Sakhalin became Russian territory.[13]

It was through those processes of division and formalization that Japan gained Hokkaido and the Kuril Islands as new territory, but lost Sakhalin, part of the empire it had imagined for itself. In its first experience of international territorial dispute, the Japanese government therefore recognized the significance of migration as a way to secure territory against Western imperialism. The Japanese had enjoyed trade relations with the indigenous people of Sakhalin long before the Russians came, but because they failed effectively to settle a Japanese population on the island they lost any territorial rights to it.

Hokkaido became the island of Japan's northern border. Having learned from experience, as soon as it assumed power, the Meiji government not only recruited free migrants to go to Hokkaido, but sent vagrants there too, and finally sought to introduce transportation of convicts. In 1868, the Meiji government designated what was then still known as Ezochi as the sole destination for transportation[14] and began to compile a penal code. From the early stages of the project, certain government officials were interested in the French model, so in 1872 the Japanese Ministry of Justice dispatched officials to Europe, specifically France, to investigate legal systems there. During that visit, the Japanese delegation succeeded in recruiting the French jurist Gustave Emile Boissonade as an adviser. In 1880, drafted by Boissonade, a new penal code was promulgated under which five categories of punishment for felony were prescribed: the death penalty (*shikei*), penal servitude (*tokei*), transportation (*rukei*), imprisonment with hard labour (*chōeki*), and imprisonment without hard labour (*kingoku*). Those sentenced to penal servitude or transportation were to be

12. Nobuhiro Satō, "Bōkaisaku", pp. 821–825; Toshiaki Honda, "Seiiki monogatari", in Shirō Yokokawa (ed.), *Honda Toshiaki Shū* (1789; Tokyo, 1935), p. 173.

13. Toshiyuki Akizuki, *Nichiro kankei to Saharintō. Bakumatsu meiji shonen no ryōdo mondai* (Tokyo, 1994).

14. Naikaku kirokukyoku (ed.), *Hōki bunrui taizen*, 26 (Tokyo, 1891), p. 14.

transported to an island for life or a finite term of from twelve to fifteen years. Although the penal code did not indicate any specific island as the destination, the prison code that was revised in 1881 stated that convicts who were sentenced to penal servitude or transportation were to be confined in *shūchikan* prisons on Hokkaido. Those sentenced to imprisonment with or without hard labour were to serve terms of six to eleven years in mainland prisons.

Shūchikan prisons were for convicted felons and political offenders. There were three *shūchikan* on the mainland, at Tokyo, Miyagi, and Miike, and there were five on Hokkaido at Kabato, Sorachi, Kushiro, Abashiri, and Tokachi. The *shūchikan* on the mainland held convicts sentenced to imprisonment without labour and, temporarily until they could be transported to Hokkaido, convicts sentenced to penal servitude and transportation.

Transportation to Hokkaido began in 1881. Among the five Hokkaido prisons four were built inland where the Japanese had not yet settled. The convicts were used to clear the land, for agriculture, and in mines. Furthermore, they were initially expected to become settlers themselves after completing their terms, in order to supplement the limited numbers of free migrants. Prisons offered business opportunities which attracted merchants and craftsmen to the prison sites, and Kabato, Sorachi, and Kushiro prisons, surrounded by dense forests, were rapidly transformed into towns.[15] From 1886 to 1893, a road across Hokkaido from east to west was constructed by convict labour to connect Sapporo, the island's capital, with the prison towns. Twenty-five *tondenhei* (farmer-soldier) towns were built along the road, with the result that it became possible for settlers on Hokkaido to move inland, and the migrant population rapidly increased in the 1890s.

TOWARDS THE ABOLITION OF TRANSPORTATION

The fluid status of Hokkaido in penal code reform

Penal transportation to Hokkaido did not last long. The penal code was revised in 1907 when the principal punishments were categorized as the death penalty (*shikei*), imprisonment with hard labour (*chōeki*), imprisonment without hard labour (*kinko*), a fine (*bakkin*), and custody (*kōryu*). Those sentenced to imprisonment with or without hard labour were incarcerated for life or for a finite term of between one month and twenty years. Those given custodial sentences were detained for between one day and a month. Transportation to an island was officially abolished under the new penal code and, in a sense, the code's revision was part of the process of the ideological incorporation of Hokkaido into the mainland.

15. Chiaki Oguchi, *"Konomarenai kūkan" no rekishichirigaku* (Tokyo, 2002), pp. 25–55.

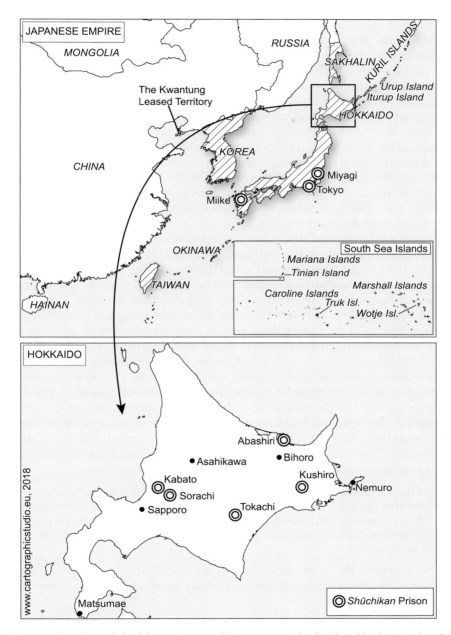

Figure 1. Locations of *shūchikan* prisons on the Japanese mainland and Hokkaido. Map based on a sketch by the author. Produced with reference to Ramon H. Myers and Mark R. Peattie (eds), *The Japanese Colonial Empire, 1895–1945*, (Princeton, NJ, 1984), p. 53; Tanaka, *Nihon shihonshugi*, p. 119.

One of the major backgrounds to the revision of the penal code and the elimination from it of transportation was the establishment of the constitution, work on which began in 1882 and which was modelled on the constitution of the German Empire because that constitution preserved the royal prerogative. France had become a republic and Britain's parliament retained strong authority, so that the Japanese, wishing to both preserve the emperor's prerogative and to introduce a Western-style legal system to gain respect as a "civilized nation", considered the German legal system to be ideal. Later, in 1886, the Japanese government began to formulate other laws and to amend the penal code,[16] and to promote consistency with the constitution those new laws, too, were modelled on German ones. Because the German penal code did not prescribe transportation, the Japanese eliminated from their new code articles relating to penal colonies.

Another background to Japan's turn towards anti-transportation was its revision of the unequal treaty that the Tokugawa Shogunate had concluded with Western powers in the mid-nineteenth century. During negotiations in 1886, Britain and Germany had asked Japan to enact Western-style laws, which they demanded should include a revised penal code as a condition for revision of the treaty. The Ministry of Justice had launched a revision of the penal code as early as 1882, early drafts containing articles envisaging enhancements of the penal colony system, such as permission to be given to the transported to settle in the penal colony with their families after a number of years of imprisonment.[17] However, under the influence of the legal reforms mentioned above, that provision was deleted from the 1887 draft. Another amendment involved the deletion of terms such as *shimachi* (island) and *naichi* (home territory or the mainland), and that was significant because the term *shimachi* distinguished Hokkaido as a destination for transportation from the mainland. Deletion of those terms therefore implied erasure of that distinction. The penal code did not fit the reality of punishment, according to the Ministry of Justice, which justified the changes as follows:

> [In the previous draft,] the destination of transportation was specified as "an island". However, Japan does not have appropriate islands. Thus, in the case of transportation, it is necessary that administrators designate a destination. The current penal code also prescribes transportation to an island. However, it does not actually seem to have occurred.[18]

The comment that "transportation to an island" did not seem to have occurred is surprising and seems to have stemmed from a series of

---

16. Fumiaki Uchida *et al.* (eds), *Nihon rippō shiryō zenshū*, 20–2 (Tokyo, 2009), p. 5.

17. "Shihōshō kaisei an (meiji 15 nen matsu–16 nen sho)", in Fumiaki Uchida *et al.* (eds), *Nihon rippō shiryō zenshū*, 20 (1883; Tokyo, 1999), p. 77; "Meiji 18 nen 'Boissonade no keihō kaisei an (nihon keihō sōan)' (1885), in *idem*, *Nihon rippō*, 20–2, p. 60.

18. "Keihō sōan shūsei setsumei (meiji 20 nen 5 gatsu)" (1887), in *idem*, *Nihon rippō*, 20–2, p. 202.

comments on the Japanese penal code written by a German jurist named Albert Friedrich Berner. Berner remarked that the current Japanese penal code was too complicated and pointed out that the German penal code referred to just four categories of imprisonment. Berner suggested, too, that no distinction was necessary between *shimachi* and *naichi*, because Japan is an island country anyway. Furthermore, an "island" for transportation should be sufficiently remote to deprive deportees of the freedom to return to their home country. Berner certainly seems to have regarded Hokkaido as part of the Japanese mainland and to have assumed that any regulation of the destination of transportation was irrelevant.[19]

According to Berner's view, the movement of convicts, which had been practised in Japan over the previous few years, was not seen as "transportation", which allowed for an easy shift of the penal system from the French model to the German model because transportation was easily re-interpreted as imprisonment. A simultaneous advantage was that the changed thinking suited the Japanese doctrine that Hokkaido was "historically" Japanese territory, which was further correlated with the reason for deleting the term *naichi* from the penal code. The 1880 penal code had prescribed that imprisonment with and without hard labour were to be served "in mainland (*naichi*) prisons", while the 1887 draft says simply that sentences with and without hard labour were to be served "in prisons". The Ministry of Justice explained the change by saying that it was because all Japanese islands were now part of the mainland, so that it was unnecessary to make a distinction. If imprisonment were restricted to *naichi* prisons, convicts sentenced to imprisonment with or without hard labour in Sapporo, Nemuro (both prefectures in Hokkaido), or Okinawa could not be incarcerated in prisons there.[20] Surprisingly, that comment implies that the Ministry of Justice regarded Hokkaido and Okinawa as equivalent to the mainland, although strictly speaking they were not.

The Ministry of Justice took the view that transportation to an island had not occurred because their view was that Hokkaido was equivalent to the mainland. The distinction between servitude and transportation originally designed as sentences for Hokkaido, and imprisonment with or without hard labour which were sentences originally designed for the mainland, therefore made no sense. In other words, the difference between transportation and imprisonment had become blurred. In the 1890 draft submitted to the Imperial Diet, servitude and transportation were eliminated and absorbed into imprisonment with or without hard labour. The Ministry of Justice explained the changes as follows:

> In the first place, the distinction between islands and the mainland is not clear in our country. [...] In countries which have colonies, this prescription means

---

19. "Beruneru shi 'Nihon keihō ni kansuru ikensho'" (1886), in *idem*, *Nihon rippō*, 20, pp. 475–476.
20. "Keihō sōan", p. 204.

removal of undesirable people from the mainland to the colonies, and it must contribute to the development of colonies. However, in our country, this is nothing but a nominal clause. Hence, in this revision, we deleted the designation of the place of punishment.[21]

It was seventeen more years before the new penal code was promulgated, but following the 1890 draft the abolition of servitude and transportation as forms of punishment and the deletion of expressions such as "transportation to an island" and *naichi* were formalized under the Japanese penal code.

Shimachi, an island, under the penal code

The reform of the penal code effectively exposed Hokkaido's ambiguous status as colony and region of the mainland, an ambiguity caused by a gap between ideology and reality. Although the 1880 penal code did not indicate a specific destination island for transportation, it was obvious in the late nineteenth-century context which island was meant. Transportation to Hokkaido was one of the policies the Meiji government sought to introduce as soon as they assumed power, and the members of the committee drafting the 1880 penal code assumed it would be the destination.[22] The 1881 prison code prescribed that *shūchikan* prisons in Hokkaido should hold convicts sentenced to servitude and transportation,[23] but in 1889, prior to the 1907 revision of the penal code along the lines of the German code,[24] that clause was modified to specify *shūchikan* as the prison for those sentenced to penal servitude, transportation, and imprisonment with hard labour according to the old law.[25] Hokkaido was now omitted as the destination of transportation,[26] a revision reflecting prison administration at the time. *Shūchikan* prisons in Hokkaido had become full and were unable to receive all the convicts who were supposed to be transported. Inevitably then, *shūchikan* on the mainland continued to confine them. Nevertheless, in his *Nihon kangokuhō kougi* [*A Lecture on the Japanese Prison Code*] published in 1890, the jurist Shigejirō Ogawa explained that convicts sentenced to penal servitude and transportation were to be transported to an island – Hokkaido.[27] Although *shūchikan* prisons on the mainland, too, held such convicts, they

21. "Keihōan setsumeisho", in Fumiaki Uchida *et al.* (eds), *Nihon rippō shiryō zenshū*, 20–3 (Tokyo, 2009), p. 202.
22. Bushō Okazaki (ed.), "Nihon keihō sōan kaigi hikki", in Waseda daigaku (ed.), *Nihon keihō sōan kaigi hikki*, I (1881; Tokyo, 1976), pp. 65, 92.
23. "Kaitei kangokusoku", in *Hōki bunrui taizen*, 29 (Tokyo, 1891), p. 164.
24. Mizuho Himejima, *Meiji kangokuhō, seiritsushi no kenkyū* (Tokyo, 2011).
25. Imprisonment with hard labour according to the old law means the severest punishment under *Kaitei ritsurei*, which was a previous penal code promulgated in 1873 and abolished in 1881.
26. *Kanpō*, 1811 (Tokyo, 1889), p. 145.
27. Shigejirō Ogawa, *Nihon kangokuhō kōgi* (Tokyo, 1890).

did so in their capacity as *Kariryūkan*, prisons the function of which was to confine convicts temporarily until they could be transferred to Hokkaido.[28] According to Ogawa's understanding, the expression "an island" in the penal code was not intended geographically but was a political concept based on the binary opposition of "island" and "mainland" (*naichi*). In practice "island" meant nothing other than Hokkaido, which was obviously not included in the mainland.

On the other hand, the revision of the prison code in 1889 allowed for a literal interpretation regarding the place of punishment for penal servitude and transportation. In his *Nihon keihō ron* [*Theory on the Japanese Penal Code*, 1894], the jurist Asatarō Okada had the following to say:

> The prison code (1889) designates *shūchikan* prisons as facilities for the incarceration of convicts sentenced to servitude, transportation, and imprisonment with labour according to the old law. Three *shūchikan* prisons are built on the mainland. Therefore, although the penal code prescribes the transportation of convicts sentenced to servitude and transportation to an island, this is not necessary according to the prison code. In practice, transportation has not always been used.[29]

According to Okada, "an island" in the penal code referred to Hokkaido.[30] However, as *shūchikan* prisons on the mainland functioned as *kariryūkan* (temporary prisons for those sentenced to servitude and transportation), their status became unclear.[31] Okada took the view that reference to transportation should be deleted as mainland *shūchikan* in practice confined convicts sentenced to penal servitude and transportation. Shigejirō Ogawa, by contrast, considered that it was mainland *shūchikan* which ought to be abolished.[32] Although Okada recognized the benefit of convict labour for the development of Hokkaido, he concluded that the penal code, which prescribed penal transportation, should be revised in view of the high cost of transportation and prison management in a barren land.[33] While Ogawa and Okada held opposite views on penal transportation, both thought that "island" (*shimachi*) in the 1880 penal code referred to Hokkaido, which both viewed as being distinct from the mainland.

---

28. *Ibid.*, pp. 6–9.
29. Asatarō Okada, *Nihon keihō ron* (Tokyo, 1894), p. 753.
30. *Ibid.*, p. 749.
31. According to Kaoru Inoue, the Home Minister from 1892 to 1894, the prison code was revised in 1889 in order to deal with the many convicts who could not be transported and so were incarcerated on mainland *shūchikan* at that time. National Archives of Japan [hereafter, NAJ], "Shūchikan seido no ken", in *Kōbun betsuroku, naimushō, meiji 19 nen–meiji 30 nen, dai 1 kan* (1893). From his description, it is not clear why they could not be transported. However, it seems that the number of convicts in Hokkaido had reached capacity.
32. Ogawa, *Nihon kangokuhō*, pp. 7–8.
33. Okada, *Nihon keihō ron*, pp. 753–754.

As mentioned earlier, the Japanese had regarded Hokkaido as their territory since the early modern period based on the doctrine that places inhabited by the Ainu were Japanese. In reality, to secure the island against Russian expansion the Japanese government found itself obliged to introduce strategies similar to those used by Western countries in their colonies. Kentarō Kaneko, who investigated Hokkaido in 1885 and proposed a policy plan for its development, which included the use of convict labour, was referring to Western colonial policies when he asserted that mainland policies and systems should not be adopted for Hokkaido.[34]

Jurists and Kaneko, the government official, clearly regarded Hokkaido as distinct from the mainland, so that Hokkaido's status as decreed by the Ministry of Justice in its reform of the penal code was not the commonly understood view of it. Only by assuming that Hokkaido was equivalent to the mainland would it be possible to deny that transportation was being practised in Japan, by re-designating as "incarceration" the continued sending of convicts to Hokkaido. In the next section, we shall see how that was done. The process of eliminating transportation in name only from the penal code therefore came about because the Japanese government sought consistency between national ideology and the legislative system.

Demand for convict labour and criticism

From 1880 to the early 1890s, just when articles concerning penal transportation were being deleted as a result of reform of the penal code, extramural convict labour was at its peak on Hokkaido. Even so, although the migrant population was steadily increasing, it was far from being enough to make up for the labour shortage. In about 1891, Teruchika Ōinoue, the Governor of Kabato prison in Hokkaido, proposed that male convicts serving sentences of imprisonment with hard labour should be sent to Hokkaido so that they could be utilized as a labour force.[35] In 1891, a petition was submitted to the House of Peers proposing transportation to Hokkaido of those convicts sentenced to more than two years' imprisonment.[36] Both those instances testify to the high demand for and poor supply of cheap labour on Hokkaido, and in the House of Peers certain members were sympathetic to the petition, for the number of migrants had not increased sufficiently. However, other members were against it, arguing that it would make Hokkaido a land of vice. That turned out to be the view of the majority, so that in the end the bill was not sent to the government.

By that time, criticism of transportation of convicts and of extramural prison labour was increasing. In 1892 and 1895, a number of members of the

---

34. Kentarō Kaneko, "Hokkaido sanken junshi fukumeisho", in Hokkaidochō (ed.), *Shinsen Hokkaido shi* (1885; Sapporo, 1936), pp. 591–644.
35. Tanaka, *Nihon shihonshugi*, p. 141.
36. *Kizokuin giji sokkiroku*, 36, 24 February 1891, pp. 547–558.

House of Representatives claimed that the policy was propagating an unfavourable image of Hokkaido as a place where felons were sent, so that potential free migrants might be disinclined to move there. Transportation was, they said, an obstacle to the development of Hokkaido.

What caused settlers' antipathy to *shūchikan* and convicts in general were the crimes of the convicts and their tendency to escape. The number of escapes from *shūchikan* in Hokkaido was much higher than from other prisons in Japan, and the more extramural prison labour was used the more convicts escaped. In 1891, 136 escapes were recorded out of a population of 6,850 convicts, and forty per cent of them were never recaptured.[37]

The government recognized the harmful effect of the transportation system. In 1893, after his inspection tour to Hokkaido, the Home Minister Kaoru Inoue[38] proposed the gradual abolition of *shūchikan* prisons on Hokkaido Island and the establishment of a prison on another island if necessary, and that convicts due to complete their terms within a year should be sent back to mainland prisons. Inoue gave two reasons for his proposal. One concerned prison administration. He explained that the number of convicts sentenced to penal servitude and transportation was increasing annually. *Shūchikan* prisons on Hokkaido had reached capacity and could not receive all of them. Therefore, the prison code had been revised to enable mainland *shūchikan* to house such convicts. Inoue concluded that, despite what the penal code said, convicts sentenced to penal servitude and transportation were not always transported to Hokkaido. The minister's other reason concerned migration policy. Inoue argued that, at that time, the number of free migrants was increasing in Hokkaido, but that they were prone to threats and even harm from escaped convicts. Moreover, he claimed that if convicts were to be officially released on Hokkaido they too might harm settlers. The cabinet approved Inoue's proposal in 1894.[39]

In fact, the transportation system went into almost complete decline following the aforementioned government decision and a subsequent amnesty offered on the occasion of the Empress Dowager's death in 1897. After 1897, the total number of convicts transported dropped by two thirds (Table 1), while repatriations meant that the number of convicts on Hokkaido *shūchikan* decreased too. That, in turn, affected the development of Hokkaido insofar as it depended on convict labour for work, such as clearing land. Indeed, by 1899, the governor of Hokkaido *shūchikan*,[40] Kingo Ishizawa, was writing to the head of the prison bureau of the Home Ministry to inform him that convicts in Hokkaido's *shūchikan* now amounted to fewer than 3,000, meaning a shortfall of 2,800 from the

37. Tanaka, *Nihon shihonshugi*, p. 139.
38. Inoue kō denki hensan kai (ed.), *Seigai Inoue kō den*, 4 (Tokyo, 1934), pp. 277–297.
39. NAJ, "Shūchikan seido no ken", in *Kōbun betsuroku, naimushō*.
40. Kabato *shūchikan* was renamed Hokkaido *shūchikan* during the period 1891 to 1903.

Table 1. *The number of convicts sentenced to servitude and transportation.*

Year	With hard labour for life	With hard labour	Without hard labour for life	Without hard labour	Total
1890	1,779	5,733	2	16	7,530
1891	1,880	6,122	2	11	8,015
1892	2,057	6,633	2	15	8,707
1893	2,252	7,000	10	14	9,276
1894	2,403	7,234	2	20	9,659
1895	2,520	7,109	2	24	9,655
1896	2,625	6,857	3	23	9,508
1897	242	2,876	0	5	3,123
1898	481	3,117	0	5	3,603
1899	674	3,307	0	5	3,986
1900	813	3,297	0	7	4,117
1901	924	3,226	0	5	4,155
1902	1,094	3,289	1	6	4,390
1903	1,285	3,458	1	8	4,752

Sources: Naimushō (ed.), *Dainihonteikoku naimushō tōkei hōkoku dai 10 kai* (Tokyo, 1895); Shihōshō (ed.), *Shihōshō kangokukyoku tōkei nenpō dai 1 kai* (Tokyo, 1901); Shihōshō (ed.), *Shihōshō kangokukyoku tōkei nenpō dai 2 kai* (Tokyo, 1905).

prison's full capacity. Ishizawa further complained, "[w]e will have difficulties to accomplish projects in the next fiscal year. Land clearing will get much more behind", and went on to request transportation of convicts from the mainland.[41] In the event, 500 convicts were sent to Hokkaido that year from Tokyo, Miyagi, and Miike *shūchikan*, but, given that fewer convicts were sentenced to penal servitude and transportation, it was impossible to prevent a chronic shortage of convicts on Hokkaido.[42]

Repatriation of convicts was an extremely financially inefficient policy. Criticism of transportation had initially arisen on the grounds of cost,[43] and repatriation only made the whole operation more expensive. From 1895, Home Ministry officials sought a way to settle convicts in Hokkaido[44] and, in 1899, the prison bureau inquired with Hokkaido's government about the possibility of releasing convicts on the island who had expressed a willingness to settle and seek proper employment. The Ministry explained

41. Japanese Correctional Association Library [hereafter, JCAL], "Hokkaido *shūchikan* e shūto hakken no ken", (1899), M092 387.
42. One possible reason for the reduction in the number of felons is the establishment of the Imperial Diet, which had been one of the most important demands of the liberty and democratic-rights movement and had prompted mass arrests in the 1880s.
43. Okada, *Nihon keihō ron*, pp. 753–754.
44. JCAL, "Hokkaido shūchikan hōmenshu torishimari ni kansuru ken" (1899), M092 387. Despite the policy proposed by the Home Minister Inoue being approved in February 1894, the Home Ministry seemed unwilling to enforce it. Inoue left his position in October 1894.

that many of the convicts sent back to the mainland subsequently moved back to Hokkaido, so the suggestion was that the state was incurring unnecessary expense for repatriation. The Ministry claimed that, unlike in the past, freed convicts could be expected to contribute to the development of Hokkaido and would be unlikely to harm free migrants. The Ministry further complained that the decline in the number of convicts on Hokkaido was causing delay to projects requiring their labour. However, the Director General of the Hokkaido government rejected the plan because there were still too few policemen on Hokkaido.[45] In fact, the Hokkaido government did not want convicts to settle there, because the number of free migrants was increasing sharply from the 1890s, and it had no real expectation that convicts would become good settlers.

Ineffectiveness of transportation as punishment and rehabilitation

In the Imperial Diet of 1895, in a reply to an inquiry from members of the House of Representatives who opposed transportation, the government explained its position on that and on the gradual closing of *shūchikan* and the repatriation of convicts.[46] That change in policy, along with the penal code reform proposed in the first Imperial Diet convened in 1890, was seen as an admission by the government that penal transportation to Hokkaido had been a failure. In the *Kangoku zasshi* [Prison Journal] in 1895 a writer, Kaneshirosei, wrote that although transportation to Hokkaido was inevitable under the circumstances of the time, "it is established knowledge that the transportation of criminals to overseas or islands is not a wise policy. As readers might admit, cases of France and Russia are such examples".[47] He briefly introduced a French jurist's essay against transportation, which argued that the appropriateness of the system should be considered from three aspects: rehabilitation of convicts, its effect on the place of imprisonment, and problems for the mainland. The essay concluded that transportation was ineffective as a means of rehabilitating convicts, that it threatened public safety, and that it placed a financial burden on the state.

Although Kaneshirosei's statements were about theoretical debates, the above points were precisely the problems mentioned in connection with the evaluation of transportation to Hokkaido, which were going on both within and outside the Japanese government at that time. We have already encountered critical voices addressing the second and third points, but on the first point I will now examine the contribution of Asataro Okada, who discussed the effects of convict labour at the Horonai coal mine (see Figure 2).

---

45. JCAL, "Hokkaido shūchikan mankishū sōkan no ken hatsugi" (1899), Mo92 387. JCAL, "Hokkaido shūchikan hōmenshū".
46. "Dai 8 kai teikokugikai shūgiin", *Dainihon teikokugikaishi*, 3, p. 632.
47. Kaneshirosei, "Tokeishū no sōkan to iunitsuite", *Kangoku Zasshi*, 6:4 (1895), pp. 1–3.

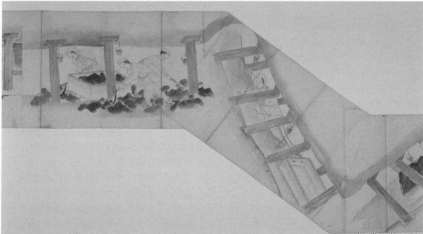

Figure 2. *Shūjin rōdō emaki* [Illustrated Handscroll of Convict Labour], c.1881–1889. Painted by a convict in Sorachi *shūchikan*. It depicts the mining process at the Horonai coal mine. *Courtesy of the National Museum of Japanese History.*

Okada visited Horonai in 1893. He first described the dreadful working environment at the mine, in which many convicts were suffering from disease and injury because of poor hygienic conditions and frequent accidents there. Okada met many convicts who had lost limbs and discovered that more than fifty people had been blinded. However, to his surprise, there were many convicts who were happy to work in the mine.

Okada then noted that the mine included many long and narrow galleries, which were rarely frequented by guards, and where convicts could therefore do as they liked – not least escape. For example, on one occasion, a group of convicts drove a tunnel up to ground level and absconded. If they did not care to escape, the convicts could still eat and drink in peace in the bowels of the mine; they brought rice to one of tunnels and used it to brew sake, while abandoned galleries were used to store tobacco, food, and illicit liquor. Gambling and sexual activity took place too.

Okada concluded that the mine had become a kind of paradise, where certain types of impenitent convicts might want to go. He saw, too, that convicts wishing to mend their ways would be exposed to the deadly situation.[48] Similar observations may be seen in official reports by the Home Ministry and in the memoirs of prisoners.[49] In general, then, *shūchikan* prisons on Hokkaido were considered ineffective or even harmful as a means of punishment and provided no rehabilitation.

FROM HOKKAIDO TO COLONIES

After the incorporation

In 1903, the vote was given to migrants to Hokkaido, which meant the completion of Hokkaido's incorporation into the mainland.[50] In the same year, the *shūchikan* prison system was abolished and each penal colony site became a general prison. Extramural prison labour was abolished around 1904, the penal code was revised in 1907, and the already dying penal transportation system was officially abolished in 1908. Hokkaido was the first successful example of the incorporation of a new territory into the Japanese mainland, a forerunner of an approach to Japanese territorial expansion later called "extending homeland ideology".

After the incorporation of Hokkaido, the concept of "the mainland" became more problematic. Even after the abolition of transportation, long-term prisoners were continually sent to prisons there. Under the new penal code promulgated in 1907, terms of imprisonment with or without hard labour

48. Okada, *Nihon keihō ron*, pp. 764–769.
49. Minako Sakata, "Japan in the Eighteenth and Nineteenth Centuries", in Clare Anderson (ed.), *A Global History of Convicts and Penal Colonies* (London, 2018), pp. 307–335.
50. Hiroyuki Shiode, *Ekkyōsha no seijishi*, p. 62.

became longer, with a maximum of twenty years, rather than the fifteen years of the 1880 penal code. As a result, the convict population increased,[51] leading, for example, Chohei Minota, a Chief Warder at Kosuge prison (the former Tokyo *shūchikan*), to write in his memoir about his experience of escorting 150 prisoners to Abashiri in 1911.[52] However, that custom was not referred to as penal transportation, because officially Hokkaido was by then part of the mainland and the transportation system no longer existed.

Extramural prison labour had been abolished, but in 1933 it was revived on Hokkaido,[53] first for railway construction by convicts from the Abashiri prison on the former penal colony site and then at Asahikawa prison, which was the successor to the Kabato *shūchikan*, closed in 1919. Asahikawa city was in central Hokkaido, and, in the late nineteenth century, was the site of a camp for convicts who built roads and military barracks. After the Seventh Division of the Japanese Army was formed in 1900, Asahikawa became a garrison city and the convicts were employed not only for public works, but for construction and farm work for the army too.

That period did not see a significant number of instances of escape attempts among the convict labourers, nor was there much convict crime. Rather, their diligence and the quality of their work impressed many people. For example, on 13 June 1938, a newspaper noted that the quality of the Asahikawa prison convicts' work on the construction of a bank far exceeded that of general labourers.[54] However, as background to such a positive evaluation we should take into account various illegal forced labour practices in use at the time on Hokkaido in the aftermath of the abolition of extramural convict labour. To supplement labour shortages, agents illegally sent Japanese vagrants and paupers to Hokkaido, who were then confined and forced by contractors to work, under violent supervision. Compared with such forced labour, convicts appeared to be more disciplined and more highly motivated. Convict labour was therefore revived not simply as a form of severe punishment for felons, but also as a kind of rehabilitation programme. Aiming to reintegrate prisoners into society, the Ministry of Justice introduced the progressive stage system in 1933, under which more diligent convicts could work towards greater freedoms in prison. In Hokkaido, extramural prison labour was rediscovered as one means to that end.[55]

After the outbreak of the Sino-Japanese war in 1937, the mainland, too, experienced a shortage of labour, so that, following the example of Hokkaido, extramural prison labour was reintroduced in other parts of the mainland.[56]

51. Kyōsei kyōkai (ed.), *Nihon kinsei gyōkeishi ko, ge* (Tokyo, 1943), p. 689.
52. Chohei Minota, "Gojū nen mae no omoide", in *Keisei*, 71:4 (1960), pp. 70–73.
53. Kyōsei kyōkai (ed.), *Senji gyōkei jitsuroku* (Tokyo, 1966), pp. 117–119.
54. *Ibid.*, p. 141; Yomiuri shinbun, 13 June 1938.
55. Kyōsei kyōkai, *Senji gyōkei*, pp. 122–123.
56. *Ibid.*, pp. 129–137.

From 1937 to 1940, convicts in Urawa prison (Saitama prefecture) constructed a rowing lake for the Games of the Twelfth Olympiad, which had been scheduled for 1940 but was not held – although, incidentally, the same lake was later improved and used in the 1964 Tokyo Olympics.[57]

After 1938, convicts became an important source of labour for the construction of naval installations. The Navy requested the use of the Abashiri prison population to construct a naval airbase at Bihoro in eastern Hokkaido; in the end, more than a thousand convicts were sent there from prisons all over Japan to join the 200 convicts from Abashiri.[58] The success of that project led to a series of instances of the use of convicts to construct naval installations and, in 1939, the Naval Ministry decided to employ convicts to construct air bases in the South Sea Islands. The Ministry requested only healthy, strong, and non-violent prisoners with few dependants and whose remaining terms were less than eighteen months.[59] The specification of "few dependants" suggests that the Navy was allowing for the possibility that convicts might die in service. In total, 2,400 Japanese convicts were sent to Yokohama and then to Tinian Island and Wotje Island (1939–1941),[60] while 1,300 were sent to the Truk Islands (Chuuk Islands) (1941–1945).[61] In the Truk Islands, construction work continued during the Pacific War, and US air raids after 1944 cut Japanese supply lines, which caused serious food shortages.[62] In such circumstances, many convicts died of starvation and, to reduce pressure on provisions, a number were killed by prison guards for trifling offences such as petty theft as well as for trying to escape. According to Sei Kubota, who survived, only fifty of 490 convicts were still alive at the end of the war.[63] Later, Akira Masaki, who was head of the penal administration bureau at the Ministry of Justice at the time, admitted that the treatment of convicts in the Truk Islands was as inhumane as it had been in nineteenth-century Hokkaido.[64] During the Pacific War, the Navy employed convict labour for shipbuilding, too, and the army began to use convicts to build air bases.

Taiwan and Korea

As in the case of Hokkaido, neither Taiwan, nor Korea were officially referred to as colonies, although, in time, the term *Gaichi* (outer territory)

57. *Ibid.*
58. *Ibid.*, pp. 136 – 167.
59. *Ibid.*, p. 175.
60. *Ibid.*, pp. 168 – 233.
61. *Ibid.*, p. 274.
62. *Ibid.*, p. 279.
63. Jun Kubota, "Nankai no shikei shikkōnin: Shihōshō tonan hōkokutai-in no shuki", *Minshū no hata*, 5 (1946), p. 65. Sei Kubota wrote this article using the pseudonym Jun Kubota.
64. Akira Masaki, *Gokuso no nakano jinken* (Tokyo, 1968), p. 275.

was introduced to refer to Japanese territories "not yet" included as part of the mainland. *Gaichi* included Taiwan, Korea, Karafuto (Southern Sakhalin), Kwantung Leased Territory, and the South Sea Islands.

In Taiwan and Korea, the Japanese mainland penal code was not formally enforced, with Governors General instead promulgating their own ordinances concerning punishment. Such ordinances were principally identical to the mainland penal code although with certain additional provisions, for example one which authorized flogging,[65] but neither transportation, nor extramural prison labour were introduced. Basing its approach on the 1880 penal code, the office of the Governor General of Taiwan sought to send convicts to Miike *shūchikan*, but when the Home Ministry refused, the focus moved to the construction of prisons.[66] At the time of Korea's annexation, transportation had already been abolished on the mainland so that in both Taiwan and Korea the chief form of punishment was imprisonment and all convict labour was principally intramural.

Throughout the war, and after its resurgence on the mainland, extramural prison labour was introduced in Taiwan and Korea, where it seems that construction work by convicts began in 1942.[67] In Taiwan, it seems to have begun in 1943,[68] when Taiwanese and Korean convicts were sent to Hainan Island to work in mines and to construct a railway for the Navy.[69]

As Japanese convicts were sent to the South Sea Islands, Korean and Taiwanese convicts were selected based on certain criteria, such as, in the case of Koreans for example, that they should be from twenty to forty years old, healthy, strong, and non-violent and with remaining prison terms of between eighteen months and three years. Those sentenced for political crimes

---

65. On the Taiwan penal system, see Takashi Koganemaru, "Nihon tōchi shoki no Taiwan ni okeru keihō tekiyō mondai", *Nihon Taiwan gakkai hō*, 13 (2011), pp. 1–24; Botsman, *Punishment and Power*, pp. 206–220. On Korea, see Chōsen sōtokufu (ed.), *Chōsen sōtokufu shisei nijūgo nen shi* (Keijō, 1935); Chōsen sōtokufu (ed.), *Chōsen sōtoku shisei sanjū nen shi* (Keijō, 1940).
66. Botsman, *Punishment and Power*.
67. Isao Asaura, "Wasureraretaru kyakka no keimu mondai sononi", *Chikei*, 20:10 (1942), pp. 14–20.
68. According to statistics from the prison in Taiwan, prison labour was intramural until 1942. In 1943, Taiwan's Governor General ordered an increase in the number of prison employees for extramural prison labour; it was planned to recruit one hundred more officials. Taiwan sōtokufu hōmubu (ed.), *Taiwan shihō ichiran* (Taipei, 1944), pp. 116–117. This was reflected in a Cabinet decision on the mainland to use Taiwanese convicts for mining and construction in Taiwan and on Hainan Island. NAJ, "Taiwan ni okeru jukeisha kōgai sagyō ni tomonau zōin ni kansuru ken o sadamu", Kōbun ruijū, dai 67 hen, shōwa 18 nen, dai 44 kan.
69. In the first plan, 2,000 Korean and 1,000 Taiwanese convicts were supposed to be sent. NAJ, "Chōsen sōtokufu jukeisha kainantō shutsueki ni tomonau kantoku shokuin tō zōin ni kansuru ken o sadamu", Kōbun ruijū, dai 67 hen, shōwa 18 nen, dai 35 kan. NAJ, "Taiwan niokeru jukeisha". In Korea, it seems at least 2,000 convicts were sent. Jung-Mi Kim, "Nihon senryōka no Kainanto ni okeru kyōsei rōdō, 2", *Sensō sekinin kenkyū*, 28 (2000), pp. 63–71, 64. The actual number of Taiwanese convicts is not clear.

were not selected.[70] For naval installations, relatively "good" convicts were selected whose remaining terms were reasonably short while still being long enough to complete the work.

The idea that extramural prison labour might be effective for prisoners' rehabilitation was spreading among prison officials in Korea too. The adoption of extramural labour in Japanese colonies was regarded not as the introduction of a new style of punishment, but as a new means of rehabilitation to turn convicts into good Japanese citizens. In the journal of the Bureau of Legal Affairs of the Korean Governor General, a number of writers argued that extramural prison labour was more effective than imprisonment for rehabilitation and that, through such labour, convicts could contribute to the Japanese Empire and become diligent imperial subjects.[71] However, it seems obvious that convicts in the colonies were exposed to harsher labour conditions. While the South Sea Islands had been a Japanese colony since 1919, Hainan was occupied by Japan in 1939 and, in 1943, conflict between the Japanese Army and Chinese guerrillas was ongoing. Prisoners in Japanese colonies were sent to more dangerous sites than their Japanese mainland convict counterparts. We also know from the testimonies of eyewitnesses and survivors that convicts were exposed to violence and ill treatment by the Japanese Army. It is unclear how many convicts were able to return from Hainan. One Korean convict said that he was sent to Hainan with 150 other convicts, and that most of them were dead.[72]

Through extending homeland ideology, transportation and extramural prison labour were initially not introduced to the colonies, but, following the same reasoning, they were introduced in World War II. Hokkaido was the point of departure of the wartime convict labour regime, which, in turn, was a legacy of nineteenth-century convict labour practice.

CONCLUSION

Japanese territorial expansion began with Hokkaido. Although Hokkaido had been regarded as a Japanese territory long before its actual annexation, the Japanese government resorted to colonial policies similar to those of the Western powers in order to incorporate the island into mainland Japan. Penal transportation was one such strategy, which enabled rapid settlement of a Japanese population to secure the new territory at its northern border. That fact betrays Hokkaido's initial status as a colony, but, in the sense that it was transformed into homeland territory through colonial policies, Hokkaido amounted to the first step towards Japanese nation-state building and the imperial expansion achieved through "extending homeland ideology".

70. Kim, "Nihon senryōka", p. 63.
71. Utarō Bandō, "Iwayuru kōgai sagyō no shisasuru ippan gyōkei no hōkō", 1–2, *Chikei*, 19:9–10 (1941); Asaura, "Wasureraretaru".
72. Kim, "Nihon senryōka", p. 65.

It was in the peak period of convict extramural labour in Hokkaido that the Ministry of Justice launched a reform of the penal code and deleted clauses concerning transportation. However, the revision was not initiated in response to the practical problems of penal transportation. In fact, the Japanese were more concerned about amending their legal system from the French to the German model, and with diplomatic matters such as the revision of an unequal treaty. During the course of penal code reform, the status of both Hokkaido and penal transportation itself were redefined. That said, even after Hokkaido's incorporation into the mainland, long-term prisoners were still sent to Hokkaido. Their sentences were now seen as amounting to imprisonment on the mainland.

High demand for labour and its low supply were continuous challenges for Hokkaido's politicians and administrators. During the 1930s, the former penal colony sites reintroduced extramural prison labour for the same reason that it was first introduced in the late nineteenth century, namely the shortage of labour resulting from a small population. However, it was not a simple revival of punitive hard labour for felons in a colony; it was reintroduced in the guise of a rehabilitation programme that had been newly introduced in mainland prisons as a part of penal reform. In a practical sense, transportation and extramural convict labour on Hokkaido continued even after the penal code's revision in 1907.

After Hokkaido's incorporation into Japan proper, the penal transportation and convict labour that had once held sway there were reframed as an imprisonment and rehabilitation programme. During wartime, the system spread from the mainland to other areas, and, in accordance with the approach of "extending homeland ideology", was introduced in Korea and Taiwan too. It was introduced not as a particular punishment for convicts in colonies, but as an extension of the new rehabilitation programme extended from mainland prisons. It was presented rather as an opportunity for convicts to contribute to the development of the Japanese Empire and thereby to become good imperial subjects.

IRSH 63 (2018), Special Issue, pp. 131–150 doi:10.1017/S0020859018000251
© 2018 Internationaal Instituut voor Sociale Geschiedenis

Exile as Imperial Practice: Western Siberia and the Russian Empire, 1879–1900*

ZHANNA POPOVA

International Institute of Social History
Cruquiusweg 31, 1019 AT, Amsterdam, The Netherlands

E-mail: zhannapop@gmail.com

ABSTRACT: More than 800,000 people were exiled to Siberia during the nineteenth century. Exile was a complex administrative arrangement that involved differentiated flows of exiles and, in the view of the central authorities, contributed to the colonization of Siberia. This article adopts the "perspective from the colonies" and analyses the local dimension of exile to Siberia. First, it underscores the conflicted nature of the practice by highlighting the agency of the local administrators and the multitude of tensions and negotiations that the maintenance of exile involved. Secondly, by focusing on the example of the penal site of Tobolsk, where exile and imprisonment overlapped, I will elucidate the uneasy relationship between those two penal practices during Russian prison reform. In doing so, I will re-evaluate the position of exile in relation to both penal and governance practice in Imperial Russia.

INTRODUCTION

This article analyses exile to Siberia at a time of reform of the Russian penal system. By adopting the "perspective from the colonies" and investigating the local specificities of exile in Western Siberia, I will discuss how tension arose between attempts at prison reform and efforts to expand and consolidate the Russian Empire.

In the Russian context, exile is often perceived as direct expulsion of criminals and political offenders from central areas of the Russian Empire to its eastern borderlands. However, closer analysis of the exile system and the chaotic arrangements that contributed to its persistence makes clear the degree to which its shape was, in fact, defined by local rather than central authorities. For this article, I have examined the history of exile from the Siberian perspective and analysed the

* The research for this article is part of the research programme "Four Centuries of Labour Camps: War, Rehabilitation, Ethnicity", based at the International Institute of Social History (IISH) and the NIOD, Institute for War, Holocaust and Genocide Studies, Amsterdam, and funded by the Netherlands Organization for Scientific Research (NWO).

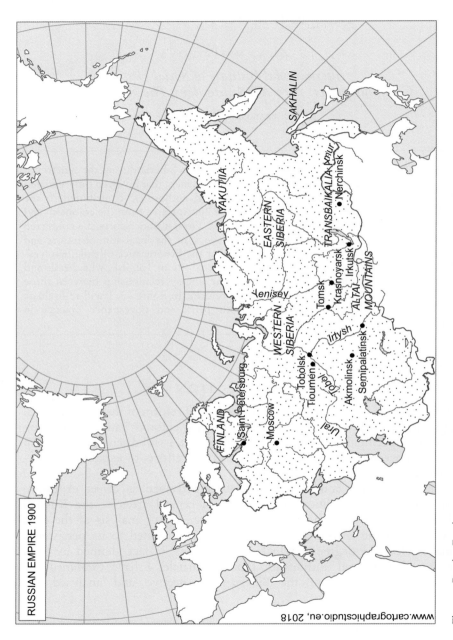

Figure 1. Russian Empire, c.1900.

role of exile within the wider repertoire of imperial policies in Western Siberia.[1]

I challenge the view that Russian exile was a simple process of expulsion by placing in the foreground the nature of exile as a spatially complex and entangled imperial practice. My focus is Western Siberia and I have traced the various punitive flows that went through that region during the last decade of the nineteenth century. At the heart of this article are two interrelated questions. What were the various goals of exile and how were they connected to the relationships of power between the central and local authorities in the Russian Empire?[2] How did exile and incarceration interact within the imperial penal architecture, especially in hinterland regions such as Western Siberia, and what impact did such interactions have on the penal system overall? This double movement foregrounds the decentralized character of exile, and, more importantly, allows the history of those Russian punitive practices to be reconnected with the wider history of Imperial Russia.

Exile implies forced displacement, so I have sought to be attentive to its spatial dimension and fluid character, instead of concentrating purely on the legal norms that prescribed it. For the same reason, it seems counterproductive to attempt to analyse it as a "system", for to do that would unnecessarily solidify it. Looking at exile as a "practice" rather than a "system" allows us to analyse the practical arrangements of exile and its political implications beyond its legal framework.

Western Siberia is a vast region to the east of the Ural Mountains, reaching from the Arctic Ocean in the north to the steppes in the south. The first Russian military colonizers arrived there at the end of the sixteenth century and, soon, a scattered network of military strongholds was constructed on the shores of the major Siberian rivers. Not long after, the first exiles from European Russia were banished to those lands and by the beginning of the nineteenth century both Western and Eastern Siberia had become traditional destinations for exiles in the Russian Empire. Within Russian pan-imperial exile architecture, Western Siberia played an important role as a convict transport hub too. Exiles from European Russia were categorized and distributed within the regions of Siberia after they had crossed the Ural Mountains. Exile's persistence over more than three centuries created the image of Siberia as "hell on earth", a "vast roofless prison".

1. For more on Russian imperial history see Jane Burbank, Mark von Hagen, and Anatolyi Remnev (eds), *Russian Empire: Space, People, Power, 1700–1930* (Bloomington, IN, 2007). For the Siberian case see Sergei Glebov, *Region v istorii imperii. Istoricheskie esse o Sibiri* (Moscow, 2013).

2. It is important to acknowledge that talking about "the central authorities" involves a significant simplification, albeit necessary for this article. The central authorities consisted of various groups with different interests, as noted in L.M. Dameshek and A.V. Remnev (eds), *Sibir v sostave Rossiiskoi imperii* (Moscow, 2007).

Exile to Siberia remained the main Russian punitive practice throughout the nineteenth century and, as in other imperial contexts, was "a key aspect of imperial sovereignty".[3] Certainly, there were considerable differences between the penal transportation overseas typical of the Western colonial empires and the internal continental exile peculiar to the Russian Empire. The differences were connected to the wider matter of colonization in Russian imperial history, and, as the prominent nineteenth-century historian Vassily Klyuchevsky famously stated, "the history of Russia is the history of a country which colonizes itself", thereby placing the colonization of Siberia within the centuries-long history of Russian peasant migrations. Indeed, debate continues on the nature of Russian policy in Siberia.[4]

The strongest evidence for understanding the interrelation between exile and imperial policy in general is provided by developments in the last third of the nineteenth century, when the penal regime of hard labour (*katorga*) fell away in the decades following the emancipation of the serfs in 1861. Experiments with various other regimes of incarceration and exile then began in the late 1870s, and there was an eventual decision to curtail exile in 1900.

EXILE WITHIN THE IMPERIAL PUNITIVE REPERTOIRE

The Russian imperial penal system was the opposite of what Michel Foucault called a "monotonous punitive system".[5] The penal system conceived by Foucault was based on control and discipline and was dominated by incarceration, whereas the Russian penal system throughout the nineteenth century included a wide range of punitive practices with very different premises. Exile stands in particularly stark opposition to Foucault's ideal of ubiquitous state control, for, in the overwhelming majority of cases, it meant not only expulsion, but also abandonment by the state.

Exile, incarceration, forced labour, and corporal punishment coexisted until the end of the Russian Empire, although they emerged under different historical conditions. For instance, exile to Siberia was first used as early as the seventeenth century, while "rehabilitative" intramural prison labour was introduced only relatively shortly before the revolution and was closely associated with the advance of modernity. During the nineteenth century, certain legal and administrative aspects of the penal system changed, but the reforms typically either had limited geographical impact, or took decades to

---

3. Christian G. De Vito and Alex Lichtenstein, "Writing a Global History of Convict Labour", *International Review of Social History*, 58:2 (2013), pp. 285–325, here 303.
4. For an overview of the debate, see Martin Aust, "*Rossia Siberica*: Russian-Siberian History Compared to Medieval Conquest and Modern Colonialism", *Review (Fernand Braudel Center)*, 27:3 (2004), pp. 181–205.
5. Michel Foucault, "La poussière et le nuage", in Michelle Perrot (ed.), *L'impossible prison. Recherches sur le système pénitentiaire* (Paris, 1980), pp. 29–39, here 30.

implement; or they were never fully realized. That was most notably the case first with the legal reform of exile designed by Mikhail Speransky in the 1820s[6] and then with the restrictions on the use of corporal punishment introduced in 1863,[7] as well as with the centralization of the prison administration that began with the creation of the Main Prison Administration in 1879. Certain regimes, such as *katorga* – the harshest punishment for common criminals – were never consistently reformed. The histories of exile and *katorga* are similarly closely interconnected.

Corporal punishment, incarceration, and exile could be used not only separately depending on the gravity of the crime committed, but also combined within a single penal regime, as was the case with *katorga*. *Katorga* was a harsh punitive regime intended for those convicts deemed the most dangerous, and it included forced labour for terms of from four to twenty-five years, followed by "eternal settlement" in Siberia. During the eighteenth century, an overlapping of different punitive measures was initially guided by a complex state agenda. The state was interested not only in the punishment of criminals, but also in the concentration of coerced convict workers in places that would benefit the state, be they naval construction sites in Petrine Russia or the Nerchinsk silver mines during Catherine's reign. In the eyes of the central authorities, exile was not purely an instrument for the punishment of convicts, for in itself the presence of exiles in the region assisted the Russian goal of colonization. On 13 December 1760,[8] the Senate passed one of the principal laws that shaped the practice of exile, by which landowners were allowed to send "unruly" peasants into exile in the region of Nerchinsk in Eastern Siberia. As noted by the historian A.D. Kolesnikov, that law was a response to the growing financial needs of the state, to satisfy which the government sought to augment the volume of silver mined at the state-owned Nerchinsk silver mines.[9] They did so by delegating to landowners the power to punish any perceived wrongdoing. Landowners were allowed to expel only healthy male peasants younger than forty-five years old, and if such men had dependent families the law encouraged the landowners to banish the men's families, too, although with financial compensation from the government.[10] That law, therefore, laid a legal foundation for two ways of coercing the peasant population, namely by displacing them and by forcing

6. Andrew A. Gentes, *Exile to Siberia, 1590–1822* (Basingstoke and New York, 2008), pp. 165–201.

7. Abby M. Schrader, "The Languages of the Lash: The Russian Autocracy and the Reform of Corporal Punishment, 1817–1893" (Ph.D., University of Pennsylvania, 1996).

8. *Polnoe sobranie zakonov Rossiiskoi Imperii*, First Series, Vol. XV (St Petersburg, 1830), no. 11166, p. 582.

9. A.D. Kolesnikov, "Ssylka i zaselenie Sibiri", in L.M. Goriushkin *et al.* (eds), *Ssylka i katorga v Sibiri (XVIII–nachalo XX v.)* (Novosibirsk, 1975), pp. 38–59, here 42–44.

10. *Polnoe sobranie*, Vol. XV, no. 11166, p. 582.

them to work for the state, while at the same time further privileging landowners. The decision to banish a peasant remained dependent purely on the whim of a landowner, thereby extending landowners' power over peasants. On the one hand, this early form of exile was a form of labour coercion in response to labour shortage; on the other, it helped facilitate the fulfilment of the "state interest in the population (*zaselenie*)" of Siberia proclaimed by the law.

The central Russian authorities were seeking to populate the vast Siberian territories with Russian peasants, and the administrative measures mentioned above provided a sizeable influx of people. According to Kolesnikov's calculations, in 1761–1781 exile had a considerable impact on the population of Siberia, with at least 35,000 male peasants arriving there during that time. Kolesnikov suggests that the number of women who followed their husbands typically constituted up to eighty per cent of the number of men, suggesting therefore that the total number of adult peasants was around 60,000.[11] According to the censuses, or *revizii*, of 1762 and 1782, the total population of Siberia in those years comprised 393,000 and 552,000 males respectively. However, the Russian state's aspiration to use the exiles as workers in the silver mines met with limited success. Only a few of them settled around Nerchinsk in Eastern Siberia, while others were settled around the Siberian Route (*Sibirskii trakt*) in the southern part of Siberia.[12] The bulk of the labour force in the Nerchinsk mines comprised criminals serving *katorga* hard labour terms. Again, according to Kolesnikov, despite the hardship of their forced displacement a number of the exiled peasants were able to settle and support their families, so that in the mid-nineteenth century in the region of Tobolsk the descendants of the exiled amounted to ten per cent of the population. In more distant regions of Eastern Siberia the percentage was higher[13] and at the end of the eighteenth century administrative exile had clearly had an impact on the colonization of Siberia, albeit a limited one.

The plurality of the punitive regimes at the end of nineteenth century resulted from the fact that, throughout the century, the authorities that implemented the various punishments were guided not only by traditional goals such as retribution, deterrence, or, later, rehabilitation. Rather, they sought to fulfil the local goals of social control through expulsions and the disciplining of offenders, as well as the imperial agenda of colonizing territory to the east of the Ural Mountains.

---

11. Kolesnikov, "Ssylka i zaselenie Sibiri", p. 51.
12. This route is a historic road that connected European Russia to Siberia. Construction of it began in the early eighteenth century and, until the construction of the Trans-Siberian Railway and the Amur cart road at the end of the nineteenth century, it was the primary connection between Russia and China.
13. Kolesnikov, "Ssylka i zaselenie Sibiri", pp. 56–57.

The official aspiration to use exile as an instrument to control and facilitate the colonization of Siberia partially explains the persistence of exile and *katorga*. Several other factors contributed to the complexity of the penal system. First, the estate system of the Russian Empire was reflected in the execution of punishment. Therefore, there existed two separate "ladders of punishment", one for the privileged estates, against whom corporal punishment was not used after 1785, and the second for peasants and urban dwellers. In 1863, the use of corporal punishment against the unprivileged was curbed, although it was still widely used as a disciplinary measure against those already serving sentences either of imprisonment or exile. That estate-based distinction persisted for the punishment of convicts, even though, on conviction, exiles of privileged origin were formally stripped of all their special rights.

Second, although the legislators' views on punishment and rehabilitation changed over time, that was rarely consistently reflected in the legislation. A growing desire to modernize the Russian Empire meant that various new laws were introduced along with new principles of organization of the penal system. However, they often contradicted the ones in use, which contributed to further complications. In the eighteenth century the ideas of revenge and deterrence guided the modalities of punishments and their execution,[14] but, in the first half of the nineteenth century, Russian penology was heavily marked by John Howard's ideas about prison reform and the moral rehabilitation of criminals.[15] On 17 April 1863, a law was passed that brought to an end the practice of branding *katorzhnye*, who had, until then, had the letters "KAT" burned into their cheeks and foreheads. The lash, too, was abolished for the majority of convicts. Later, ideas of rehabilitative convict labour attracted the particular attention of officials, for such ideas promised not only improvements in prison discipline, but also offered the possibility of easier reintegration into society for former convicts. That interest resulted in a law of 6 January 1886 that prescribed mandatory labour for all prisoners. The act did not touch upon *katorga* hard labour, which was still, at least in theory, purely retributive. In practice, however, reports by the Main Prison Administration show that *katorga* institutions were in decline and many convicts in them did no work of any kind. Organizing and maintaining convict labour in the distant regions of the empire proved to be expensive, and as the central state's

14. Sergeui Poznyshev, *K voprosu o preobrazovanii nashei katorgi* (Moscow, 1914), p. 4. For more on early-modern Russian punishments, see Nancy Kollmann, *Crime and Punishment in Early Modern Russia* (Cambridge, 2012), and Evgenii Anisimov, *Dyba i knut. Politicheskii sysk i russkoe obschestvo v XVIII veke* (Moscow, 1999).
15. John Howard was a British prison reformer. He inspected various British prisons and compiled a report, published as John Howard, *The State of the Prisons in England and Wales* (Warrington, 1780). Michel Foucault has addressed Howard's work in Michel Foucault, *Madness and Civilization: A History of Insanity in the Age of Reason* (New York, 1988), pp. 44–64.

interest in such institutions waned the local prison governors proved unable to continue enforcing convict labour.

Third, there existed a significant gap between the law, and local practice of prison and exile administration. The gap often proved to be particularly wide between the newly opened central experimental prisons, where the innovations were successful and discipline was maintained, and the decaying overcrowded prisons in distant regions. The difference was exacerbated by insufficient funding and a lack of qualified administrators and prison staff, as prison reform relied largely on the initiative of local prison governors in organizing the mandatory labour. In a number of reports from the 1870s, the Governor General of Western Siberia complained at length about the low level of education of his subordinates. Moreover, combined with the lack of first-hand information about the condition of exile, the implementation of the state's conceptions of punishment could entail additional pain for the exiles. Daniel Beer has made an important observation here: "the yawning gulf between the state's own conception of deportation as a strictly logistical operation, on the one hand, and the convicts' experience of it as a brutal ordeal, on the other, reflected the weaknesses and limitations of the autocracy".[16]

At the end of the nineteenth century, there were officially eight categories of exiles whose status differed in the extent of the deprivation of their rights and the lengths of their terms, plus the category of *katorzhnye*, the convicts deemed the most dangerous. Exile to Siberia was not only a punitive measure and therefore not only part of the criminal justice system, but also an embodiment of the state's desire to control the colonization of Siberia. To a lesser extent, it was also an instrument of communal self-governance. Rural and urban communities (*obschestva* and *meschanstva*) could expel their "undesirable" members to Siberia. Many such expelled members of communities had, in fact, been trying to return to European Russia after serving their terms within the penal system, so that administrative exile could turn out to be a second, non-judicial punishment. By law, administrative exiles became members of communities in Siberia, even though other members of those communities might consider them burdensome and more than one community opposed the practice of administrative exile by complaining to local and central authorities.[17]

Such legal categorization might lead us to assume that it was somehow reflected in the experience of the exiles themselves in Siberia. However, even the state officials admitted that, in practice, the overwhelming majority of

---

16. Daniel Beer, "Penal Deportation to Siberia and the Limits of State Power, 1801–81", *Kritika: Explorations in Russian and Eurasian History*, 16:3 (2015), pp. 620–650, here 621–622.
17. Russian State Historical Archive [hereafter, RGIA], f.1149, op.10 (D.Z.), d.60, ll.33-38. I have used the usual classification for the Russian archives. Referring to the archival documents, I have used the common taxonomy "fond–opis–delo–(list)". "Fond" is collection, "opis" is a list of files, "delo" is a file, and "list" is a page.

exiles of all categories experienced extreme hardship and were generally forced into the same condition of utter penury, which made many of them abscond from their assigned places of settlement. For example, in his annual report for 1875, the Governor General of Western Siberia complained that of 70,000 exiles more than 36,000 were not living in their designated places of exile and had not informed the authorities of their departure.[18] For the exiles, the main difference that belonging to one of the official categories entailed was the destination of their displacement. There was a distinct differentiation between regions in Siberia, for according to the view of the administrators the harsher the punishment a person deserved, the further east they should be sent.

Quantitatively, the largest category were the "administratively exiled",[19] who were generally sent to the Tomsk or Tobolsk regions – unless they asked to be sent even further east.[20] They were exiled to Siberia because their communities or, as serfs prior to 1861, their owners had banished them. They were generally allocated to rural communities in Siberia and considered by the legislators to be in a favourable situation. After terms of at least five years they were allowed to resettle or return to European Russia, although not to the communities that had expelled them. In practice, however, it appears that the radical experience of uprooting and social and geographical dislocation had a lingering and devastating effect on the majority of exiles. It also seems from the documents that those consequences were neither intended as part of their punishment, nor even predicted by the central government. In 1900, the head of the Main Prison Administration remarked,

> Even if it had been possible to make an assumption (purely theoretical and refuted by practice) that after a certain period of exile the nefarious members of society would lose their nefariousness, then what kind of correction can we expect from a person who spent only three years in exile, considering that the first years of the exile are the hardest time of settlement, the unescapable time of complete penury and extreme privation of necessary things that might engender not correction and repentance, but rather rancour.[21]

Critical remarks like those, as well as the mention of any contradiction between "theory" and "practice", were possible only at the very end of the nineteenth century; before then, the discussion of exile was dominated by abstract moral arguments. Similarly, the first consistent data on the number of exiles appeared only at the end of the 1870s. By the end of the

---

18. RGIA, *Vsepoddaneishii otchet general-gubernatora Zapadnoi Sibiri za 1875 g.*, p. 25.
19. Kolesnikov, "Ssylka i zaselenie Sibiri", p. 57.
20. Aleksandr Salomon, *Ssylka v Sibir. Ocherk eia istorii i sovremennago polozheniia* (St Petersburg, 1900), pp. 101–102.
21. *Ibid.*, p. 102.

Figure 2. Hard labour in Eastern Siberia: Exiled convicts hauling cargo from the barges to the storage facilities in Transbaikalia, 1891.
World Digital Library https://www.wdl.org/en/item/18972/. *Photo by Aleksei Kuznetsov. Used by permission.*

century (in 1897–1898), the province of Tobolsk was home to 103,102 administrative exiles, while the region of Tomsk contained 35,736.[22]

The next three categories of exiles were those banished following court decisions, and initially such "exiled settlers" constituted the second most numerous category. All except those unable to do agricultural labour were banned altogether from living in cities, and unlike administrative exiles they were legally excluded from the social system. Exiled settlers were not allocated to any particular community (*obschestvo*) but had an estate of their own (*soslovie*) as exiles.[23] In the second category were "settled workers", vagrants who had been sentenced to forced labour[24] and of whom the majority were sent to the Irkutsk, Enisei, and Transbaikalia provinces in Eastern Siberia. Finally, there was a particularly small group of people "exiled for life"

---

22. *Ibid.*, Appendix 4, pp. 14–15.

23. *Ibid.*, p. 103. Until 1822, the children of exiles and the *katorzhnye* were also attributed to this class from birth: Dameshek and Remnev, *Sibir v sostave Rossiiskoi imperii*, p. 277.

24. For more on the lives of vagrants in Siberia, see Andrew A. Gentes, "Vagabondage and the Tsarist Siberian Exile System: Power and Resistance in the Penal Landscape", *Central Asian Survey*, 30:3–4 (2011), pp. 407–421.

(*soslannye na zhit'e*). They were privileged individuals who had committed crimes for which unprivileged people would have been imprisoned.

The remaining categories were quantitatively negligible and included political exiles, those exiled for up to five years under police surveillance, and criminals from Finland[25] who had originally been sentenced to long prison terms but had chosen exile instead.

The most obvious thing about that list is the bureaucratic failure of the central administration. The categories of exiles were introduced more or less hapha-zardly, not systematically at all; moreover, the categorization had little impact on the condition of the exiles, who generally found themselves abandoned by the state rather than closely watched and controlled by its representatives.

RUSSIA AND SIBERIA: IMPERIAL TENSIONS

Exile can be understood only as part of a wider geometry of power. It was initiated by the central government, but its implementation involved actors located in different places and it was generally not centrally coordinated. Therefore, looking at exile in connection with Russian governance practice highlights the fact that penal exile was developed not only by the innovations of lawyers and ministerial administrators but also, less directly, by the tension between central and local authorities and the agenda of imperial expansion.

In their policies on Siberia, the central Imperial Russian authorities were guided by controversial desires. On the one hand, they strove to integrate Siberia better within the empire, provide it with qualified local adminis-trators, and use the economic potential of the region; on the other, they had no wish to see the region develop enough political and economic autonomy and to contest matters with the central power. Each Russian emperor approached the dilemma differently. Nicholas I's attempt to resolve the matter saw him appoint the First Siberian Committee, which, dominated by Prince Gorchakov, "made a conscious decision to keep Siberia backward and underdeveloped as the best way of bringing about the 'firm unification' and 'complete amalgamation' of Siberia with central Russia".[26] By contrast, Alexander II's government brought in a new paradigm of thinking about Siberia and how it might be possible to unify it with Russia. Their plan was to break down its administrative separateness,[27] a process accelerated under

---

25. The Grand Duchy of Finland was an autonomous part of the Russian Empire and thus its people, too, were subject to special policies. The choice on conviction of either incarceration, or exile was one of their privileges.

26. Steven G. Marks, *Road to Power: Trans-Siberian Railroad and the Colonization of Asian Russia, 1850–1917* (Ithaca, NY, 1991), p. 49.

27. S.G. Svatikov, *Rossiia i Sibir: (k istorii sibirskogo oblastnichestva v XIX v.)* (Prague, 1929), p. 76.

Alexander III until by 1887 "the very name Siberia was no longer used as an administrative term".[28] On the eve of the twentieth century, administrative unification of Siberia with Russia became the dominant policy.[29]

Despite such efforts at integration, administration of punitive exile was always dependent on local authorities, whose role was crucial because sentences of exile did not include a destination. At the beginning of the nineteenth century, in special cases individuals might be exiled within European Russia, but consistently the main flow of criminal and administrative exiles was directed to Siberia. Within Siberia exile to different regions was considered to possess differing punitive force, with exile further east perceived as constituting a harsher punishment.[30] It was, therefore, traditional for *katorzhnye* to be exiled to Transbaikalia or Yakutia, while Western Siberia received administrative exiles. The settler exiles were confined to the regions around Irkutsk and along the Amur River.[31] Distribution was arranged only after the exiles arrived in Siberia and was overseen by the Tioumen Office of the Exiled (*Tioumenskii Prikaz o Ssylnykh*), the regional Siberian prison inspectorate, and the regional offices. The Office of the Exiled was originally created in Tobolsk in 1822 as part of Speransky's reform of the system of exile,[32] but, in 1869, it was moved to Tioumen. Before the authorities began experimenting with the installation of *katorga* sites on Sakhalin in 1869, criminal exiles were sent to various places in southern Siberia, such as Nerchinsk in Transbaikalia and Krasnoiarsk in Eastern Siberia. There was also a *katorga* prison in Tobolsk, but it was much less important than Nerchinsk or Sakhalin.

The logistics of exile were complex, with exiles very unevenly distributed throughout the region. In the second half of the nineteenth century, the presence of exiles in Western Siberia was limited, but concentrated. The highest concentrations of exiles were in regions that already had the highest population density, thus both exciting discontent among the locals and prompting an otherwise unlikely shortage of usable land.

The Tioumen Office assigned precise exile locations only to those exiled to the Tobolsk region, while in all other cases it recorded only the region of destination, leaving it to the local authorities to allocate the specific places to which exiles would go. Just like the Tioumen Office, certain of the regional authorities relied on information about available land provided by local

28. Marks, *Road to Power*, p. 53.

29. Dameshek and Remnev, *Sibir v sostave Rossiiskoi imperii*, p. 138.

30. RGIA, *Vsepoddaneishii otchet general-gubernatora Zapadnoi Sibiri za 1876 g.*, p. 37. Tobolsk and Tomsk provinces received only administrative exiles while the Eastern Siberian provinces (Enisei, Irkutsk, Iakutsk, Amur provinces, Transbaikalia and Sakhalin) took criminal exiles and *katorzhnye*.

31. See art. 158 of the Code of the Exiles [*Ustav o ssylnykh 1876*].

32. Gentes, *Exile to Siberia*, pp. 179–180.

governors.[33] The area of exile changed significantly over time, and in Western Siberia in particular it gradually shrank. Initially, that was because of the organization of the Altai Mountain District (*Altaiskii Gornii okrug*) in 1808.[34] As the personal property of the emperors and a significant source of profit, the Altai District was governed directly by the Imperial Cabinet. Another limitation was related to imperial policy concerning indigenous people, for convicts were not exiled to either Akmolinsk or Semipalatinsk in the southern part of Western Siberia. That was because of the imperial authorities' conception of the local nomadic Kyrgyz tribes, whom they were gradually trying to convert to Christianity. The central government presumed that "any contact with the vicious element [*porochnyi* element] would make the Muslim Kyrgyz horde stay in the depths of the steppes, aloof from all things Russian and Christian",[35] which they considered would undermine all government efforts aimed at settlement and Christianization. Similarly, the northern regions of Western Siberia also did not host no exiles, for that would have required too much logistical effort to preserve the exiles from "dying of biting frost and hunger".[36] In other words, only a small (compared to the overall surface of Western Siberia) area still received exiles in the last third of the nineteenth century, but their concentrations there were high.

The ratio between the number of exiles and the local population, according to legal prescriptions supposed to be limited to one in five,[37] was also a matter of concern for the local administrators. On settling in Western Siberia, exiles and their families were granted allotments of three *desiatiny* (8.1 acres) of arable land per person.[38] However, research begun in 1875 by the Western Siberian Governor General Kaznakov shows that in the majority of regions that proportion of administrative exiles was far from being respected. After bringing the matter to the notice of the central government, Kaznakov stated that the relocation of those already exiled once, as well as the disposition of future exiles, should remain within the jurisdiction of local governors general.[39] That resulted in no change in the condition of the exiles, but created a legal normalization of the situation. In 1881, Kaznakov issued an instruction that the new normal proportion of exiles to the local population (*starozhily*) should be one in three.[40]

33. Salomon, *Ssylka*, p. 117.
34. *Ibid.*, p. 121.
35. RGIA, *Vsepoddaneishii otchet general-gubernatora Zapadnoi Sibiri za 1877 g.*, p. 29.
36. RGIA, *Otchet za 1877 g.*, p. 29. Exiles were indeed sent to the north of Western Siberia in Soviet times; for a case of the catastrophic and deadly failure of this endeavour, see Nicholas Werth, *Cannibal Island: Death in a Siberian Gulag* (Princeton, NJ, 2007).
37. Salomon, *Ssylka*, p. 122.
38. *Ibid.*, p. 123.
39. Journal of 27 September to 4 October 1879 of the Council of the Main Administration of Western Siberia, IAOO, Historical Archive of the Omsk Region), f.3, op.9, d.15872.
40. Salomon, *Ssylka*, p. 125.

Local authorities sought to change the position of Siberia as the main exile destination in the Russian Empire, but they failed to do so and power over the definition of punishments remained firmly in the hands of the central government. Siberian authorities therefore remained obliged to accommodate exiles and adapt to their growing numbers.

KATORGA AND THE CHANGING ROLE OF SIBERIA

Among all the flows of punitive relocations to Siberia, the cases of those sentenced to *katorga* were the most complex, but they allow us to trace the interrelation between punitive relocation and imprisonment. The case of the Tobolsk *katorga* prison, therefore, deserves closer inspection. Tobolsk prison was an imperial institution where exile and detention overlapped, so that a study of the history of its establishment and functioning will highlight the uneasy relationship between those two types of punishment.

Before the arrival of the railways in Siberia, rivers were the main routes of commerce and communication. The town of Tobolsk, situated at the confluence of the Irtysh and Tobol rivers, had been one of the main outposts of the Russian presence in Siberia since the end of the sixteenth century. However, the choice at the end of the nineteenth century of a "Southern route" for the Trans-Siberian Railway led to the growing importance of more southerly towns such as Tioumen and Omsk and brought the economic development of Tobolsk to a halt. Over the first few decades of the twentieth century, Tobolsk then completely lost its commercial and administrative influence to Tioumen.

Nevertheless, at the end of the 1870s, Tobolsk was still the seat of the governorate and the site of a number of distinctly imperial institutions, including two relatively new *katorga* prisons built in response to overcrowding in European Russia.[41] With the growth of the prison population in the 1860–1870s after the emancipation of serfs and curtailment of corporal punishment, the existing *katorga* prisons had become insufficient to cope with the influx of new convicts.

The decision to create new *katorga* prisons in Tobolsk dates to 1874, when a former wine cellar was supposed to be refurbished as a huge prison cell. It is unclear exactly whose decision that was, but it most probably originated within the Ministry of Internal Affairs. However, before construction work could even begin 250 *katorga* convicts were sent to Tobolsk. As a transport hub for prisoners to be sent further east, Tobolsk had a prison stronghold (*tiuremnii zamok*) with space that could be utilized as a temporary jail for those inmates. In September 1876, a new and bigger *katorga* prison was opened in another part of the stronghold that had

41. State Archive of the Russian Federation (GARF), f.122, op.5, d.743, 1.11.

previously been a military prison, which, in June of that year, had been moved to the town of Ust-Kamenogorsk. The new *katorga* prison could accommodate 550 convicts and the temporary jail was transformed into its special section. The construction of a second *katorga* prison, for 300 prisoners, was completed at the end of 1878.

Large groups of *katorga* prisoners from European Russia were confined in Tobolsk prison for the first part of their punishment. The principles of sorting those convicts who would stay in the European part of the empire and those who would have to be displaced further to the east were outlined in an ordinance of 18 April 1869 drafted by a Special Committee responsible for exile reorganization.[42] Once again, these principles reflected the use of convicts as the embodiment of Russia's imperial expansion into Siberia. The mere presence of Russian men and, especially, women in Eastern Siberia was considered sufficient to fulfil the goal of colonization. Therefore, male convicts with families were sent to Siberia directly after their conviction, while single convicts remained to serve their term in Europe: convicts with families were deemed more capable of settling down and becoming well-established colonists after their release from confinement in a *katorga* prison. Regardless of their marital status, female convicts from all over the empire were also sent to Eastern Siberia. Abby Schrader discusses in detail the conception senior officials had of the socio-sexual order of the Siberian exiles and the instrumentalization of women for the purpose of domesticating male exiles. That underlines the role of views of gender in the policy of using exiles as colonists in Siberia.[43] Unmarried prisoners and married convicts unaccompanied by their families generally remained in European Russia to serve at least the initial periods of their sentences.

Unlike some *katorga* prisons in Eastern Siberia, such as the one at the silver and lead mines of Nerchinsk, Western Siberian *katorga* prisons were not dedicated to one particular type of forced convict labour in the interest of the state. Despite forced labour constituting the core of the punitive regime of the *katorga*, the organization of convict labour in those prisons was clearly of less importance than their accommodation of incoming convicts. The author of the report on the condition of the Tobolsk *katorga* prisons, junior official [*mladshii chinovnik*] Merkushev, mentioned that discussions about the necessity of well-established convict labour began as early as 1875 with the opening of the temporary *katorga* jail. One type of work discussed was that needed for the canalization of the town, a typical example of extramural convict labour. However, the discussions had had no

42. "O predstoiashchem preobrazovanii katorgi", *Tiuremnyi vestnik*, 6–7 (1910), pp. 897–922.
43. Abby M. Schrader, "Unruly Felons and Civilizing Wives: Cultivating Marriage in the Siberian Exile System, 1822–1860", *Slavic Review*, 66:2 (2007), pp. 230–256.

actual outcome at the time the report was written in February 1882 and the convicts were mostly set to work inside the prisons, doing tasks such as cleaning, cooking, and laundry. There were artisanal workshops, but their production was limited and destined mostly for private customers.

The overall impact of forced labour on prison life at the time of the Merkushev report was very limited. Both prisons together could accommodate 1,100 prisoners, but, unlike most in the Russian Empire at that time, were not employed at full capacity.[44] However, the report states that the number of people forced to work both in the workshops and on prison maintenance almost never exceeded 250 in total, while other prisoners did no work at all. In other words, although prison governors in Tobolsk were not confronted with overcrowding they were nevertheless unable to ensure full employment for their charges.

The reports from the local prisons show the lack of coordination between the different parts of the penal system, with the practice of exile putting additional strain on the *katorga* prison. That convicts were sent to Siberia in spite of insufficient facilities awaiting them was just one example of such mismanagement. More importantly, discrepancies and shortfalls seem to have been inherent in the prison and exile management system as a whole, rather than specific to Tobolsk. The condition of prisons on the eve of reform was largely defined by problems of administration and communication. Bureaucratic inconsistencies together with fragmented and insufficient funding clearly produced a penal system within which conditions might differ dramatically depending on where prisons were.

Normal prisons were intended to house convicts serving shorter terms, while exile and especially *katorga* were designed as longer and harsher punishment. By the beginning of the twentieth century the condition of the *katorga* regime was considered critical and provoked a public outcry[45] as the gap widened between new attitudes to punishment and the theoretical premises of *katorga*. Together with the continuous protests of the Siberian authorities and communities, that mismatch made the crisis of the whole system of *katorga* colonies more and more visible. The absence of any consistency in reform of *katorga* in the nineteenth century was ostensibly related to the installation of the penal colony on Sakhalin Island, for rather than reforming the regime of punishment officials of the Main Prison Administration opted to establish that major new site. In other words, they believed that in the 1860s and later the *katorga* system was still valid and needed only to be employed more consistently and with better conditions. Some of those officials, most notably the head of the Main Prison

44. GARF f.122, op.5, d.743.
45. The public discussions of *katorga* were prompted by the publication of Chekhov's *Sakhalin Island* (1893), Doroshevich's *Sakhalin* (1903), and Tolstoy's *Resurrection* (1899).

Figure 3. Katorga convicts in the Due coal mine on Sakhalin, 1890s.
World Digital Library https://www.wdl.org/en/item/18468/. *Photo by Innokentii Pavlovskii. Used by permission.*

Administration Mikhail Galkin-Vraskoi, considered Sakhalin Island to be the ideal location for a penal colony due to its remote geographical position, hostile weather conditions, and relatively small local population. In practice, however, it turned out that the establishment of a stable penal settlement based on the agricultural labour of convicts was scarcely possible. The weather was too unfavourable, the settlers needed constant supplies of food, and transport was expensive as, prior to the opening of the Suez Canal in 1869, the convicts had to be shipped the long way round Africa from the Black Sea. Moreover, escapes turned out to be less rare than the officials of the Main Prison Administration had expected. The case of Sakhalin was just one example, although probably the most striking, of the gap between the imagination of Russian state officials and reality.

PENAL REFORMS AND THEIR LIMITS

The economic backwardness of the Russian Empire became painfully evident after its defeat in the Crimean War. Shortly after 1856 "the tsarist regime [embarked] on radical policies of economic, administrative and social modernisation",[46] beginning with the emancipation of serfs and followed by judicial, educational, and administrative reforms. However, not all the reforms introduced in European Russia were introduced in Siberia, too, for as a border region Siberia existed under a different regime of governance, and the rhythm of change was different there as well.

The prison reform of 1879 was aimed at centralization of prison management in the Russian Empire. It did not bring immediate changes to the condition of the prisons or to the system of exile, but it did begin a long process of organizational change. The ultimate goal of the reform was to create a uniform prison system based on rehabilitation through obligatory artisanal labour in prison workshops. However, prison officials were confronted with the reality that prisons permanently lacked both funds and qualified officers, and that prison administrators preferred to employ convicts for unskilled extramural labour. Meanwhile, local authorities, preferring to rely on exile instead, were unwilling to build new prisons. Nevertheless, the spread of prisons in the last third of the nineteenth century remained consistent, if slow, and was much more prominent in European Russia than in Siberia, especially in densely populated regions. The whole architecture of exile proved less susceptible to attempts to centralize it and it effectively impeded the adoption of imprisonment as the dominant punishment.

Exile in general proved to be largely untouched by reform until the beginning of the twentieth century, for only then had it lost its appeal as an instrument to colonize Siberia. Natural population growth and especially the explosive increase in the rates of peasant colonization during the last decade of the nineteenth century eventually played a far more important role in that.

Throughout the nineteenth century, the remoteness of Siberia, both physical and in the imagination, was one reason for the persistence of the regime of sending convicts into exile both administratively and after trial. The central administrators could argue that the practice would make the "real" Russia, by which they meant its European part, safer. However, although as early as the nineteenth century dissenting voices considered the system brutal and costly, as it led to social dislocation and many deaths and injuries of people on their way to Siberia,[47] pleas to curb it did not bring about a quick solution. Initial attempts in 1835 to reform the exile system continued sporadically and inconsistently for more than sixty years. For example, administrative exile of peasants banished by their communities or their

46. Dominic Lieven, "Russia as Empire and Periphery", in: Dominic Lieven (ed.), *The Cambridge History of Russia, Volume 2. Imperial Russia, 1689–1917* (Cambridge, 2006), pp. 7–26, 12.

47. For more on conditions in exile, see Sarah Badcock, "From Villains to Victims: Experiencing Illness in Siberian Exile", *Europe-Asia Studies*, 65:9 (2013), pp. 1716–1736.

masters was at one time abolished, but then reintroduced less than two years later. The exile system was considered problematic and more than once the tsars suggested resolving matters,[48] but a major shift in the perception of exile was needed before agreement could be reached to curtail it.

At the end of the nineteenth century, the efforts of the Russian state to reinforce its position in Siberia were channelled into strengthening the region economically. Those efforts included improving communications by building the Trans-Siberian Railway and facilitating peasant resettlement from the European part of the empire. In the final decades of the Russian Empire's existence, primacy in empire-building was ascribed neither to the military, nor to administrative officials but to peasant colonists.[49] Unprecedented waves of free migration, with approximately three million people arriving in Siberia in just fifteen years (1895–1910),[50] swept away the lingering image of Siberia as a barren place of exile. High-ranking officials such as the Prime Minister Piotr Stolypin (1863–1911) as well as middle-ranking technocrats[51] and scholars like Matvei Liubavskii (1860–1936) defined the degree of integration of regions within the Russian state by their extent of peasant colonization.[52] Promotion of peasant colonization of Siberia was therefore connected to administrative changes to the position of the region within the empire and the shift from administrative separation to integration. In discussions of reform, the changes provided administrators with convincing arguments for the abolition of exile[53] as they first insisted that exile was now less punitive and then that Siberia was becoming steadily more "Russian". Peasant colonization should, therefore, be encouraged instead of forcibly populating the region with convicts. Finally, a law of 12 June 1900 abolished judicial exile and curtailed the administrative variety. According to some estimates, those two categories together constituted eighty-five per cent of all exiles.[54] Subsequently, exile to Siberia was preserved only in the form of the administrative exile of political and religious offenders.

---

48. A.D. Margolis, *Tiurma i ssylka v imperatorskoi Rossii: Issledovaniia i arkhivnye nakhodki* (Moscow, 1995), pp. 15–21.

49. Anatolii Remnev, "Vdvinut Rossiiu v Sibir: imperiia i russkaia kolonizatsiia vtoroi poloviny XIX. Nachala XX veka", in Glebov, *Region v istorii imperii*, p. 48.

50. P.A. Stolypin and A.V. Krivoshein, *Poezdka v Sibir' i Povolzhie* (St Petersburg, 1911), p. 2.

51. Peter Holquist, "'In Accord with State Interests and the People's Wishes'": The Technocratic Ideology of Imperial Russia's Resettlement Administration", *Slavic Review*, 69:1 (2010), pp. 151–179.

52. Matvei Liubavskii, *Obzor istorii russkoi kolonizatsii s drevneishikh vremen i do XX veka* (Moscow, 1996).

53. Extensive discussions on the abolition of exile can be found in *Zhurnaly vysochaische uchrezhdennoi Komissii o meropriiatiakh po otmene ssylki. Zasedaniia 3 iunia, 9 i 16 dekabria 1899 g., 10 ianvaria i 7 fevralia 1900 g.* (St Petersburg, 1900).

54. Dameshek and Remnev, *Sibir v sostave Rossiiskoi imperii*, p. 288.

So significant a reduction in the number of exiles facilitated the advance of prison reform. Over the ensuing decades prison administrators were able to achieve increasing uniformity in conditions between prisons in European Russia and in Siberia, especially in Western Siberia. In 1913 the head of the Main Prison Administration could still lament conditions at the *katorga* sites in Transbaikalia, but he found the Tobolsk prisons acceptable.[55] Despite the fact that exile and *katorga* existed until the 1917 Revolution, they lost their importance as standard punishments and, especially after 1905, became more prominent as instruments of repression against political militants.

CONCLUSION

The final decades of the nineteenth century were a time of rapid social and economic change in the Russian Empire, and the penal system, too, was changing, albeit at its own pace. Exile remained the cornerstone of punitive practice throughout the nineteenth century, despite attempts by prison administrators to promote prison as the dominant punitive regime. Even though exile had de facto a limited impact on the colonization of Siberia, the central authorities still relied on its alleged potential as they used exile forcefully to displace thousands of peasants and their families. Only as Siberia acquired a new role within the Russian Empire did exile lost its appeal for the central administrators. With unprecedented peasant migration during the last third of the nineteenth century, Siberia, and especially Western Siberia, increasingly came to be considered part of Russia's "core" rather than a colony. The changes were embodied in the law of 1900, which curtailed administrative exile.

Looking at exile from the Siberian perspective provides a number of otherwise impossible insights. First, an analysis of the precise geographical organization of exile demonstrates the multitude of flows of punitive displacement and how those flows were differentiated, with exile further east considered more punitive. In other words, a Siberian perspective demonstrates how hinterland regions were organized within the imperial hierarchy and so underscores the variety of goals exile was supposed to fulfil, whether as punishment, to provide coerced labour, or for the colonization of border territories. Second, the case of the Tobolsk *katorga* prison demonstrates the limits of central government control as well as how the persistence of exile thwarted the advance of prison reform. Reform was impeded simultaneously by severe bureaucratic inefficiency and failed experiments. Finally, there was strong asymmetry in administrative and political structures, while local practice persisted.

---

55. P.K. Gran, *Katorga v Sibiri* (St Petersburg, 1913), p. 7.

IRSH 63 (2018), Special Issue, pp. 151–167 doi:10.1017/S0020859018000263
© 2018 Internationaal Instituut voor Sociale Geschiedenis

The *Depósito de Degredados* in Luanda, Angola: Binding and Building the Portuguese Empire with Convict Labour, 1880s to 1932

TIMOTHY J. COATES

History Department, The College of Charleston
66 George Street, Charleston, SC 29424, USA

E-mail: coatest@cofc.edu

ABSTRACT: After ignoring its holdings in Africa for the first half of the nineteenth century, the European scramble for colonies in the 1880s forced the Portuguese state to adopt a new policy to cement its tenuous hold on its two largest African colonies: Angola and Mozambique. This challenge occurred just as the penal reform movement of the nineteenth century was arriving in Portugal, with a new penitentiary in Lisbon and new legal codes aimed at reforming convicts through their labour. This article examines the rationale and impact of the *Depósito de Degredados* (Depot for Transported Convicts) in Luanda, Angola, the larger of the two prisons established to supervise the work of convicts sent from Portugal and Portugal's Atlantic colonies of Cape Verde, Portuguese Guinea, and São Tomé.

INTRODUCTION

In January 1891, Portugal and its "ancient ally" Great Britain had reached an impasse regarding their mutually exclusive plans to occupy and colonize southern Africa. Great Britain forced the issue with the Portuguese, presenting an ultimatum to agree to British terms. The resulting loss of face and national prestige in Portugal led to riots against the government and even the monarchy itself, both popularly perceived as weak at a time of national crises.[1] While many Portuguese who favoured the establishment of a republic used this crisis to further their cause, the writings of a journalist (and later politician) provide a unique insight into the day-to-day workings of Portugal's largest overseas prison. His experience (below) highlights the

---

1. A lingering memory of the ultimatum is the marching song "A Portuguesa", composed by Alfredo Keil with lyrics by Henrique Lopes de Mendonça. Written for the Republican movement at the time, when Portugal became a republic in 1910 it became the new (and is the current) national anthem. Buried in the third stanza, the lyrics recount this reaction in Portugal in 1891, "Let the echo of an insult be the signal for our revival".

themes of penal reform, "development" and occupation of Portugal's African colonies, and forced labour, which are the focus of this article. Convicts sent to Angola, such as Chagas, in the period up to 1900 formed two thirds of all whites in the colony, and, for the later period of 1902 to 1914, many more convicts entered Angola than free European colonizers.[2]

JOÃO PINHEIRO CHAGAS – A UNIQUE SOURCE

João Pinheiro Chagas, a pro-republican journalist, wrote for several newspapers, including the (aptly named) *A República Portuguesa*. He was arrested for inciting an uprising in Porto in January 1891 against the British ultimatum and tepid response from the Lisbon authorities. Along with other conspirators, he was sentenced to six years in Portugal's penal colony in Angola. João Chagas, a highly educated journalist, was no ordinary prisoner and his writings about his time in Angola are unique.[3]

Convicted and sentenced, João was taken aboard the ship *São Tomé*, and after twenty-five days at sea he arrived at the port of Luanda. On this, his first time in Angola (see below), João was remanded to a secondary facility, a dependency in Mossamedes, further south on the Angolan coast. His one night in Luanda (they removed him overnight from the ship to prevent his escape) drew a scathing comment from him in his notes. "In this facility [speaking of the *Depósito*] one finds inept and impertinent staff which should not be allowed even in penal colonies because they are the worst of men and everything that is inferior in agents of authority."[4] By the first of November that same year (1891), he had escaped from Mossamedes and made his way to Paris and eventually back to Portugal the next year. Apprehended a second time, he was again sent to Angola to complete his sentence. This second time, he would remain under closer watch in Luanda.

Once the ship arrived in Luanda, João Chagas, like so many prisoners before him, was taken to the prison overlooking the city, his name inscribed

2. Gerald Bender, *Angola under the Portuguese: The Myth and the Reality* (Berkeley, CA, 1978), pp. 87–88.
3. Chagas' work is the only primary source from a Portuguese prisoner. This is in contrast to the comparative wealth of such material for the British in Australia, such as Lucy Frost and Hamish Maxwell-Stewart, *Chain Letters: Narrating Convict Lives* (Carlton South, 2001), or the French in Guiana. The latter includes René Belbenoit, *Dry Guillotine: Fifteen Years among the Living Dead* (New York, 1938), and, by the same author, *Hell on Trial* (New York, 1940), and George John Seaton, *Isle of the Damned: Twenty Years in a Penal Colony of French Guinea* (New York, 1951). Chagas wrote two works that touched on his time in prison in Angola: *Trabalhos Forçados*, 2 vols (Lisbon, 1900), and *Diário de um Condenado Político* (Porto, 1913).
4. Chagas, *Diário*, p. 24.

in the master register of prisoners, he was assigned a number and company, and issued the regulation indigo-coloured prison uniform, including boots, items made by the convicts within the confines of the *Depósito*. João had some disparaging comments about the uniform:

> The cloth for the jacket does not appear to be measured correctly, and it closes across the chest with slender porous buttons made of bone, the type that are normally used for cloth made from raw cotton. At first glance, it appears to be a dish towel like those that appear on kitchen tables. Once you put it on, it has little shape, tight in the waist, loose in the shoulders with shoulder pads like those in soldiers' uniforms. These are its best features. The pants are grotesque and make you laugh as if they were some child's creation. They appear to be made in a girl's school for teaching sewing.[5]

This prison, the *Depósito de Degredados*, was established as an urban penal colony at the edge of Luanda (1866–1932), but it did not function with any regularity until its second or third administrative reorganization by 1885.[6] The fort had a long history of being used as a prison; in the eighteenth century, it had been the home for those sentenced to the galleys (public works). It had a parallel institution on the island of Mozambique, established at the same time. Both were administered by special units of the army and both operated under identical guidelines. The prison in Mozambique received inmates from Portugal as well as those sentenced by courts in Portuguese Asia (Portuguese India, Macau, and Timor). By the turn of the twentieth century, the two prisons also exchanged their local inmates; those from Mozambique were sent to Angola and vice versa, preventing any prisoner from having local connections. However, the prison in Mozambique was a much smaller operation than the Luanda *Depósito*, and it received approximately twelve to fifteen per cent or around 2,500 of the 16,000 to 20,000 prisoners sentenced to time in Portuguese Africa from the 1880s to 1932.[7]

Orlando Ribeiro, Portugal's outstanding historical-geographer of the twentieth century, described the Angola João Chagas must have experienced at the turn of the century:

> The atmosphere of the colony was not attractive: a bad climate, dangerous diseases, a complex population, where on the one hand there was an elite *mestiço* element with which not all of the whites wanted to live, and on the other hand former convicts who after completing their sentences, some shortened by amnesties, had risen to social positions which those who were more scrupulous did not appreciate. Angola was the main locale for *degredo*: at

---

5. *Ibid.*, pp. 107–108.
6. See Hermenegildo Augusto de Faria Blanc Junior, *O Depósito de Degredados* (Luanda, 1916), p. 19; *Angolana, Documentação sobre Angola, 1883–1887, vol. II* (Luanda, 1971), pp. 483–484.
7. Timothy J. Coates, *Convict Labor in the Portuguese Empire, 1740–1932* (Leiden, 2014), pp. 131–132.

the end of the nineteenth century, convicts represented twelve per cent of the white population, living in Luanda with a shocking liberty. Many owned restaurants.[8]

Other travellers in the nineteenth century, including George Tams (writing in the middle of that century) and Mary Kingsley (observing Luanda in 1890s), were more generous in their descriptions of the city.[9] Kingsley felt Luanda was the only "real" city on the west and southern African coast, probably because Luanda had been founded and planned by Europeans. Thus, she would have felt it had a more familiar urban pattern than other African ports. What made Luanda (and Mozambique Island) unique was that they were both not just colonial capital cities, but also urban penal colonies.

The interlocking rationales in Lisbon for the creation of these two penal colonies are complex. The mid- to late nineteenth century saw the convergence of three (seemingly) unrelated issues in Portugal. The first of these was legal reform and new theories of the goals and methods of incarceration. The second issue was the European contest for colonies in Africa, a process commonly referred to as "New Imperialism". Third was the gradual end of slavery in Angola and Mozambique and the consequent need for cheap labour.

During the nineteenth century, Portugal revisited and updated its archaic legal codes dating from the early 1600s, revising them several times in the 1860s and 1870s, reflecting changing ideas of punishment. Significantly for Angola and Mozambique, these codes linked the traditional Portuguese punishment of *degredo* (exile or banishment) with then current ideas of reforming the prisoner (i.e. penitence in the new Lisbon penitentiary) followed by forced labour performed in the colonies. *Degredo*, that is having one's legal status "degraded" in the Portuguese legal tradition, meant being exiled for a specific period of time to some distant location. The distance from the sentencing court was determined by the nature of the crime: the more serious the offence, the more distant the location. This punishment dates from the Portuguese legal codes of the Middle Ages.

This linkage of an old punishment with a new objective was a sure-fire method to ensure the "effective occupation" demanded by the Treaty of Berlin in the division of most of Africa among various European powers. This second issue meant that these prisoners would first build the infrastructure needed in the colonies and ideally also become the colonizers, farmers, or settlers themselves. Their presence (so the government believed) would assist in the ongoing transition away from slavery in Portuguese

---

8. Orlando Ribeiro, *A colonização de Angola e o seu fracasso* (Lisbon, 1981), p. 132. By "mestiço", Ribeiro here means people of mixed European and African background.
9. George Tams, *Visita ás possessões portuguezas na costa occidental d'África*, 2 vols (Porto, 1850); Mary Kingsley, *Travels in West Africa (Congo Français, Corisco, and Cameroons)* (London, 1897).

Africa. While these three are the most important and relevant, there are additional aspects as well, such as a growing urban population in Portugal, the government wishing to encourage emigration to the colonies rather than to (now-independent) Brazil, ending vagrancy through forced colonial labour, the promise of extracting mineral wealth from Angola (and to a lesser extent Mozambique), and national pride in maintaining a global empire.

AN URBAN PENAL COLONY AND ITS INMATES

The typical penal colony in the nineteenth and twentieth centuries was located in a remote setting, often on an island far away from urban populations. Juan Fernández Island, used by the Chilean authorities, and Fernando de Noronha Island for Brazil are two such examples.[10] This is one of the many aspects that make these two Portuguese penal colonies distinctive: their urban locations in the capital cities of Portugal's two largest and most promising African colonies. As noted above, the larger prison in Luanda accounted for the vast majority of prisoners sent to Africa, and the remainder of this essay will focus exclusively on it.[11]

"Prison" is probably the wrong word to describe the *Depósito de Degredados* in Luanda, since a prison is a place from which prisoners cannot leave. However, in Luanda many convicts would daily come and go through the *Depósito*'s gates, working in the city of Luanda and returning at night. Others worked under military supervision in the interior of the country, far away from Luanda. Perhaps "Hub of Convict Activities" would be (an awkward but) a more accurate term.

Reflecting its military administration, prisoners in the *Depósito* were organized in five companies. The first two were for male prisoners from Portugal. The third was for male prisoners from the Atlantic colonies of Cape Verde, Portuguese Guinea, and São Tomé (as well as any foreigners).[12]

---

10. For Juan Fernández, see Ricardo D. Salvatore and Carlos Aguirre, "Colonies of Settlement or Places of Banishment and Torment? Penal Colonies and Convict Labour in Latin America, c.1800–1940", in Christian G. De Vito and Alex Lichtenstein (eds), *Global Convict Labour* (Leiden, 2015), pp. 273–309. On Fernando de Noronha, see Peter Beattie, *Punishment in Paradise: Race, Slavery, Human Rights, and a Nineteenth-Century Brazilian Penal Colony* (Durham, NC, 2015).

11. Much more on the Angolan prison is available in the Lisbon archives and libraries than a few shreds of evidence regarding the Mozambique prison. See Coates, *Convict Labor*, pp. 189–201.

12. Foreigners are rare, but some do appear in the records here and there. For the most part, "foreigners" means Spaniards, largely from Galicia. However, George Tams noted the presence of a group of Italian convicts deported from Portugal in 1818, sent to the coast of Novo Redondo, Angola. During his visit, Tams found that six of the original group of twenty-three or twenty-four were still residing there and a total of nine or ten Europeans lived in the town. Tams, *Vista ás possessões portuguezas*, 1, p. 180.

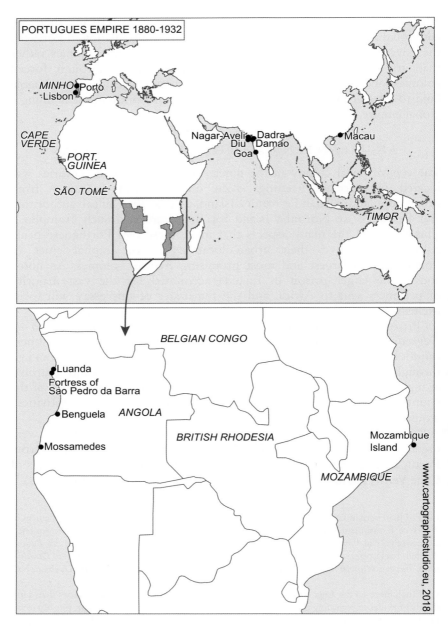

Figure 1. The Portuguese Empire 1880–1932, and the *Depósito de Degredados* in Luanda and its dependent facilities.

Women composed the fourth company and male vagrants formed the fifth. As noted above with the case of João Chagas, the *Depósito* maintained dependent facilities in Mossamedes and Benguela, two coastal cities south of Luanda, for its first twenty years, closing Mossamedes in 1884 and Benguela in 1907.[13] The *Depósito* also administered a place of secondary punishment, the fortress of São Pedro da Barra in the Luanda harbour. In any given year, the *Depósito* might oversee more than 1,000 prisoners or as few as 400. The commander also had no way of knowing in advance how many convicts to expect with the arrival of each steamship or the lengths of their sentences. As a result, he had to be flexible and creative in assigning housing and work.

Typically, male prisoners were guilty of murder, theft, or assault, or a combination of these. Their sentences ranged from four to six years of *degredo* to Angola. Male prisoners formed between ninety and ninety-five per cent of the prison population and, again typically, were under forty and not married. Female inmates were a radically different group. Largely guilty of infanticide, theft, or murder, female prisoners had much longer sentences and their ages ranged more widely. The company of male vagrants came and went, depending on vagrancy laws at the time. The bulk of prisoners came from Portugal; more specifically, the city of Lisbon and the Minho, the densely populated far north of the country.

In addition to common criminals or *degredados*, there were several other categories of prisoner, each with a special label and all counted separately. *Deportados* were persons convicted of political crimes, such as João Chagas. This distinction was of sufficient importance that a police sergeant met João Chagas at the boat to accompany him to the *Depósito*, telling him he offered this courtesy "so that you do not have to walk with the levy of *degredados*".[14] Vagrants or *vadios* were normally counted apart from the others. Their only crime was not working, and the state alternated between ignoring them or attempting to make them useful. In the period 1905 to 1914, the *Depósito* received 50 to 240 new vagrants annually, or a total of 1,155, all but fifteen of them men.[15] Vagrants were younger than convicts, with 49 per cent under the age of twenty-five, and 63 per cent under thirty. The vast majority were single (87 per cent) and illiterate (67 per cent), although 24 per cent were able to read and write. Most vagrants remained in the *Depósito* for sentences of four years or less, and their death rates were higher than any other group; 20 per cent died before completion of their sentences.[16] They were also a troublesome lot; 30–40 per cent of the entire

---

13. Junior, *O Depósito*, p. 21.
14. Chagas, *Diário*, p. 20.
15. Junior, *O Depósito*, chart opposite p. 88.
16. *Ibid.*, p. 89.

group of vagrants faced disciplinary actions each year, mostly for attempting to avoid work.

Given their backgrounds of being homeless, none of these statements appears out of the ordinary. It would be logical to expect vagrants to be illiterate, in poor health, and idle. Attempts to control vagrancy in Portugal (a process begun as early as 1375) appeared in numerous pieces of nineteenth-century legislation. First were attempts to outlaw it (1835, 1836), control it, move vagrants to special asylums (1780, 1836, 1867), create special vagrant agricultural colonies (1894), impress vagrants into military service (in Cape Verde, 1877), banish them overseas, and, as a last resort, forbid them from returning to Portugal (1897). The *Depósito* was a sometimes-used tool in this much larger picture of attempted social control of vagrancy in Portugal, and its commander tells us clearly that, by 1915, Company 5 (vagrants) was almost extinct because "they are no longer sent here".[17] We also know, because of the numerous complaints from those supervising them, that vagrants were the most problematic group within the *Depósito*. António Leite de Magalhães (a career military man who served in several colonies) provides a good example of this when he made a sharp distinction between convicts and vagrants: "Many times I had convicts under my command and to give them justice, I never had better or humbler workers. The incorrigibles were the vagrants."[18] George Tams mentions one vagrant/criminal sent from Portugal to Angola who, "educated in the streets of his native city", was able to acquire wealth and status in Luanda. How this occurred is a mystery, but profits from the (then ongoing) slave trade are the most probable source of his new-found wealth.[19]

Addidos were recidivists, normally counted separately, but sometimes blended with *degredados*. They had more liberty than ordinary convicts and were sent to Angola only after committing a series of crimes, none of which alone would have triggered transportation. This provision in Portuguese law was undoubtedly modelled on a similar French provision, which banished recidivists to French Guiana.[20] The Portuguese were close students of both the French and British experiments with transportation and had nothing but admiration for what the British had achieved in Australia. The greatest differences, however, between British Australia and Portuguese Angola was that convict labour had real value (i.e. there was a demand) in the former and such a demand was absent in the latter. Angola had a very large native population, especially when contrasted to the

---

17. *Ibid.*, p. 24.
18. António Leite de Magalhães, *A colonização e desenvolvimento de Angola* (Lisbon, 1925), p. 38.
19. Tams, *Vista ás possessões portuguezas*, 1, p. 226.
20. See Jean-Lucien Sanchez, "The Relegation of Recidivists in French Guiana in the Nineteenth and Twentieth Centuries", in De Vito and Lichtenstein, *Global Convict Labour*, pp. 222–248.

number of native Australians. The Portuguese had the added advantage of hindsight in that the Australian experience was earlier (1788–1868) and had concluded by the time they established their two prisons in Africa.

Military deportees were present in large numbers in Angola, but they were sentenced and supervised by the military itself and do not make their way into documentation from the civil judicial system. It is quite possible that some of the personnel supervising the convicts were themselves military deportees, but there is no proof of that. We occasionally get glimpses into a convict/military connection that was surprisingly wide-spread, such as this comment from a Minister of the Colonies:

> The colonies which up to that point [1843] had been a nest of slaves then became an exclusive nest of convicts. The detestable system of populating the African colonies with criminals produced, as its first result, the inability of the governors of each of the provinces to depend on the loyalty of the troops because they were largely composed of convicts.[21]

Although referring to Portuguese Guinea, this statement applied equally to all of Portuguese Africa. Nor was this connection unique to Portugal; the French used their convicts in the military as well.[22]

This link between *degredados* and the military in Angola was strong. Gerald Bender, in his fundamental work on the Portuguese in Angola, claims that they formed the majority of the military in the colony. However, it is not clear from his statement whether these were civilians impressed into military service or military personnel punished with *degredo* to Angola.[23] These troops "rarely amended their notorious behaviour [...] official missions into the interior to foment or protect the slave trade, collect taxes, or procure forced labourers often gave the *degredado* troops an open license to murder and plunder the African populations [...] this pattern continued throughout the century [...]".[24] The police were equally riddled with *degredados* among their ranks and were noted for their corruption and incompetence.[25]

CONVICT LABOUR

These prisoners were sent to Angola to redeem themselves through labour, and the state attempted a number of distinct schemes to extract and direct convict labour in the colony. First, perhaps the most privileged convicts were leased to individuals under a bond and worked anywhere in the colony. This option was available only to those who had completed at least

---

21. Manuel Pinheiro Chagas, *As colónias portuguezas no século XIX* (Lisbon, 1890), p. 86.
22. See Dominique Kalifa, *Biribi: les bagnes coloniaux de l'armée française* (Paris, 2009).
23. Bender, *Angola under the Portuguese*, p. 68.
24. *Ibid.*
25. *Ibid.*, p. 69.

one fifth of their sentences and were not recidivists. These individuals had to present themselves periodically before the local police authorities as a precaution against escape. In the 1901 listing (see below), only twenty-seven convicts were so licenced, but, of those, fourteen faced disciplinary charges. The bulk of the prison population worked either in Luanda for a municipal and state agency or in one of the workshops within the prison.

Escape into the interior of the colony was apparently a well-worn path for many convicts from Luanda, and as long as the *Depósito* functioned it would appear it produced escapees who made their way into the interior. This was especially true for the first half of the nineteenth century. Bender makes the point that "[t]he end of the slave trade forced most of the *degredados* out of the interior".[26] *Degredados* had to survive by participating in the colonial workforce, and when the slave trade was one (if not the primary) economic activity in Angola it is not surprising to find *degredados* (and former *degredados*) supplying and supervising slaves.

The 1901 statistical summary for the colony includes a listing of the assignments for the 993 convicts assigned to the *Depósito* that year:[27] Fifty-seven were delegated to work with the troops in Benguela (building infrastructure?); twenty-four were being punished in the fortress of São Pedro da Barra, thirty-three were working for the telegraph company of Luanda; another thirty-four laboured for the town council of Luanda (cleaning streets?); twenty-seven worked at the army's storage depot; twenty-two were in the hospital; and 127 were absent. While concentrated in Luanda, it is fair to say they worked throughout the colony as clerks, maids, and in many other positions. João Chagas makes the comment that, at the turn of the century, many convicts performed public works in pairs, chained together. The townspeople of Luanda complained that the sight of chained convicts coming and going through town was a disgrace. The *Depósito* stopped this practice as a result.

By 1915, the *Depósito* had added a third possibility for work when it created a series of workshops within its walls. The *Depósito* had already been making the uniforms and boots for its own convict population as well as for the military. New workshops were added to these tailors and cobblers to bind books, and make locks and items from tin; a carpentry shop was created and the inmates made bookcases, beds, and other pieces of furniture. The *Depósito* also created a barber's workshop and a section for street sweepers. Female inmates worked in the tailor's shop or in the laundry, the laundry reception area, washing, starching, and ironing clothes from the

26. *Ibid.*, p. 66.
27. *Annuário Estatístico da Provincia de Angola* (Luanda, 1905), pp. 150–170.

prison and from town. In short, the convicts performed a great variety of tasks under supervision, ranging from very light (when leased under bond) to constant (within the walls of the *Depósito*). The type of work they performed also varied greatly, from the hard labour of building docks to semi-skilled work in a prison shop or clerical desk work.

Some of these prisoners were paid, but the methods used to calculate their salaries were extremely complex and not totally clear. All prisoners paid at least twenty-five per cent of their salaries into an obligatory repatriation fund, and probably paid more into other obligatory funds supervised by the commander. Men working in one of the first eight workshops listed above received a wage based on the workshop's monthly profit divided by the number of workers. Women were paid in a similar manner except that they were also subject to a behaviour classification system, which rewarded those who had not broken any of the rules.[28]

THE PRISON AS A LOCAL INSTITUTION

The rationale for the creation of this prison is relatively clear when viewed from Lisbon and an imperial perspective. However, what impact did the *Depósito* have on Angola? What was the perspective when viewed from Luanda? Just about every author who visited Luanda during this period mentioned the presence of convicts in their distinctive uniforms throughout the city. Commentary came from a wide range of visitors to the colony, such as Protestant missionaries working in the interior of the country to Portuguese government officials conducting official business in Luanda. The fact that virtually every visitor to the colony mentioned them makes it all the more unusual that no one went beyond these comments to inquire as to their numbers, the organization of their labour, the goals of the *Depósito*, or the success or failure of this redemptive effort (to list but four possible questions). The colonial government itself vacillated between providing a great deal of data about the *Depósito* and its prisoners (such as the 1901 data or the 1915 published annual report) or offering little or nothing, such as details about its budget or expenses. We do know that during the early years of its organization in 1885, in a letter to the Lisbon authorities, the Financial Council of Angola stated that the expenses for the *Depósito* were ruinous, costing the colonial government over fifty thousand *milréis*

---

28. The terminology for these classifications was based on Crofton's "Irish Method" of gradation of behaviour. "First class" (also referred to as "improved") was an inmate who had never received any disciplinary action or who had been in second class for eighteen months with no new infractions. "Second-class" (a.k.a. "suspicious") inmates had received one such action or had been in third class for eighteenth months with no new charges. "Third class" ("incorrigible") were those who had committed a new crime or received two disciplinary actions while in custody. This system was in place until 1915 but it seems to have been phased out afterwards. See Coates, *Convict Labor*, pp. 92–105, for a detailed discussion of the work of convicts and their salaries.

(50,000$000) annually.[29] The *Depósito* and its inmates were, in fact, the proverbial elephant in the room. Everyone saw them, was aware of them, and yet avoided saying anything of consequence about them. Unfortunately, as a result of this avoidance, the impact of the convict presence in Angola is murky and becomes a matter of guesswork and assumption. Other than Bender's work, there is no discussion of the prison in the secondary literature.[30] The documentation produced by the state itself does little to clarify the role or importance of the *Depósito* since its budget and expenses are blended with the total colonial military budget.[31]

We know that supervision was relatively lax, which allowed for many convicts to escape from this system. We also know that convict mortality was relatively high, reflecting their difficult living and working conditions. A third method of escaping the prison system was by way of a pardon, and convicts were well aware of this possibility. The medieval and early modern Portuguese monarchs periodically issued pardons on special occasions, such as marriages or births of royal children. This practice continued after 1910 with the Republic; the President publishes a list of those fortunate convicts pardoned each 5 October, the anniversary of the Republic. While convicts did request pardons before 1910, the number and frequency accelerated after 1910, no doubt fuelled by the republican rhetoric of "equality, fraternity, liberty". However, requesting a pardon was a tricky matter and required a scribe (since most prisoners were illiterate) and official paper with fiscal stamps. Thus, a prisoner would have had to pay to make such a request. By 1915, the prison commander had developed a standardized form for this purpose and these completed forms made their way through his office, to the military commander of Angola, to the governor, then to Lisbon for the attention of the Overseas Minister, the Minister of Justice, and finally to the President. This was obviously a slow and cumbersome process. In the turbulent and unstable years of Portugal's First Republic (1910–1926), with numerous changes of

---

29. Arquivo Histórico Ultramarino (AHU, in Lisbon) Angola *caixa* (box) 789, letter dated 10 February 1885. One interesting detail in this letter is that Lisbon insisted on forcing the colonial government to pay the expenses for the *Depósito*. Thus, from the perspective of Lisbon, they were free of the convicts *as well as* of any expenses to maintain them. This would change by 1915, but letters from Angola at that time complained of numerous late or partial payments.

30. While this is true about the secondary literature, I should mention that the best overall description of day-to-day life in Luanda c.1900 is in David Birmingham's *A Short History of Modern Angola* (New York, 2015), ch. 2; "The Urban Culture of Luanda City", pp. 13–26.

31. This last point is especially problematic since it is impossible to distinguish what the *Depósito* cost or what profit it netted (if any). In order to answer these questions, it would be necessary to find the master register of convicts and the accounting books maintained by the commanders, perhaps now located in the National Archives of Angola in Luanda.

government, it is not surprising that bundles of petitions sat unanswered at each stage of the process.[32]

One such collection is a batch of sixty-eight petitions from 1915, frozen in the archives of the Ministry of Justice.[33] Since we know little about the individual convicts, these petitions offer welcome details. Of these, sixteen are from women and fifty-two are from men; women represented only five per cent of the prison population, so how do we explain the fact that their letters account for almost a quarter of the total? João Chagas tells us that female convicts in the 1890s believed a republic would be more merciful and grant more pardons.[34] Here, we see that female prisoners obviously had higher expectations of this process than their male counterparts.

These sixteen women were guilty of first degree murder (six cases), infanticide (five), poisoning (three), theft and murder (one), and simple theft (one). An equal number were married and unmarried (six each) and four were widows. This group is a good example of the characteristics of female convicts in general: their average age was thirty, the oldest was sixty, and the youngest eighteen, and all were from the north of Portugal. Some of them had very long sentences of more than twenty years in Angola, which had been shortened with previous commutations. With one exception, all appear to have been model prisoners with no disciplinary actions taken against them. The exception, Mathilde de Jesus, had violated prison rules three times with an insolent attitude, insulting guards.

The fifty-two men were more diverse in age and crimes committed. The oldest was sixty-three and the youngest was eighteen, with an average age of thirty-two. Almost all were from the north of Lisbon, about half were married (twenty-three), and they were overwhelmingly guilty of theft, murder, or attempted murder. Their sentences were typically time in prison (four to eight years), followed by transportation to Angola for years of work, typically eight to twenty. Several also had obligatory fines and many were not model prisoners; in some cases, the commander needed a second sheet of paper to list all their infractions. In both cases of male and female inmates, it would appear they were out of luck. Few, if any, received a pardon from the President of the Republic.[35]

---

32. A good indication of the slow progress of such petitions and how they were often ignored: bundles of these petitions were tied with cord and sealed with red wax and then placed in the archives and never forwarded. The author found several of these unopened bundles in the AHU and opened them in 2010 for the first time since 1915.

33. Arquivo Nacional da Torre do Tombo (Lisbon), Ministério de Negócios Eclesiásticos e Justiça, *maço* [bundle] 729, *documento* [document] 5.

34. Chagas, *Trabalhos Forçados*, 2, p. 282.

35. In order to know for certain, it would be necessary to review the master register maintained by the prison commander. However, an examination of the lists of pardoned convicts published in newspapers from the era revealed no prisoners held in Angola. Many subjects from one of the

The *Depósito* was a major purchaser of foodstuffs for its population, so it is safe to say that merchants who supplied it with food had a large and steady customer. Two lists of purchases for food for the *Depósito* were uncovered in archives in Lisbon detailing purchases for August and September 1931. They show monthly purchases from ten individual providers of foodstuffs, plus purchases from the state's bakery and butcher's shop.[36] This would have been a very lucrative contract indeed, assuming prompt payment from the state. As early as 1915, the commander noted the rising costs of food and the difficulties of staying within his budget while also providing sufficient sustenance for his charges. The only other evidence that we have regarding the prisoners' diet are the photographs from the published 1915 commander's report, which shows rail-thin prisoners blankly staring at the camera, contrasted with a smiling and well-fed military administration. We also know from the commander's published report that European and African prisoners were given two distinct sets of rations, yet the photographs of both groups show very thin men, in many cases with oversized uniforms hanging on them. Meanwhile, the officers appear to be a contented lot and are clearly better fed.

The prisoners – or at least some of them – were paid for their labour. On payday, another safe assumption is that those who were able to temporarily leave the *Depósito* for a visit to Luanda (and many were allowed this privilege) did so. The fact that so many inmates were listed as "absent" in 1901 (127 of 993, or almost thirteen per cent) underlines their relatively lax supervision in Luanda. The fact that none appear to have been pardoned partially explains their reasoning for running away. Of course, the simple fact that they had fled could have resulted in several outcomes. They could return, meet their deaths, continue living in the interior, or escape to another colony.

This payday and its impact would have meant that certain days of the month were probably not as safe as others for the citizens of Luanda to wander out in the streets, especially at night, and this would have been common knowledge among the townspeople. Not just the inmates, but the guards themselves (as well as all other military personnel) were paid, and payday for them would have been equally problematic in Luanda, given the large number of military stationed in the city. The town itself had a long-standing reputation as a rough place filled with convicts who were friends of drink. Alcohol in Angola has a long history among the European

colonies also petitioned for pardons, but not in this specific batch from 1915. See Coates, *Convict Labor*, Appendix 6, pp. 170–185, for extended examples of requests for pardons.

36. These are located in the Arquivo Histórico Militar (in Lisbon), second division, second section, *caixa* 161, *documento* 22. Unfortunately, without more information, these lists of purchases do not tell us how much each inmate was allotted. African and European inmates (as well as dependent children) were provided with different rations. The *Depósito* also maintained a small garden, but we do not know what it provided or in what quantities.

population as being indispensable for the tropics. It was the *only* item produced by a series of planned agricultural/settlement colonies during the nineteenth century that made a profit and it had long been a staple trade item in the slave trade itself, Brazilian rum being traded for African slaves. As a result, alcohol has a powerful and dark history in Angola associated with slavery and convict labour.[37] Bars, taverns, and restaurants, by association, were convict-friendly environments in Luanda and this would have been common knowledge among the locals as well. We know from the lists of infractions that many returned drunk or late. Other visitors commented that the bars and restaurants in Luanda were largely run by former convicts. As a result, there was obviously a large network of former and current inmates within Angola centred on these bars and taverns. It would have been there that current inmates would have been able to obtain the name of someone willing to provide a bond (for work outside the prison), send or receive correspondence from home (outside the scrutiny of the prison authorities), borrow money, learn the identity of sympathetic guards, or arrange an escape to the interior or neighbouring Belgian Congo or British Rhodesia.

Many of the inmates spent time recovering from illnesses in the Luanda hospital, and such medical expenses were substantial. George Tams visited the military hospital, where convicts were also treated, describing it as "showing signs of excessive economizing". Soldiers treated there, he claimed, were "mostly criminals" who had received severe punishments of whippings.[38] In 1898, the hospital had 800 admissions from inmates during the year, in all likelihood not 800 separate individuals but times admitted. The governor of the colony complained in a letter to his superiors that each convict in the hospital cost the state 300 *réis* daily. Prisoners largely suffered from fevers and other symptoms of malaria, but gastrointestinal illness, anaemia, and bronchitis were also widespread.

In spite of the best efforts of the military authorities, supervision of the convict population was spotty at best and non-existent for many. Both of the sub-depositories in Mossamedes and Benguela were closed because adequate supervision was impossible, given the lack of funds and personnel. The result was that convicts roamed the streets of both towns and escaped into the interior. Convicts in the period up to 1900 formed two thirds of all whites in the Angolan colony, and for the later period of 1902 to 1914 many more convicts entered Angola than free European colonizers.[39] The reality on the ground in Luanda (and elsewhere throughout Angola) was that being a European meant that you could be assumed to be a convict or former convict; the terms were synonymous. This would continue until the

---

37. On the role of alcohol, see José Curto, *Enslaving Spirits: The Portuguese-Brazilian Alcohol Trade at Luanda and its Hinterland, c.1550–1830* (Leiden, 2004).
38. Tams, *Vista ás possessões portuguezas*, 2, p. 12.
39. Bender, *Angola under the Portuguese*, pp. 87–88.

post-World War II period, when Portugal had some success encouraging free immigration to both Angola and Mozambique. When one examines the overall demographic picture of Angola up to World War II, white "colonizers" were (largely) convicts or former convicts, and this would have been common knowledge to all Angolans as well as to people remaining in Portugal. This underlines the fact that Brazil was more attractive as an emigration destination for the Portuguese. It was not strictly for economic reasons; "Angola" meant "penal colony" for the white population.

RATIONALES FOR THE PRISON AND ITS END

Perhaps another way of examining this question is that we know that the anticipated outcomes from establishing the *Depósito* never materialized. The authorities in Lisbon wanted the convicts to marry, cultivate land, and produce children, to thus create a stable European presence in the colony. We know they did none of these things. Although the majority were not married, there is no evidence of convicts marrying each other or Africans in any significant numbers. Marriages between convicts were unlikely given the nature of their crimes: men were common criminals guilty of murder, theft, etc., while women were normally guilty of a one-time crime (today it might be called "a crime of passion") – killing an unfaithful husband or boyfriend or ending the life of an unwanted baby. The state was eager to give or lease land to convicts to encourage commercial agriculture in the colony, yet there were fatal problems with this plan as well. Most of the convicts came from an urban setting and had no background or interest in farming. Quite the opposite. In nineteenth-century Portugal many single men left the countryside for the cities to escape a life of rural poverty working with their hands as a farmer. Why would they want to return to a farmer's life in Africa?

How many convicts remained in the colony after the completion of their sentences? This is one of a series of questions that are difficult to determine with any certainty, but it appears that the vast majority of these convicts did not remain in the colony. An obligatory percentage of their earnings went into a transportation fund to help repay the state for their journey home, and every indication is that most convicts used it to return. One of the major complaints of the *Depósito*'s commander in his 1915 report was that the year-long grace period enjoyed by a former convict to request transport home should be eliminated. In fact, he felt that only a handful of carefully screened ex-convicts should be allowed to remain in the colony. One has to admire the tenacity of a prison commander suggesting in print to his superiors that one of the initial goals of creating the prison and of state policy was a total folly. However, this also demonstrates that state officials were of two minds about this population. On the one hand, sending them to Africa meant "cleansing" the European homeland of criminal undesirables and any expenses associated with them. However, allowing them to remain in Angola then linked "Angola" with "penal colony", making free immigration less attractive and burdening the colonial budget. Was it better for former convicts to remain in the colony or return to Europe? We see evidence of both goals (in spite of their contradictions) in the documentation.

Thus, the major goals of the state – marriage, cultivation of land (by former convicts), and children (in a stable environment) – were illusions. The other goals of penal reform, i.e. penitence and redemption, were equally distant from reality. In fact, convicts were sent thousands of miles from their sentencing courts (at state expense) to conduct work that could easily and much more cheaply have been accomplished by local wage labour. They lived under difficult conditions, with questionable diets and in poor health. Many died and those who survived returned to their homeland "broken down by their sufferings".[40]

In spite of all this, convict labour was responsible for the Portuguese meeting two critical objectives in the late nineteenth and early twentieth centuries in Africa. First, the consolidation of Portuguese colonial presence by means of military supervision and control, effectively defining the geographical extent of modern Angola (and Mozambique). Second, the creation of infrastructure to facilitate the influx of free European immigrants who would follow in the post-1945 period. However, even though it is true that Portuguese emigrants to Angola and Mozambique increased sharply after World War II, such emigration in the twentieth century was largely to Brazil, France, and the United States (in that order).[41] This was *in spite of* the best efforts by the Lisbon authorities to direct it to Portuguese Africa.

The entire issue of vagrancy and its punishments, especially reforming efforts and attempted uses of vagrants for public works, military conscripts, overseas colonizers, etc., remains unexplored and a fertile subject for future study. The same can be said for the military-convict connection, especially as it applies to Angola and Mozambique. Our understanding of both the prison in Mozambique as well as in Angola would be greatly enhanced by a focused institutional study of each, using local archival materials (assuming these are available).

Several late nineteenth-century institutions, such as the Sociedade de Geografia de Lisboa (Lisbon Geographical Society, a private organization) and the state-sponsored Instituto de Investigação Científica Tropical (Tropical Research Institute), were central to planning and implementing colonial policies in Africa. Institutional studies on them as well as other related bodies, such as the Lisbon Penitentiary, and even the Overseas Council itself, would clarify many issues surrounding convict labour in Portuguese Africa.

---

40. *Ibid.*, p. 87. He is citing the report by Francisco Xavier da Silva Telles, *A Transportação Penal e a Colonização* (Lisbon, 1903).
41. See Cláudia Castelo, *Passagens para África* (Lisbon, 2007), pp. 90, 97, and 183.

IRSH 63 (2018), Special Issue, pp. 169–189 doi:10.1017/S0020859018000275
© 2018 Internationaal Instituut voor Sociale Geschiedenis

Punitive Entanglements: Connected Histories of Penal Transportation, Deportation, and Incarceration in the Spanish Empire (1830s-1898)*

CHRISTIAN G. DE VITO

School of History, Politics and International Relations
University of Leicester
University Road, Leicester LE1 7RH, UK

E-mail: christian.devito@gmail.com

ABSTRACT: This article features a connected history of punitive relocations in the Spanish Empire, from the independence of Spanish America to the "loss" of Cuba, Puerto Rico, and the Philippines in 1898. Three levels of entanglement are highlighted here: the article looks simultaneously at punitive flows stemming from the colonies and from the metropole; it brings together the study of penal transportation, administrative deportation, and military deportation; and it discusses the relationship between punitive relocations and imprisonment. As part of this special issue, foregrounding "perspectives from the colonies", I start with an analysis of the punitive flows that stemmed from the overseas provinces. I then address punishment in the metropole through the colonial lens, before highlighting the entanglements of penal transportation and deportation in the nineteenth-century Spanish Empire as a whole.

On 28 November 1896, two ships left the port of Havana in the midst of the cries, waved handkerchiefs, and threatening screams of the crowd on the dockside. More than one hundred men, chained in pairs, were being brought to the steamship *Ciudad de Cadiz* for deportation to various destinations across the Spanish Empire. They included two dozen "unfaithful" (*infidentes*) individuals allegedly involved in the Cuban War of Independence (1895–1898), seventy-four cattle rustlers (*cuatreros*), and a considerable number of *ñáñigos*, or members of the Abakuá mutual aid society. The latter were primarily slaves and ex-slaves from West Africa. Manuel María Miranda, an anarchist who worked at the Don Quijote de la Mancha tobacco factory, was on board as well. A military court had sentenced him to deportation to Fernando Poo, a Spanish colonial possession in the Gulf of Guinea, for his opposition to the compulsory

* The research leading to these results has received funding from the European Research Council under the European Union's Seventh Framework Programme (FP/2007–2013) / ERC Grant Agreement 312542.

contribution for the Spanish navy during that time of war. In San Juan, Puerto Rico, twenty-five more deportees embarked on the *Ciudad de Cadiz*. In Spain, they were joined by Cuban, Filipino, and Spanish men destined for the Chafarinas Islands, Ceuta, and Fernando Poo. During his forced residence in Fernando Poo, Miranda worked for several landowners, including a man named Mellizo, a "criminal" from Cadiz.[1]

In order to unravel the complexity of punitive relocations such as those experienced by Miranda, we need to address the connected histories of punishment from an imperial perspective. To this end, I aim to foreground three levels of entanglement in punitive relocations across the Spanish monarchy during the nineteenth century. First, this article looks simultaneously at punitive flows stemming from the colonies and from the metropole. Second, it brings together the study of penal transportation and other forms of punitive relocation that originated from states of exception, that is, administrative deportation and sentences of transportation pronounced by military courts. Third, the article discusses the relationship between punitive relocations and imprisonment. Its ambition is to locate the contested rise of the penitentiary in the last third of the nineteenth century, within a broader picture of coexisting, conflicting, and related penal regimes.

The following sections are organized in such a way as to foreground the "perspective from the colonies", and to allow a connected history of punitive relocations. I start by analysing the punitive flows that stemmed from the overseas provinces; I then address punishment in the metropole through the colonial lens, before going on to highlight the entanglements of penal transportation and deportation in the nineteenth-century Spanish Empire as a whole.

COLONIAL PUNITIVE FLOWS

The Napoleonic Wars (1808–1814) and the related process of independence in Latin America (1810–1820s) created a deep discontinuity in the history of the Spanish Empire. The incipient liberalism that emerged from resistance to French occupation and that developed from the 1830s posed questions about the legal status of the monarchy's subjects. It did so both within the Peninsula and in the remains of the overseas empire – the "system of the three colonies", which included Cuba, Puerto Rico, and the Philippines. The Constitution of Cadiz (1812) envisaged a path of legal convergence across the empire, but the preservation of slavery in the overseas provinces and the limitations imposed on the provinces' representation in the metropolitan Cortes (the legislative assembly) clearly undermined that promise. By 1837, the new Constitution sanctioned the divergence of legal regimes, with article 2 stating that "The overseas provinces will be ruled by

1. Manuel María Miranda, *Memorias de un deportado* (Havana, 1903).

special laws". In fact, the metropolitan authorities never created a coherent set of colonial laws. The legal framework for the overseas provinces depended on the old *Recopilación de las Leyes de Indias* (Collection of the Laws of the Indies), selected and filtered peninsular laws, and new laws issued for each colony. Furthermore, the Captains General were given "all-encompassing faculties" (*facultades omnímodas*). Indeed, the construction of their "supreme authority" (*mando supremo*) proved the basis of a new type of governance of the colonies. This presented relevant differences vis-à-vis the model inherited from the previous three centuries of colonial rule: as the Captain General had both military and civilian powers, the traditional role of the *audiencias* (Higher Courts) to check and balance the power of the first authority was substantially limited.[2]

The punitive regimes applied during the nineteenth century in the overseas provinces, and especially convict transportation and deportation, reflected that new mode of colonial rule. Convicts continued to be sentenced to transportation by local courts and the *audiencias*, as they had been in the past. However, the "all-compassing faculties" of the Captains General included the power to relocate colonial subjects by administrative order. Moreover, the broad militarization of the colonies allowed for the extensive use of military courts to legitimize exile, confinement, and deportation. Taken together, penal transportation, administrative deportation, and military relocation provided the authorities with a broad toolkit to maintain colonial order, discipline subaltern labour, and prevent or curb anti-colonial insurgencies. They formed a flexible instrument, which additionally allowed government to cope with the specific and changing circumstances of each province, and to differentiate repression by class, ethnicity, gender, and type of crime or disorder.

The case of punitive flows from Cuba is telling in this respect.[3] From the 1830s to 1868, the priority was to protect the thriving sugar plantations. In that context, sentences to transportation to Puerto Rico, Santo Domingo, and Ceuta complemented the planters' use of "domestic" justice, including detention in public prisons and *depósitos* for the plantation workforce of African slaves and Chinese contract labourers. Free blacks based in the urban centres were the main targets of the brutal repression led by the military commission in the aftermath of the *Escalera* conspiracy of 1843. That institution, created in March 1824, additionally curbed the aborted secessionist expeditions that punctuated the 1850s and 1860s. Meanwhile,

---

2. Josep M. Fradera, *Colonias para despues de un imperio* (Barcelona, 2005). See also Javier Alvarado Planas, *La Administración Colonial española en el siglo XIX* (Madrid, 2013).
3. For a detailed study of the Cuban case, and related information on primary and secondary sources, see Christian G. De Vito, "Punishment and Labour Relations: Cuba between Abolition and Empire (1835–1886)" (forthcoming).

exile and administrative deportation provided a swift means of expelling abolitionist agents from the surrounding British colonies, as well as those viewed as "internal enemies". These included "incorrigible" vagrants and lumpenproletarians, and members of the Abakuá mutual aid societies. Fernando Poo, Ceuta, and the Philippines were the destinations of those convicts and deportees, while shorter-distance relocations headed to the Isle of Pines, located just to the south of Cuba.

The Ten Years' War, which started in 1868, changed Cuba's political and military situation, and the punitive strategies of its Spanish administration. Repressing the insurgents, isolating them from potential supporters in the rural areas, and preventing rebellion from spreading from the eastern to the western part of the island were the new priorities. Military courts sentenced many rebels to death and ordered the transportation of hundreds more to Hacho Castle in Ceuta. Preventive measures against civilians in eastern Cuba included "warnings" and administrative confinement on the Isle of Pines. Finally, urban supporters of the insurgency, or *laborantes*, were relocated administratively to the Peninsula, the Baleares Islands, Ceuta, and Fernando Poo. A similarly repressive scheme was applied during the Little War (1879–1880) and in the course of the military conflict of 1895–1898. In the latter, anti-insurgency policies against civilians took on a mass scale: between February 1896 and November 1897 around 300,000 individuals were forcibly "re-concentrated" to fortified Spanish towns along the military lines. Between 155,000 and 170,000 of them died of starvation and epidemics.

The period between the Little War and the military conflict of 1895–1898 witnessed the abolition of slavery (1880) and the introduction of the *patronato*, or apprenticeship of emancipated slaves (1880–1886). The need to prevent ex-slaves from leaving the plantations and the imperative to discipline the workforce at large triggered anti-vagrancy laws that were applied to rural bandits and the urban unemployed and underemployed. The Isle of Pines was once again a site of confinement and, during the 1870s, of imprisonment in the Correccional de vagos (Reformatory for vagrants).

Punitive policy in other colonial territories followed different paths and had diverse chronologies, depending on different political circumstances and goals. Yet, there too, the flexible combination of penal and military transportation and administrative deportation proved to be a recurring feature of repression. In Puerto Rico, for example, a group of convicts was sentenced to penal transportation to the North African *presidio* of Peñon de la Gomera in 1865.[4] Two years later, in the aftermath of the mutiny among troops in the barracks of San Francisco, in San Juan, eighty military convicts were transported to Cuba. The Governor General

---

4. Archivo General Militar, Madrid [hereafter, AGMM], 5154.1, Real Orden 21 August 1865.

used those circumstances to also deport to Cuba fourteen "enemies of Spain, agitated and disturbing the public order", in part for their abolitionist propaganda.[5]

Securing the colony was a central goal in the Philippines as well, and spatial relocation proved a key strategy in removing unwanted internal enemies. In the aftermath of the insurrection of Cavite of 20 January 1872, the War Council sentenced forty-one men to death and many others to transportation to the North African *presidios*, while the Governor General deported twenty civilians to the Mariana Islands.[6] The anti-colonial war of 1896–1898 also generated flows of military transportation and deportation from the Asian archipelago to various destinations across the empire. On 10 December 1896, for example, a group of 148 Filipinos temporarily held in Barcelona prison were redirected to Hacho Castle in Ceuta and to the islands of Chafarinas and Fernando Poo.[7]

In the Philippines, repression had other goals too: disciplining native rural labour; impressing Filipinos into the army; reducing overcrowding in the *presidios* of Manila and Cavite; and colonizing the southern islands of Mindanao and Jolo. Starting in 1871, those aims combined to produce one of the most significant institutional innovations in the field of punishment in the nineteenth-century Spanish Empire: military penitentiary colonies manned by the native troops of disciplinary battalions.[8] They represented the majority of the few penal colonies that the Spaniards ever set up in four centuries of empire, a departure from the mixed-populated military outposts (*presidios*) that had previously been the primary destinations of the convicts. The new agricultural penal colonies first emerged on the island of Paragua and in San Ramón (Zamboanga), and then spread to Balabac, Davao, Jolo, the province of Isabela de Cagayan, and Bonga (Cottabato). They also hosted non-military prisoners and "vagrants, useful beggars, moneyless orphans and those who reoffend in behaviours like drunkenness".[9] In the 1890s, the total number of deportees in those destinations

5. Archivo Historico Nacional, Madrid [hereafter, AHN], Ultramar, 5110, exp. 23, Gobierno Superior Civil de la Isla de Puerto Rico, Secretaria oficial, Reservado, Puerto Rico, 14 July 1867. See also exp. 24.

6. AHN, Ultramar, 5230, exp. 36.

7. Lucía Segura and María Josefa Parejo, "Filipinas en el Archivo del cuartel general de la Región militar sur. Deportados y confinados (S. XIX)", in *El lejano Oriente español. Filipinas (siglo XIX). Actas VII Jornadas Nacionales de Historia Militar, Sevilla, 5–9 de mayo de 1997* (Coslada, 1997), pp. 121–122.

8. See especially AHN, Ultramar, 456, exp. 13; AHN, Ultramar, 612, exp. 7; AHN, Diversos-Coleciones, 202, exp. 68. See also Alicia Castellanos Escudier, "Las Compañias disciplinarias en la colonización de Mindanao", in *El lejano Oriente español*, pp. 541–554. See also Juan Salcedo, *Proyectos de dominación y colonización de Mindanao y Joló* (Gerona, 1891).

9. AHN, Ultramar, 5230, exp. 8, Gobernador Superior Civil of the Philippines to Ultramar, 1 March 1871.

ranged from a few dozen convicts in the Carolina Islands to almost 1,000 convicts in the disciplinary battalion of Mindanao. By then, secondary deportation served the purpose of disciplining convicts within that punitive network, as in the case of nearly 200 rebellious inmates of the disciplinary battalion of Mindanao who were deported for the second time to the Mariana Islands in December 1896.[10]

Disciplinary battalions, such as those created in the Southern Philippines and, to a lesser extent, in Cuba, clearly connected punishment to the military. Conversely, in the course of the nineteenth century, urban prisons in the overseas provinces increasingly became administratively independent of the military, though largely militarized as far as the personnel and the internal regime were concerned.[11] Yet, that (partial) transition from military to penal *presidios* did not anticipate the transformation of colonial prisons into penitentiaries, as penal reformists had hoped. The persisting connection between prisons and extramural forced labour prevented that from happening. Indeed, throughout the century the prisons of Manila, San Juan, Havana, Puerto Principe, and the Isle of Pines remained hubs of penal transportation for a flexible convict workforce used for public works.[12] In Puerto Rico, between 1857 and 1886, Chinese contract labourers and enslaved Africans from Cuba, military convicts from Spain, and local prisoners built the Carretera Central, the 134-kilometre-long road that connected the northern and southern parts of the island.[13] In Cuba, prisoners were used in the construction of the Havana-Güines railway during the 1830s and the railway between Cardenas and Tucano forty years later.[14] They worked in stone quarries and in the construction and repair of Havana's streets and buildings, sewers, and the aqueduct. Moreover, to a much larger extent than in Puerto Rico, from 1867 to 1887 the convicts of the three major penal institutions in Cuba were leased out to sugar planters to complement and partly replace enslaved workers.[15]

10. AGMM, 6309.7, Polavieja to Ultramar, 20 January 1897.

11. *Reglamento para el presidio de la Plaza de Puerto-Rico* (San Juan, 1850); *Reglamento que establece y manda observar en los presidios de la siempre fiel isla de Cuba* (Havana, 1858).

12. For Manila see, for example, AHN, 438, exp. 10.

13. AHN, Ultramar, 5104, exp. 10, *Memoria de la visita de inspección*; Joseph Dorsey, "Identity, Rebellion, and Social Justice Among Chinese Contract Workers in Nineteenth-Century Cuba", *Latin American Perspectives*, 31:3 (2004), pp. 18–47; Fernando Picó, *El día menos pensado. Historia de los presidiarios en Puerto Rico, 1793–1993* (Río Piedras, 1994); Kelvin Santiago-Valles, "'Bloody Legislations,' 'Entombment', and Race Making in the Spanish Atlantic: Differentiated Spaces of General(ized) Confinement in Spain and Puerto Rico, 1750–1840", *Radical History Review*, 96 (2006), pp. 33–57.

14. Manuel Moreno Fraginals, *El ingenio. Complejo económico social cubano del azucar* (Barcelona, 2001), pp. 241–242.

15. AHN, Ultramar, 1833, caja 1; AHN, Ultramar, 1833, caja 1, "Liquidación de los ingresos y gastos"; AHN, Ultramar, 1833, caja 2, exp. 451; AHN, Ultramar, 1927, caja 1. See also Balboa

METROPOLITAN PUNISHMENTS

In the first two thirds of the nineteenth century, the prison system in Spain converged with that of the colonies in two key respects. First, a transition took place from military to penal *presidios*.[16] This emerged especially after the *Ordenanza general de los presidios del Reino* (General Order of the *Presidios* of the Kingdom) of 1834, but was part of longer-term trends. Indeed, the abolition of sentences to the mines of Almaden (1800), the galleys (1803), and the arsenals (1835) for non-military convicts were early steps in that direction. Second, due to the influence of penal utilitarianism, the prison system was strongly connected with extramural public works. In the 1830s, thousands of peninsular convicts worked on the Canal of Castile and in building new roads in Andalusia. This trend was confirmed in the *Reglamento de obras publicas* (1843) and the Penal Code of 1848. Extramural work did not start to decline until the 1850s, due to increasing competition from free labour and partly to changes in penological thought. Indeed, the penitentiary model implied the centrality of work within the walls of penal institutions. Artisanal and industrial workshops had opened in the prison of Valencia as early as the 1840s, under the direction of the prison governor and penal reformer Manuel Montesinos. However, this phenomenon remained localized, as did the diffusion of the penitentiary itself, due to a mix of budgetary and political reasons. As a result, in 1888, the first systematic prison statistics revealed the existence of only seventeen cellular penitentiaries and the persistence of fifteen *presidios* in a sea of 416 non-cellular local prisons, half of which were hosted in buildings described as "absolutely unreformable".[17] The construction of cellular institutions in Spain, planned in the early 1870s, proceeded much more slowly than had been expected. Moreover, they were not altogether successful. If the "modern" penitentiary was never implemented in the overseas provinces, the situation towards the end of the century did not look much better in the metropole.

The limited dissemination of the penitentiary accentuated another important characteristic of the prison system, namely its marked connection with spatial relocation. In fact, the logic of the system linked distance to the perceived gravity of crime.[18] For this reason, prisoners awaiting trial and

---

Navarro, "Presidiarios por esclavos. Mano de obra cautiva en la transición al trabajo libre", in José A. Piqueras (ed.), *Trabajo libre y coactivo en sociedades de plantación* (Madrid, 2009), pp. 253–279.

16. On the prison system in nineteenth-century Spain, see Justo Serna Alonso, *Presos y pobres en la España del XIX. La determinación social de la marginación* (Barcelona, 1988); Pedro Trinidad Fernández, *La defensa de la sociedad. Cárcel y delincuencia en España (siglos XVIII–XX)* (Madrid, 1991); Fernando José Burillo Albacete, *La cuestión penitenciaria. Del Sexenio a la Restauración (1868–1913)* (Zaragoza, 2011).

17. Quoted in Burillo Albacete, *La cuestión penitenciaria*, p. 14.

18. *Ibid.*, p. 47.

those sentenced to up to six years' imprisonment remained within the jurisdiction of their place of trial. Those sentenced to between six and twelve years were sent to specific penal institutions across the Peninsula, and in the Baleares and the Canary Islands. Men sentenced to imprisonment for life, or periods of twelve to twenty years, were sent to the *presidios* in North Africa. Indeed, the flows of convicts to Ceuta and the so-called minor *presidios* of North Africa – Peñon de Velez, Alhucemas, Melilla, and Chafarinas – were continuous and on a large scale. In the 1880s, as in 1901, those institutions hosted an average of 3,000 convicts out of a total male prison population in the peninsular system of approximately 20,000 individuals.[19]

The North African *presidios* had a peculiar status in the context of the Spanish punitive system. On the one hand, in those outposts located outside the Peninsula, extramural work for the state continued to be compulsory, and military authority was the rule. On the other hand, the North African territories were viewed as part of the metropolitan legal space, rather than as overseas provinces or "colonies". For this reason, convict transportation from mainland Spain to those *presidios* was seen as an extension of the peninsular prison system.[20] Conversely, the spatial relocation of sentenced convicts from the metropole to the overseas provinces was discontinued during the nineteenth century. Penal transportation to Cuba, Puerto Rico, and the Philippines was first suspended by royal decree in December 1836, as a consequence of the "critical circumstances" experienced in those dominions. That prohibition remained in force throughout the rest of the century. Indeed, the plans of Positivist criminologists to extend again penal transportation from the metropole to the overseas space were repeatedly rejected in the final quarter of the century, on the grounds that this would have meant a unification of the legal regime across the empire.[21] Therefore, when several hundred peninsular prisoners were transported to the colonies, this happened under a different legal regime. Those metropolitan convicts formally "volunteered" to join the colonial army in the midst of the mass mobilization of troops at the time of the attempted reconquest of Santo Domingo (1861–1865) and during the Cuban War of Independence and the Spanish-American war (1895–1898).

19. *Ibid.*, p. 187; Trinidad Fernández, *La defensa de la sociedad*, p. 212.
20. The Canary Islands were similarly considered part of the legal region of the metropole, and the legislation accordingly allowed for penal transportation to those territories. However, no penal institution was ever activated in the Canary Islands for the purpose of receiving peninsular convicts.
21. On the debates in the 1870s, see Burillo Albacete, *La cuestión penitenciaria*, pp. 62–67; Luis Gargallo Vaamonde and Pedro Oliver Olmo, "Desarrollo y colapso del penitenciarismo liberal", in Pedro Oliver Olmo (ed.), *El siglo de los castigos. Prisión y formas carcelarias en la España del siglo XX* (Barcelona, 2013), pp. 18–23.

The suspension of penal transportation from the metropole to the overseas provinces during the nineteenth century marked a major break with a
tradition of relocating sentenced prisoners from Spain that began at the start
of the Spanish Empire. The criminal justice system, however, was not the
only source of punitive relocations. As in the colonial settings, in the
Peninsula military justice and administrative power produced significant
flows of convicts and deportees throughout the nineteenth century. Indeed,
while the spatial scope of the penal flows from mainland Spain was now
limited, military transportation and administrative deportation significantly
expanded, both spatially and quantitatively.

This aspect has received insufficient attention in the scholarship so
far. On the one hand, important research centred on the prison systems has
marginalized the importance of military and administrative deportations.[22]
On the other, those who have addressed deportations in detail have
focused on specific events and groups, and even when they have provided a
broader overview they have not discussed their connections with
the legal and political systems.[23] Conversely, I would like to suggest
the need to write back military and administrative deportations into the
history of nineteenth-century punishment. In the case of Spain, this is
especially important. Indeed, it foregrounds a fundamental aspect
of the construction of the Spanish nation in the nineteenth century, which
Manuel Ballbé and Eduardo González Calleja have described as the "permanent use of the technique of the declaration of the state of exception",
based on the "primarily military configuration of the bureaucratic organization of the national state", especially in the realm of public order.[24]
Declarations of the "state of siege", the "state of war", and the "state of
prevention and alarm", as well as the concession of "extraordinary powers"
to prime ministers and local Captains General, accompanied all major
events in the history of Peninsular Spain during the nineteenth and the
early twentieth centuries. Frequently, the suspension of constitutional
rights outlived specific events and lasted years, or the length of entire
governments.

In other words, the exception was not only out there, in the colonial
space. It was also a key feature of "normal" rule in the metropole.
Indeed, the "norm" contained the "exception".[25] The faculty to suspend

22. Burillo Albacete, *La cuestión penitenciaria*.

23. See the otherwise very important Pere Gabriel, "Más allá de los exilios políticos. Proscritos y
deportados en el siglo XIX", in Santiago Castillo and Pedro Oliver (eds), *Las figuras del desorden.
Heterodoxos, proscritos y marginados* (Madrid, 2006), pp. 197–221, 211–221.

24. Manuel Ballbé, *Orden público y militarismo en la España constitucional (1812–1983)* (Madrid,
1983), p. 20; Eduardo González Calleja, "La política de orden público en la Restauración",
Espacio, Tiempo y Forma, 5:20 (2008), p. 94.

25. For important interventions on the role of states of exception in history, see Nasser Hussain,
The Jurisprudence of Emergency: Colonialism and the Rule of Law (Ann Arbor, CT, 2003);

constitutional rights was inscribed in the liberal constitutions themselves. Its contents were further detailed in legislation such as the Law of 17 April 1821 and the public order laws of 20 March 1867 and 23 April 1870.[26] On that basis, depending on the circumstances, the scope of military justice was extended to include civilians, special courts were set up, and Captains General were entitled to take administrative measures. Besides the application of death sentences and temporary incarceration, intermittent, yet frequent and sometimes large, flows of deportation resulted. They were characterized by the sudden and collective nature of the initial relocation and by their relatively short duration, until the states of exception were discontinued and amnesties accorded. As in the colonies, their social and political targets were multiple, and single events often gave the authorities the opportunity to expel diverse groups by manipulating blurred categories.

In the aftermath of the mutiny of the gunners at the barracks of San Gil in Madrid on 22 June 1866, approximately 800 individuals were sentenced by military courts to six to ten years' *presidio* and impressment in the army.[27] Their destinations literally spanned the whole empire. The lists of deportees comprised soldiers directly involved in that attempt to replace the monarchy by a democratic regime. However, they also included a large group of men whose profiles included the following: Ramon Grebot, aka Bisbe, "great propagator of republican ideas in a revolutionary direction"; Romualdo Pipian Pepenim, aka Rampè, "vagrant, gambler, and of bad records"; and Agustín Torrens y Sala, "vagrant, undocumented, and with no fixed address, one of those who advise workers not to hire themselves unless they are given everything they ask for".

That variegated world of subaltern workers, lumpenproletarians, and "furious democrats" – in the words of the authorities – was the target of multiple political regimes throughout the century. It provided the bulk of the hundreds sentenced to death, imprisonment, and deportation by the provincial military commissions created under the monarchy of Ferdinand VII between 1824 and 1825 and re-established under the regents in 1836–1838. It offered the political prisoners and subversive republicans sent to the Philippines in revolutionary 1848. It also included the rural labourers who revolted in Loja on 28 June 1861 against their living and

Francesco Benigno and Luca Scuccimarra (eds), *Il governo dell'eccedenza. Poteri straordinari e di guerra in Europa tra XVI e XX secolo* (Rome, 2007).

26. Carmen Serván, *Laboratorio constitucional en España. El individuo y el ordenamiento, 1868–1873* (Madrid, 2005), pp. 271–295.

27. AGMM, 5936.1, *Relaciones de artilleros sentenciados por los sucesos del 22 junio de 1866 en Madrid*; Archivo General de la Administración, Alcalá de Henares [hereafter, AGA], 81.6941 (including the lists and profiles of deportees).

working conditions, and who were subsequently deported to Fernando Poo and elsewhere.[28] In 1873, it was the turn of the republican government, supported by generals with extensive colonial experience, such as Arsenio Martínez-Campos and Manuel Pavía, to curb the federalist revolts of Murcia and Cartagena. In that context, over 1,600 *cantonalistas* and *internacionalistas* were deported administratively, some to Ceuta and Fernando Poo, and the vast majority to the Philippines and the Mariana Islands.[29]

The state of exception declared by the republican authorities in the aftermath of the *cantonalista* revolt lasted until January 1877, well into the first Restoration government. Paradoxically, therefore, it was the leader of the Conservative Party, Antonio Cánovas del Castillo, who amnestied the revolutionary leftists. In the northern provinces of the Peninsula, however, the suspension of constitutional rights was further extended in order to repress the insurrection of the traditionalist monarchists, or *carlistas*. Indeed, as in the 1830s and 1848, the 1870s witnessed the constant overlapping of deportation of members of conflicting groups that fell outside the spectrum of the liberal regimes.[30] In the course of the Third Carlist War (1872–1876), *carlista* prisoners of war were imprisoned in various peninsular institutions (Cartagena, Burgos, Santoña, Avila) and transported to the Baleares and the Canary Islands, to Ceuta and Fernando Poo, to the Philippines and the Marianas.

Even beyond those periods of sustained political conflict and civil war in the Peninsula, administrative deportation from Spain had a broad reach. A rare overview issued by the Ministry of Overseas Territories in the early 1880s listed 1,181 peninsular deportees across the empire, including 134 in Cuba, forty-one in Puerto Rico, 130 in Fernando Poo, and over 800 in the Philippines and the Mariana Islands.[31]

IMPERIAL ENTANGLEMENTS

When nineteenth-century penal transportations, military relocations, and administrative deportations stemming from the metropole and the colonies are visualized simultaneously, as in Figure 1 below, we see a thick network spanning the whole Spanish Empire.

28. Segura and Parejo, "Filipinas en el Archivo", pp. 105–121; Gabriel, "Más allá de los exilios políticos", pp. 211–212.
29. AGA, 81.6942, exp. 1; AHN, Ultramar, 5222, exp. 1.
30. AGMM: 5969.9; 5972.33; 5970.8; 5948.14; 7149.77; 6027.4; 6636.22. AGA: 51.53; AHN, Ultramar: 5227, exp. 56. On the deportation of over 1,600 *carlistas* to Cuba in the 1830s, see AHN, Ultramar, 4603, Havana, 6 October 1835.
31. AGA, 81.6946, exp. 13, *Resumen de deportados de la Península*.

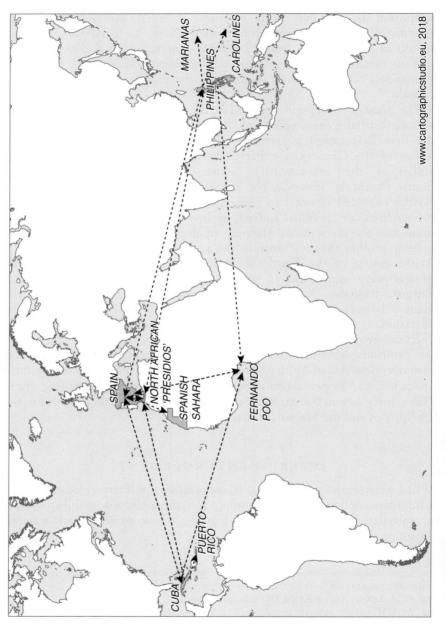

Figure 1. Punitive relocations in the Spanish empire, 1830s–1898

A key element in the construction of those punitive entanglements lay in the highly mobile careers of the imperial officials who decided upon them. Indeed, the lives of leading political and military figures of the nineteenth-century Spanish Empire were strongly intertwined with the history of penal transportation and deportation from both the metropole and the colonies. General Juan Prim y Prats, for example, took part in the First Carlist War (1834–1840), curbed the radical revolt of the *Jamància* during his charge as Governor of Barcelona (1843), was Captain General of Puerto Rico, contributed to the repression of the slave revolt on the nearby Danish colony of Saint Croix (1848), and then participated in the War of Morocco (1860), the Spanish expedition in Mexico (1861), and the Glorious Revolution of 1868 in Spain. At the same time, he was himself threatened with deportation to the Marianas for six years for his participation in a coup, confined in Ecija, and later exiled to Switzerland in connection with the insurrection of the gunners in June 1866. He was killed by a republican in 1870, when he was President of the Council of Ministries and Minister of War.

During their career, the same officials were often responsible for punitive relocations from several sites across the empire. General Camilo García Polavieja decreed the deportation of 265 *libres de color* (free blacks) to Fernando Poo when he was military commander and Governor of Santiago de Cuba in 1880; he ordered the imprisonment, confinement, and deportation of hundreds of civilians through the anti-banditry Gabinete Particular he set up as Captain-General of Cuba in 1890–1892; and then, as Governor General of the Philippines during the War of Independence, he oversaw the court martial of José Rizal and other Filipino insurgents and ordered administrative deportations to the Marianas, Spain, and Fernando Poo.[32]

Taking a perspective that spans the empire also reveals important features regarding the selection of destinations of punitive relocations. Indeed, while the expulsion of convicts and deportees from a certain territory emerged primarily from local circumstances, the logic that guided the choice of their destinations usually stemmed from broader imperial goals. Starting from the 1860s, for example, punitive flows of various types were consistently directed to sites of new colonization. It was part of the response of the Spanish monarchy to growing imperialist competition in the Caribbean, the Pacific, and Africa.

The attempt of the Spanish authorities to take advantage of the American Civil War and reannex Santo Domingo was accompanied by significant relocations of convicts and deportees. During the first years of operations

32. Archivo General de Indias, Seville [hereafter, AGI], Diversos, 8; AGA, 81/6942, exp. 7, 8, and 9; Camilo Polavieja y Castillo, *Conspiración de la raza de color descubierta en Santiago de Cuba el 10 de Diciembre de 1880* (Santiago de Cuba, 1880); AHN, Ultramar, L. 666.

(1861–1863), over 1,000 prisoners were "voluntarily" transferred from Spain, and various brigades of convicts headed there from Cuba in order to fortify Samaná Bay, build other infrastructure, and exploit the island's coal mines and forests. Later on, hundreds of prisoners of war and deportees were relocated from Santo Domingo to Cuba, Puerto Rico, and Ceuta. Finally, following Spain's defeat, in mid-1865 they were gathered in Puerto Rico and exchanged for Spanish POWs.[33] In the Pacific, the second half of the nineteenth century witnessed the occupation of the islands of Mindanao, Jolo, and Paragua in the Philippines, and the consequent punitive flows from Spain and the northern islands of that archipelago to the newly created penal colonies and disciplinary battalions. Similar developments took place in the Marianas, which attracted flows of deportees from the Philippines and Spain. From the same territories, individuals were deported to the disciplinary battalions created in the Carolina Islands from 1885 onwards, in order to cope with the growing German and US penetration in the region.[34] In North Africa, following the 1860 War of Morocco the Spanish sent convicts and deportees from Cuba and the Philippines to the Chafarinas Islands. After the peace treaty extended Spanish sovereignty to parts of the Western Sahara, deportees were sent to that region. Meanwhile, imperial efforts to colonize the island of Fernando Poo were supported by the deportations of rural labourers from Loja in 1861, the rebellious gunners of Madrid in 1866, Cuban *incorregibles* in 1866, and *laborantes* from the same island in 1868–1869.[35]

In those cases, convicts and deportees were viewed as useful agents of colonization, primarily as a temporary workforce for building infrastructures and to serve in the military, and at times as settlers. However, punitive relocations raised considerable problems. In fact, certain flows were carefully avoided, including those to Spain of sentenced slaves during the decades between the abolition of slavery in the Peninsula (1837) and its abolition in Puerto Rico (1873) and Cuba (1880): the legal discontinuity between the colonies and Spain would have entitled them to claim their freedom. Broader legal, political, and logistic difficulties emerged vis-à-vis the status of the deportees. A clear example lies in the administrative expulsion from Cuba in 1866 of hundreds of *incorregibles*, or individuals

33. AGMM: 5654.2; 5654.3; 5661.6; 5661.7; 5661.9; 5661.10; 5774.10.
34. Carlos Madrid, *Beyond Distances: Governance, Politics and Deportation in the Mariana Islands from 1870 to 1877* (Saipan, 2006); María Dolores Elizalde Pérez-Grueso, *España en el Pacífico. La colonia de las Islas Carolinas, 1885–1899* (Madrid, 1992). On the disciplinary battalions in the Carolinas, see AHN, Ultramar, 5365, exp. 1, and 5867.
35. Mariano L. de Castro and Maria Luisa de la Calle, *Origen de la colonización española de Guinea Ecuatorial (1777–1860)* (Valladolid, 1992); Ibrahim K. Sundiata, *From Slaving to Neoslavery: The Bight of Biafra and Fernando Po in the Era of Abolition, 1827–1930* (Madison, WI, 1996); Dolores García Cantús, "Fernando Poo. Una aventura colonial española en el África Occidental (1778–1900)" (Ph.D, Universitat de Valencia, 2004).

deemed by the local Captain General to be "incompatible with public tranquillity", due to their repeated crimes and acts of insubordination. Wherever the group arrived, local authorities complained. In Spain, the President of the Section of Ultramar argued that "if there are justified reasons to expel the above individuals from that Antilles, similar reasons exist not to tolerate their presence in the Metropole".[36] The Governor General of the Philippines was predisposed to temporarily incarcerate them in the prison at Bilibid and unsuccessfully tried to hire them out to the Navy and the tobacco manufactures; these rejected his offer for security reasons. The high officer was especially worried that the presence of those black and mulatto Cubans would threaten the "good opinion that Europeans, and especially all Spaniards, enjoy among these simple peoples, whose limited intelligence generally doesn't reach beyond defining the deportees as *Peninsulares negros*". Finally, he decided to re-deport each of them to a separate province of the archipelago.[37]

The Governor of Fernando Poo initially sought a similar solution for the dozens of deportees he received from Cuba, but relocation to the nearby Spanish islands of Annobón and Corisco was made impossible by the lack of effective colonization there.[38] During their two years of permanence on the island, the deportees were physically isolated from the rest of the population and detained as a single group in a prison hulk. When they left Fernando Poo in 1869, the problems they took with them transcended the boundaries of the empire. Re-labelled as voluntary exiles, most were able to reach the destinations they had selected, including Monrovia, Madera and Principe, Mexico City, and Montevideo. Their fluid legal status, however, caused a diplomatic clash with the British authorities, who refused to admit them in Sierra Leone and Nigeria: the governors general of the West African colonies and the British diplomatic officers assumed that those individuals must have been "great criminals" to deserve such a serious punishment. They consequently argued that, "since England has decided not to receive her own convicts and political prisoners in the Colonies, it would be inconsistent to accept or host those from other Nations". For their part, the Spanish authorities first tried to highlight the legal difference between administrative deportation and penal transportation; then they opted for the easier solution of redirecting those *incorregibles* to new destinations of their own choice.[39]

---

36. AHN, Ultramar, 4718, exp. 5, Presidente Sección de Ultramar to Ultramar, Madrid, 26 June 1866.
37. AHN, Ultramar, 4718, exp. 5, Gobernador Superior Civil de Filipinas to Ultramar, n. 325, Manila, 16 September 1867.
38. AHN, Ultramar, 4718, exp. 5.
39. AHN, Ultramar, 4718, exp. 5, Fernando Poo to Ultramar, 26 October 1868; AHN, Ultramar, 4718, exp. 5, Ministro de Estado, 19 December 1868.

The convergence of penal, military, and administrative flows frequently transformed each destination into a contact zone, where individuals from various colonies and the metropole forcibly met. We know very little about the interactions among those groups. The memoirs of contemporaries tend to foreground distance and mistrust, if not open conflict. Juan José Relosillas, who served as inspector of works in Ceuta between April 1873 and August 1874, for instance, described four separate groups of prisoners. Two main factions (*bandos*) were represented by the dominant group of the *andaluces*, which included convicts from Andalusia and some of the Cubans, and the *aragoneses*, comprising prisoners from Aragon, Castile, Catalonia, Valencia, and the Basque countries. The black Cubans formed a third group, and the Chinese Cubans another. Relosillas wrote of the latter: "the rest of the confined look down on these poor people, but exploit their clear passion for gambling".[40] In a similar fashion, Manuel María Miranda expressed admiration for the Filipino anti-colonial leader Rizal, but decided to search for work on the farms of Fernando Poo because of his "disgust" at having to share barracks with "such rude and uneducated people".[41] Similarly, the anarchist activist described the *ñañigo* deportees as "odd" and their ritual singing as a "savage noise", echoing the arguments concerning their supposed "barbarism" that were used by the Cuban authorities to legitimize their repression. Paradoxically, his exclusion from the amnesty of 17 May 1897, which incorporated many Cubans and Filipinos, was motivated by the belief that his presence in Cuba was "at least as harmful as that of the *ñañigos* and cattle rustlers, excluded from the amnesty".[42]

While long-standing racial and class stereotypes proved difficult to break, punitive relocations strengthened the identity of each group and triggered processes that reached beyond the repressive settings. A fascinating example of this is their impact on members of the Abakuá societies. The Cuban *ñañigos* kept their rituals alive during their captivity, for example in Ceuta.[43] Moreover, their deportation to Fernando Poo brought them in close proximity to their homelands in Old Calabar. Their interactions with the local population produced an unexpected "return to Africa" of their rituals. Indeed, the deportees passed on to the local Creoles the use of the sacred drum named *Ékwe*, which reproduced the voice of the leopard and was central to their faith.[44]

40. Juan José Relosillas, *Catorce meses en Ceuta* (Ceuta, 1985), p. 40.
41. Miranda, *Memorias de un deportado*, quotes on pp. 15 and 29.
42. AHN, Ultramar, 5007, exp. 25.
43. Rafael Salillas, "Los ñáñigos en Ceuta", *Revista General de Legislación y Jurisprudencia*, 49:98 (1901), pp. 337–360.
44. Isabela de Aranzadi, "El viaje de un tambor. África de ida y vuelta en Annoboneses y Fernandinos. Instrumentos musicales de Guinea Ecuatorial", *Revista valenciana d'etnologia*, 5 (2010), pp. 201–215.

Meanwhile, nineteenth-century penal and military transportations and administrative deportations introduced new forms of collective agency. This was the consequence of the primarily political nature of the punitive relocations of those decades. Traditionally, convict transportation in the Spanish Empire had been operated through, and legitimized by, the apparently neutral functioning of the criminal justice system. The growing recourse to exceptional measures during this period made it clear that those relocations were directly aimed at political repression. To be sure, the colonial and metropolitan authorities frequently denied the status of political prisoner to deportees and convicts, especially if they came from non-elite groups. However, their political goal could hardly be missed – and surely not by those who were targeted.

Corresponding to this politicization of repression was a politicization of convicts. This can be observed in the insurrections that took place at various sites during the second half of the nineteenth century, including Zamboanga in 1872, Ceuta in 1878 and 1880, Peñon de Velez in 1887, and on the Isle of Pines in July 1896. These were distinct from the joint revolts of convicts and (impressed) soldiers and sailors in the late eighteenth century, which had been primarily motivated by appalling living conditions. These new collectives of prisoners attempted coups to overthrow peninsular governments, launched insurrections shouting "Spain must die", and wrote political manifestos with the slogans "God, Fatherland, People, and Freedom" and "Long Live the Spanish Brothers, Long Live the National Party".[45]

Political networks within and beyond the punitive sites allowed deportees and convicts to escape, or at least to enhance their conditions. In January 1874, for example, Cuban military officers put the repeated escapes of *carlista* prisoners from the Castle of La Cabaña down to the existence in Havana "of a *junta* or Centre that facilitates [them], considering that these people are unfamiliar with the country, yet no deserter has ever been captured".[46] In a similar fashion, the eleven *carlistas* who ended up in the Philippines in the late 1860s enjoyed the solidarity of the reactionary local clergy.[47] First housed in the local fort, they were soon moved to monasteries and allowed considerable freedom of movement within the city of Manila. Conversely, liberal activists built some support around the two Spanish republicans who were deported to the Philippines and then to the Mariana Islands in the same years.

The network of support around Cuban deportees was particularly extensive, for it included Cuban exiles in the US and in Europe. It was very significant within Spain, too, where the precise boundaries between

---

45. AGMM: 5321.6 and 5321.8 (Zamboanga); 5929.10, 5929.11, 5929.12, and 5931.5 (Ceuta); 5915.5 and 5914.1 (Peñon de Velez).
46. AHN, Ultramar, 4374, exp. 20, Estado Mayor, Havana, 15 January 1874.
47. Madrid, *Beyond Distances*, p. 37.

deportees and exiles were often blurred. Indeed, due to their higher social circumstances and their legal status as administrative deportees, elite *laborantes* were usually allowed to choose where they wanted to live and their occupations in the Peninsula; this gave them scope to establish contacts with other Cubans and even escape altogether. An intensification of surveillance, a prohibition on residence in coastal cities, and attempts to confine them in more isolated villages in the interior were as frequent as they were ineffective, given legal limitations and the lack of supervision.[48]

The networks established in support of anti-colonial prisoners and deportees sometimes overlapped with those of the freemasonry. Broad connections existed, for example, between the Gran Oriente Español (GOE) led by Miguel Morayta and the Filipino anti-colonial movement. In Madrid, the *La Solidaridad* lodge gathered the Filipino community of the Peninsula, including exiles and deportees, together with Spaniards, Cubans, and Puerto Ricans, with the specific goal of supporting the rights of the Filipinos. Starting in 1889, the influence of the GOE extended to the native population in the Philippines. Moreover, cultural and political organizations, such as the Asociación Hispano-Filipina and the Liga Filipina, provided platforms where Spanish freemasons and Filipino activists could meet, and actively promoted campaigns in favour of exiles and deportees.[49]

The anarchist movement was similarly involved in the support of Cuban and Filipino anti-colonial struggles, through the exchange of information and books, personal contacts, and shared political campaigns.[50] In addition, it mobilized transnationally to support its own activists in the frequent events of repression. In the aftermath of the bombing of the Corpus Christi procession in Barcelona on 7 June 1896, at least 300 anarchists, radical republicans, and progressive intellectuals were imprisoned in the local fortress of Montjuich. In the following months, a broad campaign was unleashed in Europe and across the Atlantic to secure their liberation. The Cuban Creole Fernando Tarrida del Mármol published several articles in Paris in which he compared the repression of Cánovas with that of the Inquisition.[51] In Britain, the "Spanish Atrocities Committee" organized a demonstration that attracted 10,000 people in Trafalgar Square, London, on 30 May 1897. The pressure exercised by the activists temporarily isolated

---

48. See especially AHN, Ultramar, 4777, exp. 1 and 2.
49. Maria Asunción Ortiz de Andrés, *Masoneria y democracia en el siglo XIX. El Gran Oriente Español y su proyección político-social (1888–1896)* (Madrid, 1993), pp. 271–311.
50. Benedict Anderson, *Under Three Flags: Anarchism and the Anti-Colonial Imagination* (London and New York, 2005), esp. pp. 169–233. See also Richard Bach Jensen, *The Battle against Anarchist Terrorism: An International History, 1878–1934* (Cambridge, 2014), pp. 111–113.
51. Fernando Tarrida del Mármol, *Les Inquisiteurs d'Espagne. Montjuich, Cuba, Philippines* (Paris, 1897).

the Spanish Prime Minister. However, it was unable to influence the military courts, which sentenced five individuals to death and nineteen to long periods of imprisonment. Although acquitted, sixty-three men were exiled or administratively deported to the Spanish possession of Western Sahara.

CONCLUSION

Before the Napoleonic occupation of Spain and the independence of Latin America, penal transportation was the primary form of punitive relocation across the Spanish Empire.[52] In the context of a polycentric monarchy, regional systems of convict transportation emerged, consistently complemented by interregional flows of sentenced convicts that connected the empire at large. Penal transportation from the metropole played a fundamental role in those interregional relocations. The advent of liberalism in the Peninsula and the transition to the system of the three colonies changed the structure and nature of punitive relocations. Penal transportation took on an exclusively regional character. Convicts were still exchanged between the two Caribbean provinces, and transported separately within the Philippine archipelago (and to the dependent territories of the Marianas and Carolinas) and within the region including Peninsular Spain, the Baleares (and, more rarely, the Canary Islands), and the North African *presidios*. Unlike the Portuguese and French empires, and as in the German Reich, in the case of the Spanish Empire penal transportation from the metropole no longer extended to the rest of the empire in the nineteenth century.[53] This was the consequence of the legal gap between the metropole, ruled according to liberal constitutions, and the overseas provinces, governed by "special laws". Accordingly, plans to reintroduce penal transportation across the empire from the metropole were consistently rejected.

Military transportation and administrative deportation provided a solution where penal transportation was not permitted. These spanned the whole empire, with flows from the metropole and from Spain's overseas provinces. They even prompted significant flows from the colonies to the metropole, albeit usually restricted to elite and explicitly "political" deportees: it was a feature seldom seen in the previous history of the Spanish Empire.

Military and administrative relocations stemmed from "states of exception". These, in turn, reflected the limits of liberal citizenship in two

---

52. Christian G. De Vito, "The Spanish Empire, 1500 to 1898", in Clare Anderson (ed.), *A Global History of Convicts and Penal Colonies* (London [etc.], 2018), pp. 65–95.
53. For a comparative analysis, see the introduction to this special issue.

connected ways.[54] On the one hand, they excluded the slaves and natives of the colonies, by first denying and then limiting the representation of the provinces in the Cortes. The construction of the *mando supremo* and the related "all-compassing" punitive powers of the Captains General derived from that political choice made in the first few decades of the nineteenth century. On the other hand, in the metropole, members of the "dangerous" subaltern classes and advocates of "subversive" political alternatives were targeted through the repeated recourse to the states of siege, war, and alarm. Prime ministers and the Captains General of the peninsular provinces made extensive use of them to legitimize repression. That double exclusion produced the basis for broad networks of punitive relocations that spanned the whole empire. It also produced a significant shift in their nature: relocations based on states of exception explicitly politicized punishment and triggered (or perhaps responded to) the growing politicization of convicts' collective agency.

Meanwhile, in the metropole, as in the overseas provinces, "exception" was never a synonym for illegality, or anti-legality. On the contrary, it was a way to govern political and social exclusion without breaching liberal legality. In fact, "exception" was embedded in the liberal constitutions and in specific laws. Military transportation and administrative relocation were therefore an integral part of the punitive system, not beyond it. For this reason, this article has argued for the need of an integrated study of all forms of punishment in the metropole and in Spain's overseas provinces. In that connected perspective, I have also suggested that the history of the prison in Spain and its colonies should be rewritten in a way that questions the idea of the "birth of the prison" as a defining moment in the history of punishment, and of the nineteenth century as "the age of the triumphant prison".[55] I have sought to show that, in the Peninsula, a strong continuity existed between military *presidios* and the prisons until at least the 1850s, and up to 1898 in the overseas provinces. In both cases, an increased discontinuity with the military took place, but the prison regime maintained a strikingly military character (and personnel) and a consistent connection with extramural work. For that reason, the penitentiary never became established in Spain's overseas provinces. But even in the metropole, its emergence in the 1870s met with widespread criticism and its effective diffusion remained very limited by the

---

54. I follow here the general argument adduced by Josep M. Fradera, *La nación imperial (1750–1918)*, 2 vols (Barcelona, 2015), I (especially the introduction). See also *idem, Colonias para después de un imperio*. For a similar argument, see Stefan Berger and Alexei Miller, "Introduction: Building Nations In and With Empires: A Reassessment", in *idem* (eds), *Nationalizing Empires* (Budapest and New York, 2015), pp. 12–13.

55. Michel Foucault, *Discipline & Punish: The Birth of the Prison* (New York, 1977); Michelle Perrot, "Délinquance et système pénitentiaire en France au 19e siècle", *Annales ESC*, 30 (1975), pp. 67–91, 81; Rudolph Peters, "Egypt and the Age of the Triumphant Prison: Legal Punishment in Nineteenth Century Egypt", *Annales Islamologiques*, 36 (2002), pp. 253–285.

end of the century. "Model" prisons also rapidly became unbearable and often deadly places for those who were incarcerated.

The relationship between penal transportation and the penitentiary model was ambivalent. Penal experts tended to view them as alternative institutions, both when they foregrounded the "modernity" of the penitentiary over the "backwardness" of convict transportation and when they praised the virtues of spatial relocation vis-à-vis overcrowding and the lack of work in the penitentiaries. Officials on the spot had more fluid perspectives, revealed by the fact, for example, that they used the term "penitentiary" (*penitenciaria*) to refer to institutions hosting transported convicts. That fluid interpretation reminds historians of the complex spatiality of imprisonment. Indeed, convicts were rarely immobilized in a single institution for the whole length of their sentence; more often, they were moved from one establishment to another across the prison system, often beyond their region of origin. Moreover, one could hardly define whether long prison sentences to the North African *presidios* were a form of imprisonment or penal transportation. Indeed, they were both, as were most punitive relocations in the colonies, where prisons were little more than deposits for the convicted workforce.

The legal status of one individual could also change across time. Prisoners of war could be imprisoned, then deported, and finally exchanged as captives. Convicts could be moved out of the penitentiaries and "voluntarily" impressed into the military in the event of colonial wars. And deportees could be detained in penal establishments, exiled, or relocated, and put under surveillance within a city or a province. From that perspective, too, penal transportation, military relocation, administrative deportation, and imprisonment in the Spanish Empire of the nineteenth century really do share a deeply connected history.

IRSH 63 (2018), Special Issue, pp. 191–210 doi:10.1017/S0020859018000287
© 2018 Internationaal Instituut voor Sociale Geschiedenis

Fearing the Flood: Transportation as Counterinsurgency in the US–Occupied Philippines

BENJAMIN D. WEBER

American Council of Learned Societies (ACLS)
Mellon Postdoctoral Fellow
1307 Oretha Castle Haley Blvd., Suite 203
New Orleans, LA 70113, USA

E-mail: bendavidweber@gmail.com

ABSTRACT: Examining intra-colonial punitive relocations during the first decade of US occupation in the Philippines, this article shows how colonial police and prison officials used incarceration and transportation in tandem to suppress incipient populist revolutionary movements. They exploited historic regional and religious tensions in their effort to produce new modes of racialized and gendered prison and labor management. Finally, while colonial officials sought to brand certain imprisoned subjects as criminal outlaws, rather than political prisoners, many of these anticolonial fighters actually sharpened their ideas about freedom through their experience of being criminalized, incarcerated, and forcibly relocated.

> Bilibid prison in fact could be likened to a faucet
> which though used day and night was never without water.[1]

In the days leading to the outbreak of war between the United States and the newly independent Philippine Republic, anticolonial revolutionaries planned a revolt inside Bilibid Prison. In late January 1899, prison physician Manuel Xeres Burgos informed Philippine President Emilio Aguinaldo, "it is absolutely necessary that an order be received here permitting the uprising of those in prison before the movement is begun anywhere else".[2]

---

1. "Casunod nang buhay na Pinagdaan ng Ating manga Capatid", trans. Reynaldo C. Ileto, *Pasyon and Revolution: Popular Movements in the Philippines, 1840–1910* (Quezon City, 1979 [2003]), Appendix 4, p. 263.
2. Manuel Xeres Burgos to Aguinaldo, January, 1899, quoted in Dean Worcester, *The Philippines Past and Present* (New York, 1914), p. 135. See also J.R.M. Taylor, "The Philippine Insurrection Against the United States: A Compilation of Documents with Notes", in US National Archives and Records Administration, Record Group 350, File 2291–38; *idem et al.*, *Compilation of Philippine Insurgent Records: Telegraphic Correspondence of Emilio Aguinaldo* (Washington, DC, 1903); *idem et al.*, *Report on the Organization for the Administration of Civil Government*

Jacinto Limjap, imprisoned for financing the revolution against the Spanish colonizers, drew up the plan for arming prisoners with rifles taken from the US Army barracks opposite the prison. As commander of the volunteers inside the penitentiary, he coordinated with Aguinaldo's General, Teodoro Sandiko, on the outside.[3] Aguinaldo and Sandiko stationed 600 troops, called *sandatahan*, on the outskirts of Manila in preparation. US officials, who had intercepted their communications, feared a simultaneous attack from inside and outside the city before reinforcements could arrive.[4] On 4 February 1899, US troops fired on a *sandatahan* patrol on the edge of Manila; they returned fire, and the exchange marked the start of war. The ensuing US attack left 500 Filipinos dead and pushed Aguinaldo's forces out of Manila.

During the war, the US military captured scores of revolutionary leaders and nationalist political writers. Those who refused to swear a loyalty oath to the US, such as Apolinario Mabini, Artemio Ricarte, Maximo Hizon, Pio del Pilar, and Pablo Ocampo, were exiled to Guam.[5] In so doing, US officials were clearly following the precedent set by the Spanish system of deporting political prisoners to far-flung islands, such as Guam and the Marianas Islands.[6] Yet, while US colonial officials exiled better-known figures, they also sought to reclassify significant portions of the ongoing anticolonial struggle as bandits, rather than members of lesser-known and long-misunderstood movements led by those who refused to assimilate into either US colonial, or Filipino nationalist regimes.[7]

Instituted by Emilio Aguinaldo (Washington, DC, 1903); and *idem*, *The Philippine Insurrection against the United States: A Compilation of Documents with Notes and Introduction* (Pasay City, 1971).

3. Worcester, *Philippines Past and Present*, pp. 135–139. Limjap asked Sandiko to authorize a battalion of 600 *sandatahan* to seize the American armaments, listing the commanding officers. Sandiko passed the list on to Aguinaldo, and they mustered their troops at Calcoocan Station on the outskirts of Manila

4. *Ibid.*, p. 139; Philip P. Brower, "The U.S. Army's Seizure and Administration of Enemy Records up to World War II", *The American Archivist* (1961), pp. 191–207.

5. See, for example, Apolinario Mabini, *La Revolucion Filipina (con otras documentos de la época)* (Manila, 1931); Vicente Rafael, "The Afterlife of Empire: Sovereignty and Revolution in the Philippines", in Alfred W. McCoy and Francisco A. Scarano (eds), *Colonial Crucible: Empire in the Making of the Modern American State* (Madison, WI, 2009), pp. 342–352; Honeste A. Villanueva, "Apolinario Mabini: His Exile to Guam", *Historical Bulletin*, 8:1 (1964), pp. 1–37; Atoy M. Navarro, "Philippines–Marianas Relations in History: Some Notes on Filipino Exiles in Guam", *Asian and Pacific Migration Journal*, 8:1–2 (1999), pp. 117–130.

6. See Greg Bankoff, *Crime, Society, and the State in the Nineteenth Century Philippines* (Quezon City, 1996).

7. Ileto, *Pasyon and Revolution*; Dylan Rodriguez, "'Not Classifiable as Orientals or Caucasians or Negroes': Filipino Racial Ontology and the Stalking Presence of the 'Insane Filipino Soldier'", in Martin F. Manalansan and Augusto F. Espiritu (eds), *Filipino Studies: Palimpsests of Nation and Diaspora* (New York, NY, 2016), pp. 151–175.

Continually afraid that revolts would trigger widespread uprising, US officials used transportation within the archipelago to dissipate revolutionary pressure. In this way, penal transportation came to be used not as a commuted sentence, as an alternative to death or life imprisonment, as it had been in British, French, and Iberian empires. Rather, it was designed to work in concert with incarceration. This, too, was not wholly without precedent. Indeed, Spanish officials had used intra-colonial transportation within the Philippine archipelago to try and incorporate non-Christian regions, such as Mindanao and Palawan, and thereby expand their political and territorial jurisdiction.[8] Thus, according to historian Greg Bankoff, Spanish colonial governors used a "policy of enforced migration under the guise of penal deportation" to send "undesirable" Christian Filipinos to coastal sections of Mindanao and Palawan.[9] Strikingly, when US officials took control of the prison system in the Philippines at the dawn of the twentieth century, they used transportation for the purposes of counterinsurgency and racial management under the guise of prison labor transfers. In fact, in some instances, they intentionally reversed the flows by using non-Christian Moros from Mindanao as prison guards to oversee Filipino prisoner labor.

Bilibid Prison was the hub of the network of prisons US colonial officials inherited from the Spanish. Under US colonial rule, that network included the San Ramon Penal Farm in Mindanao, the Iwahig Penal Colony on the Island of Palawan, Bontoc Prison in the Mountain Providence of Northern Luzon, Fort Mills on Corregidor Island, and a host of provincial jails, temporary facilities, and detention sites listed in colonial reports merely as "other stations". Historians have generally characterized these prisons as "colonial laboratories" for experiments in racial classification, benevolent assimilation, and work discipline, and for good reason.[10] Yet, just as this essay is concerned more with the forcible transport of

---

8. Bankoff, *Crime, Society, and the State*, p. 12; *idem*, "Deportation and the Prison Colony of San Ramon, 1870–1898", *Philippine Studies*, 39:4 (1991), pp. 443–457. Bankoff argues that this was in part a response to Spanish legislation abolishing deportation to and from the colonies in 1842. While judicial sentences of deportation were forbidden, the colonial Governor General retained the authority to expel persons considered prejudicial to the state and found ways to forcibly move people around for other purposes.

9. *Idem*, "Deportation and the Prison Colony of San Ramon, 1870–1898", p. 443.

10. On racial classification see Paul A. Kramer, *The Blood of Government: Race, Empire, the United States and the Philippines* (Chapel Hill, NC, 2006); on benevolent assimilation see Aaron Abel T. Mallari, "The Bilibid Prison as an American Colonial Project in the Philippines", *Philippine Sociological Review*, 60 (2012), pp. 165–192; on work discipline see Michael Salman, "'Nothing Without Labor': Penology, Discipline and Independence in the Philippines Under United States Rule", in Vicente L. Rafael (ed.), *Discrepant Histories: Translocal Essays on Filipino Cultures* (Philadelphia, PA, 1995), pp. 113–129; and Michael Salman, "'The Prison That Makes Men Free': The Iwahig Penal Colony and the Simulacra of the American State in the Philippines", in McCoy and Scarano, *Colonial Crucible*, pp. 116–130.

populist leaders, rather than the deportation and exile of well-known political prisoners, it likewise focuses on these prisons as nodes in an intra-colonial transport system, rather than on the social history of life inside the prison itself.

Looking behind the official rationale of transporting prisoners merely to use their labor on public works, it becomes clear that transportation and incarceration were conjoined strategies of carceral colonialism driven by the constant fear that prison revolt would trigger a flood of wider uprisings. For anticolonial fighters, on the other hand, prison revolt catalyzed opposition to US occupation, and escape from forced transport became a powerful act of resistance. For both sides, the revolutionary impulse was carried forward in the metaphor of the flood. Thus, by re-examining the connected histories of revolt and transportation as counterinsurgency from the perspective of the colony, this article also shows how experiences of incarceration shaped anticolonial leaders' freedom dreams and practices.

FEARING THE FLOOD: TERRAINS OF COUNTERINSURGENCY

The Bilibid revolt was a cornerstone of US justifications for war. When explaining the outbreak of hostilities to the US War Department back in Washington, DC, for instance, Major John R. Taylor put the prison plot at the heart of a coordinated uprising in Manila that would have slaughtered every American in sight. It was not difficult for Jacinto Limjap to find volunteers to "rob, to burn, to rape, and to murder", Taylor claimed, because that was why they were sent to prison in the first place. He argued that, as the uprising spread from Bilibid across Manila, servants would rise up and kill their masters, insurgents disguised as civilians would attack US Army barracks, and white people would be massacred in the streets. "If the plan had been carried out", Taylor reported, "no white man and no white woman would have escaped".[11] For officials like Taylor, the narrative that dangerous prison revolt would lead to widespread anticolonial uprising figured prominently in what historian Ranajit Guha elsewhere called the "prose of counterinsurgency"; that is, the need to characterize subaltern insurrection as irrationally violent to justify colonial law and order.[12]

Other US officials, like Dean Worcester, who had just been appointed to the First Philippine Commission by US President William McKinley, relied heavily on Taylor's narrative to assert that the Filipinos had brought war

---

11. J.R.M. Taylor, quoted in Worcester, *Philippines Past and Present*, p. 140; *idem et al.*, *Compilation of Philippine Insurgent Records*.
12. Ranajit Guha, "The Prose of Counter-Insurgency", in *idem* and Gayatri Chakravorty Spivak (eds), *Selected Subaltern Studies* (New York, 1988), pp. 45–84.

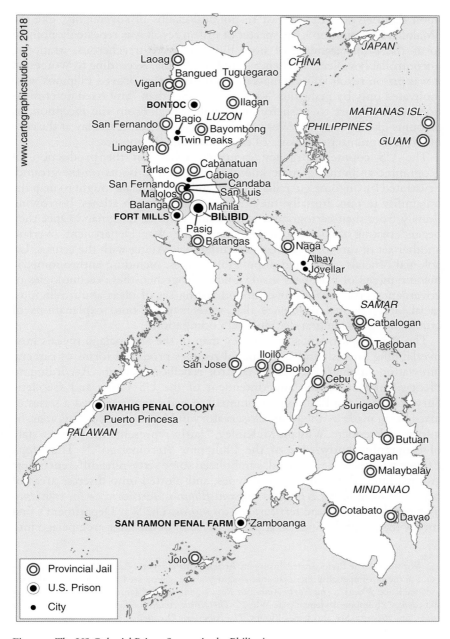

Figure 1. The US Colonial Prison System in the Philippines.

upon themselves.[13] In contrast to political claims of sovereignty, like the "Malolos Constitution", the specter of prison revolt was repeatedly pointed to as the prime example of how Filipinos were treacherous, irrational, uncontrollably violent, and hence unfit for self-rule. According to Worcester, it was prison revolt igniting mass urban uprising that proved Filipinos were motivated only by malicious "savagery", rather than "any fixed determination on their part to push for independence".[14] From the inception, as accounts like Taylor's and Worcester's illustrate, prison revolt lay at the core of white-supremacist fantasies of race war in the Philippines.

The US counterinsurgency campaign relied on the production of geographic and ethnographic knowledge as well as boots on the ground. Frustrated by ongoing guerrilla warfare, military officials sought to map the unfamiliar terrain. Initially, they used existing Spanish atlases, borrowing heavily from their cartographic lexicon and colonial imaginary. Once they began creating their own survey maps, the War Department overlaid another set of categories of regional difference. Along with the census, US colonial officials conducted population studies, including anthropometric measurements of prisoners inside Bilibid. Together, these technologies of governance produced a powerful and lasting set of ideas about religious, racial, and regional difference that were mapped onto explanations of criminality over the first decade of US occupation.

The War Department's first survey map of the archipelago reveals how overlapping Spanish and US imperial regimes produced forms of carceral innovation in their attempt to control rebellious terrain. According to Henry S. Pritchett, the Superintendent of the US Coast and Geodetic Survey Office, the Philippine Commission had commandeered a series of maps being made by the Jesuit Observatory in Manila in 1899. This atlas, he informed President William McKinley, "fairly represents the present state of geographic knowledge of the Philippine Archipelago".[15] The *Mapa Ethnographico*, as it was called, symbolized some sixty-nine different ethnic groups, lumped into three racial types, and plotted onto discrete areas of land: *territorio de los cristianos hispano-filipinos, territorio de los cristianos nuevos y los infieles*, and *territorio de los moros*. The War Department's first survey map kept the Spanish tripartite division of the same archipelago into

---

13. Worcester, "The Premeditated Insurgent Attack", in *Philippines Past and Present*, pp. 127–151. For the anti-imperialist interlocutor he sought to argue against, see James Blount, "Philippine Independence When?", *The North American Review*, 184:607 (18 January 1907), pp. 135–149; and *idem*, "Philippine Independence Why?", *The North American Review*, 185:617 (21 June 1907), pp. 365–377. See also James Blount, *The American Occupation of the Philippines, 1898–1912* (New York, 1913).

14. Worcester, *Philippines Past and Present*, p. 151.

15. *Report of the First Philippine Commission Atlas/Atlas de Filipinas. Colección de 30 Mapas. Trabajados por delineantes filipinos bajo la dirección del P. José Algue, S.J., director del observatorio de Manila* (Washington, DC, 1899), p. 3.

degrees of religious conversion, even retaining the same color to represent the Moro, predominantly Muslim, provinces in the South. It also split the archipelago into North and South, shading some areas as controlled by "civil provincial government" and others as controlled by "Moro and other non-Christian tribes".[16]

At the same time, census takers under the direction of the Philippine Commission surveyed the islands' peoples. The *Census of the Philippine Islands* presented a series of carefully staged photographs of people from various islands arranged along a gradient of supposed "civilization".[17] The census proved to be a devastating tool of imperial governance, with far-reaching social consequences for the construction of criminality. Other forms of ethnographic knowledge were produced by officials like Dean C. Worcester and anthropologists like Daniel Folkmar, whose *Album of Philippine Types* set out to classify the inmates of Bilibid Prison. The operative spatial category for these men was a static North–South binary and Folkmar sought to sort his subjects into northern (whom he considered generally "tall and long-headed") and southern ("short and broad-headed") types.[18] His theories rested on broader anthropological and social-scientific ideas of the day, particularly the belief in physiognomy and phrenology, that the outer surface of the head bore signs of inner character. What is especially striking is the eerie parallel between imagining the topography of the skull, with its presumed regions of localized mental faculties, and the topography of the land, with presumed regions of localized deviance.[19]

The conflation of theories about geography with natural history, climatology, and racial science was central to the emergent fields of criminology and penology at the dawn of the twentieth century. The Attorney General's massive multi-volume study, *Criminality in the Philippine Islands*, sought to compile crime statistics in order to advance regionalized explanations for what he came to call the "propensity to crime".[20] He was especially

---

16. Bureau of Insular Affairs, War Department, *Map of the Philippines* (Washington, DC, 1902). National Archives and Records Administration, Record Group 350.3; Gen. J.P. Sander, Dir., *Census of the Philippine Islands: Taken under the Direction of the Philippine Commission in the Year 1903*, 4 vols (Washington, DC, 1905).

17. See Vicente Rafael, *White Love and Other Events in Filipino History* (Durham, NC, 2000), pp. 19–51.

18. Daniel Folkmar, *Album of Philippine Types (Found in Bilibid Prison in 1903)* (Manila, 1904), p. 3.

19. *Annual Report of the Philippine Commission, 1900–1903*, p. 609. By 1903, the Philippine Commission's "Bureau of Non-Christian Tribes" reported that their ethnological survey led by David P. Barrows of the Igorot people of Bontoc, taken to be the most representative of the mountain region, would prove of great importance to "governing these very primitive tribes".

20. Ignacio Villamor, *Criminality in the Philippine Islands, 1903–1908* (Manila, 1909); *idem*, "Propensity to Crime", *Journal of the American Institute of Criminal Law and Criminology*, 6:5 (1916), pp. 729–745.

preoccupied with the "influence of local conditions on crime", and sought to show how "aggressive tendencies" produced crimes against persons (parricide, murder, homicide, physical injuries), "nutritive tendencies" caused crimes against property (robbery, theft, embezzlement), and "genesial tendencies" resulted in crimes against public morals (adultery, rape, abduction, seduction, corruption of minors). These tendencies, moreover, became mapped onto an imagined geography that artificially cut the archipelago into three distinct regions, identified in terms of the pre-valence of certain types of criminality. This new tripartite regional division formed a hybrid of older Spanish geographies of religious classification and the rigid American North–South geography of racial simplification and hierarchy. These areas were chosen, he insisted, because of the "ethnological and geographic affinity between the inhabitants".[21] Mapping and the census as technologies of rule were combined with the rise of criminal statistics to produce a carceral geography that regionalized supposed deviance and targeted alleged perpetrators.

This kind of geographic knowledge, like the Attorney General's collec-tion of regionalized crime statistics over the first ten years of US colonial rule, constructed a cartographic imaginary that fused criminality to discrete territories. According to this explanatory scheme, Mindanao and the islands of the southern archipelago were seen to be overly aggressive and insur-rectionary, the islands of central and southern Luzon symbolized the moral degeneracy associated with rapidly growing urban centers like Manila, and the far north was seen as dangerously poor, hungry, and in need of improvement. Genesial crimes in the cities, reasoned the Attorney General, were surely the result of "the loosening, if not breaking up, of religious beliefs, which leads to the relaxation of customs".[22] Ultimately, differently classified peoples – civilian, subject, criminal, insurgent – were seen to necessitate distinct modalities of rule, authorizing drastically different scales of violence.

The early reports of the Secretary of Commerce and Police reveal how this kind of thinking about regionalized criminality informed counterinsurgency strategy. Writing in 1903, for example, Secretary Luke E. Wright described the fear that *ladrones* and gangs of robbers would swoop down and prey on the rest of the population before taking refuge again in the "mountain fastnesses".[23] Formidable bands of "considerable magnitude" had sprung up in the provinces of Rizal, Cavite, Albay, Iloilo, Cebu, Suriago, and Misamis according to Wright. Their leaders managed to evade capture by concealing themselves in the

21. *Ibid.*
22. *Ibid.*
23. Luke E. Wright, "Report of the Secretary of Commerce and Police", in *Annual Report of the Philippine Commission, 1903* (Washington, DC, 1904), p. 611.

remote mountains.[24] In this paranoid environment, officials blurred the lines between pre-emption and retribution, killing and incarceration. As Wright put it: "the speedy killing and arrest and punishment [...] of outlaws has already produced a most beneficial effect and has borne in on the minds of those likely to depart from the path of peace in future".[25]

BEING THE FLOOD: ANTICOLONIAL FREEDOM DREAMS AND PRACTICES

Given this context of mass criminalization, escape and prison revolt became two central currents running through revolutionary struggles against US occupation. Social historians of popular independence movements in the Philippines have long warned against subsuming their various aims into a singular elite-nationalist narrative of seeking political rights in the nation state. By focusing on the meaning of revolution to the masses, for instance, Reynaldo C. Ileto focuses instead on the vitality of the messianic and millennial visions within these movements.[26] He shows how revolutionary ideas that surfaced in poetry and political street theater were channeled into a "revolutionary style" by brotherhoods like the *katipunan*, and erupted in people's uprisings against Spanish and US rule. Vicente Rafael meanwhile suggests that these revolutionary movements opened a new experience of sovereignty, based in *kayalaan*, understood as "freedom from the necessity of labor and the violence of law", in contrast to US and elite-nationalist doctrines of sovereignty claims.[27] Following this line of argument, prison revolt in the Philippines can be seen not only as an affront to US sovereignty claims, but as an alternative practice of radical freedom itself.

Breaking out of prison as an act of individual liberation leading to collective salvation was a recurrent theme throughout the various waves of revolutionary activity in the Philippines. Consider the case of Felipe Salvador in 1902. That year, US officials tried to propagate the fiction that war had ended by declaring a handover from military to civil government. Governor General William Taft led the Philippine Commission in passing legislation to try and render abstract sovereignty into actual jurisdiction on the ground. The Sedition and *Bandolerismo* laws of 1902 provided the legal architecture for hunting down and locking up all remaining "insurgents", suddenly reclassified as outlaws and bandits rather than anticolonial freedom fighters.[28] Felipe Salvador was legendary.

---

24. *Ibid.*, p. 613.
25. *Ibid.*, p. 616.
26. Ileto, *Payson and Revolution*.
27. Rafael, "Afterlife of Empire", p. 349. See also *idem, White Love and Other Events in Filipino History*.
28. These laws, as Ileto puts it, made revolutionaries into "bad men" and "bandits" as if overnight. Ileto, *Payson and Revolution*, p. 172.

He had defeated 3,000 Spanish with an army of 300 at the battle of San Luis in Pampanga in 1896, captured 100 Mauser rifles from the Spanish, and led a triumphant march through Candaba after Pampanga had been liberated from the Spanish in 1898.[29] He had amassed an enormous following, causing him to be routinely tracked by US intelligence forces. Ensnared by the new laws, he was captured in Nueva Ecija on charges of sedition and transported to Bilibid Prison in 1902. But when they passed Cabiao en route, he escaped.

To his followers, Salvador's escape was seen as an individual act toward communal freedom. He had predicted it, telling his followers he went to jail voluntarily and would walk free when he chose.[30] It was also one among a series of prophecies featuring imprisoned leaders as harbingers of liberation that had deep roots in the original *katipunan*. During the war against the Spanish, Salvador promised the return of revolutionary hero Gabino Cortes along with seven archangels to shield them from the bullets.[31] In preparation for war against the Spanish, Andrés Bonificio and other *katipunan* leaders had ascended Mount Tapusi to write "long live Philippine independence" in chalk on the wall of the Cave of Bernardo Caprio. King Bernardo, "hero of the Indios", was said to be "imprisoned in the cave, awaiting the day when he would break loose and return to free his people".[32] During Felipe Salvador's escape, he too ascended a mountain top. After wandering in the nearby forests and swamps, Salvador climbed Mount Arayat and returned with a prophecy: "a great flood would wash away nonbelievers and precipitate the impending battle for independence".[33]

The years following the US transfer from military to colonial government in 1902 were marked by what the Philippine Constabulary referred to as the

---

29. *Idem*, "The *Payson* of Felipe Salvador", in *idem*, *Payson and Revolution*, pp. 209–252; Vic Hurley, *Jungle Patrol: The Story of the Philippine Constabulary, 1901–1936* (Salem, OR, 2011 [1938]), p. 121; Philippine Commission, *Fifth Annual Report of the Philippine Commission* (Washington, DC, 1905), p. 64.

30. Ileto, *Payson and Revolution*, p. 228. Or, as Vic Hurley put it, "Even if he was captured, his followers believed that he would escape or that he would have a second life after death" (Hurley, *Jungle Patrol*, p. 121).

31. Ileto, *Payson and Revolution*, p. 215.

32. *Ibid.*, pp. 99–101; Damiana Euginio, *Philippine Folk Literature: The Legends* (Quezon City, 2002), pp. 4–5. See also, Teodoro A. Agoncillo, *The Revolt of the Masses: The Story of Bonificio and the Katipunan* (Quezon City, 1956).

33. Ileto, *Payson and Revolution*, pp. 210, 222; Hurley, *Jungle Patrol*, p. 121; Henry J. Reilly, "Filipino Bandit Terror in Luzon: Career of Felipe Salvador Shows Danger of Such Uprisings in Islands", *Chicago Tribune*, 2 August 1914. See also Salvador's autobiographic writings, *Tatlong Tulisan*, quoted in Ileto, *Payson and Revolution*, p. 225. See also "Narrative of the Feelings and Supplications of the Accused Major Felipe Salvador", quoted in Ileto, *Payson and Revolution*, p. 215.

period of "papal resistance".[34] These militant religio-political movements were led by messianic figures like Felipe Salvador, called "Popes", and traced their origins to the *katipunan*. According to the Constabulary, in addition to Salvador's Santa Iglesia, other resistance organizations included the Tulisans, Dios-Dios, Colorados, Cruz-Cruz, Cazadoes, Colorums, Santo Niños, Guardia de Honor, Hermanos del Tercio Orden, and Babaylane.[35] Vic Hurley, honorary Third Lieutenant and chronicler of the Philippine Constabulary, carefully recorded the messages and movements of these Popes. He also uncovered visions of freedom defined in opposition to imperial notions of law and order.

Describing the Tulisan movement led by Ruperto Rio, self-proclaimed "Son of God" and "Deliverer of the Philippines", Hurley focused on the meaning of independence to the organization. While being interrogated, a wounded Tulisan prisoner spoke about a box inscribed with the term *independencia*; it *was* in the box, he told his captors, but had now flown away back to the Pope to be enclosed again in a new box. "The fanatic rolled his glistening eyes as he drank in the thought of the approach of the millennium", wrote Hurley. "When independence flies from the box, there will be no labor, *señor*, and no jails and no taxes [...] and no more *constabulario*", explained the prisoner.[36] Here was an understanding of freedom predicated on the abolition of policing, prisons, taxation, and labor. Messianic leaders like Ruperto Rios and Felipe Salvador were promising total revolution in the Philippines, social transformation rooted in reversing the collective experience of criminalization.

The revolutionary impulse carried forward the metaphor of the flood. Two years after Felipe Salvador's escape en route to Bilibid, for example, the Philippine Commission intercepted a call to arms. Writing to Dionisio Velasquez and all members of the Santa Iglesia, estimated to be 50,000 strong, Salvador asked them to assemble the brothers of the *katipunan* and ready the soldiers: "I therefore request that you do all you can in order that we may have our self-government within the month of October".[37] The Constabulary believed he was using the old Spanish Weather Bureau's infrastructure to circulate predictions of floods.[38] The Detective Bureau believed Manila to be continually in danger. "This city has always been the storm center of these political typhoons, and the least variance of sentiment or feeling of unrest

---

34. See, for example, Hurley, *Jungle Patrol*, pp. 125–127.
35. *Ibid.*, p. 127. Hurley notes that the Constabulary had made concerted efforts to eliminate these "messiahs".
36. *Ibid.*, p. 126.
37. *Fifth Annual Report of the Philippine Commission*, p. 64.
38. Hurley, *Jungle Patrol*, p. 121.

is at once noted", wrote Secret Service Chief C.R. Trowbridge.[39] Although Salvador's plan for an uprising did not come to pass in 1904, revolutionary forces continued to muster and would again break loose in the "People's Rising" of 1910. By that time, it was clear that it was not only Salvador's followers who believed the prophecy of the great flood, but US colonial officials were also thinking about revolutionary currents in terms of fluid dynamics. If Manila was the storm center, Bilibid would again be its epicenter.

CRIMINAL TRANSPORTATION AS VALVES OF REVOLUTIONARY PRESSURE

As US officials consolidated geographic and ethnologic knowledge to produce cartographies of criminality, they increasingly relied on incarceration and convict transportation in their counterinsurgency strategy. First, they exiled political prisoners to Guam. Then, over the first decade of US rule, they built a network of prisons around the archipelago and moved prisoners to different locations in order to separate them from regional affiliations and bases of support. As they developed more elaborate transport systems, officials began strategically creating and exploiting regional antagonisms as a way of managing convict labor. Justified as labor transfers, it was clear that US officials were seeking to rationalize counterinsurgent racialization through the mechanism of capitalism.

Police and Commerce Secretary W. Cameron Forbes became obsessed with transportation and prison administration as twin hallmarks of governance. Read alongside police and prison reports, Forbes' personal journal reveals the extent to which he saw himself as a mastermind of convict transportation in the Philippines.[40] Beginning with the establishment of the Iuhit penal colony on Palawan Island, later renamed Iwahig, Forbes began using Bilibid as a valve, redistributing revolutionary pressure around the islands. Officially, the colonial government used convict transportation to relieve the overcrowding at Bilibid that they blamed for the unsanitary conditions and rampant disease that periodically killed hundreds of prisoners.

Tracing the plans for prisoner transportation through Forbes' journal also shows how he imagined it as a way of fixing the "labor problem" and building the requisite infrastructure to maximize economic penetration of

---

39. US War Department Bureau of Insular Affairs, *Annual Report of the Philippine Commission* (Washington, DC, 1904),Part 1, p. 201. Trowbridge was referring to their fear of Artemio Ricarte, another revolutionary threat, who had just landed in Manila.
40. See W. Cameron Forbes Papers, Journals, First Series, vols 1–5, MS Houghton Library, Harvard University.

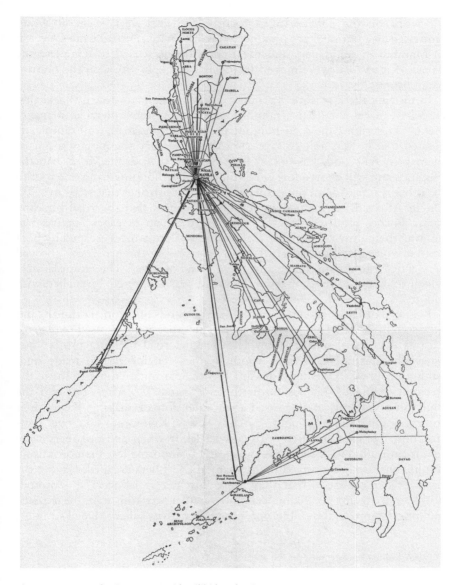

Figure 2. Bureau of Prisons Map with Bilibid at the Center.
Bureau of Prisons, Catalogue of Products.

regions he deemed unproductive or underproductive. In the fall of 1904, for instance, he had promised to send 1,000 prisoners to General Wood to build roads in Mindanao and another 500 to General Allen in Albay for work on the Tabaco-Ligao road.[41] The next year, General Wood requested an additional 250 prisoners to work on his railroad from Overton to Marahui in Mindanao, and the 1,000 prisoners used to complete the Tabaco-Ligao road were moved to Jovellar to begin work on the Guino-batan project.[42]

In moving these prisoners around, Forbes sought to destroy local ties, exploit regional antagonisms, and design new systems of racial management.[43] Describing the road-building project in Mindanao, for example, he gloated that he was able to save the Insular treasury the money to guard them: General Wood "has an easy time guarding them as the Moros hate the Filipinos and will be standing along the dead line hopping from one foot to the other waiting for an opportunity to kill any prisoner that steps over".[44] Or, in Albay, when forty-two starving prisoners fled the road-building camp, Forbes reported that they enlisted the help of eager "natives" in hunting them down.[45] Similarly, when thirty-six prisoners escaped by boat from a work detail on Malahi Island, "natives" in the province "showed very active interest" in recapturing them "dead or alive". The escape launch, which soldiers had fired on from the shore, was recovered "drenched with blood".[46]

Regional differences were racialized in the minds of colonial officials, and they sought to create civilizational hierarchies that could be used to manage various degrees of unfree labor. The Benguet road-building project was especially illustrative of this. Begun in 1901, engineers had made only halting progress in pushing forward earlier Spanish attempts to make the Benguet highlands "accessible to the white man".[47] After Taft and the Philippine Commission declared their intention of making Bagio their summer capital, they brought in Major L.W.V. Kennon to take over construction. He experimented with convict labor when 200 prisoners were sent from Bilibid to Twin Peaks that year, but reported less than promising results. Disease had ravaged them, many died, others escaped, leaving the rest so "demoralized" that they were "useless as laborers".[48] Another problem according to Major Kennon was that working them near road-building Camp 3, above the 900-foot sheer drop called "Devil's Slide",

41. *Ibid.*, vol. 1, October 1904, pp. 88, 94.
42. *Ibid.*, vol. 1, March 1905; September 1905, p. 322.
43. On the term racial management, see David Roediger and Elizabeth Esch, *The Production of Difference: Race and the Management of Labor in U.S. History* (New York, 2012).
44. Forbes Papers, Journals, vol. 1, February 1905, p. 159.
45. W. Cameron Forbes, "Report of the Department of Commerce and Police", in *Sixth Annual Report of the Philippine Commission, 1905* (Washington, DC, 1906), Part III, p. 19.
46. *Ibid.*, p. 20.
47. L.W.V. Kennon, "Report of the Officer in Charge of Construction of the Benguet Road", Appendix H, in *Sixth Annual Report of the Philippine Commission, 1905*, Part III, p. 359.
48. *Ibid.*, p. 379.

meant that they could not be shackled while working without risk that they might fall off the cliff.

The larger population of unshackled workers were also racialized and criminalized in Kennon's view, and the two were co-constitutive. American Camp foremen had been given police powers, he wrote, and "considering the class of workers there – Japanese, Chinese, Filipinos, Igorrotes [sic], and Americans including negroes – it is surprising to me that there is so little crime".[49] Quoting his predecessor's view of their supposed racial capacities to labor, he reflected on the idea that Filipinos only worked under the direct charge of a white foreman: "they quit or go idle the minute the eye of the white man is off them". The inclination to "lay off", he continued, was common to the Filipino and the "American negro".[50] These road engineers had figured that the Filipino was equal to about one-fifth the amount of work of a "good white laborer", while the "Igorrote was a 'vastly superior animal' and equaled 'three Ilocanos or Pangasinans in wage value'". Working parties of "different tribes", Kennon concluded, "were sometimes pitted against each other and a spirit of emulation was fostered which increased the output of their labor". The rivalry between Tagalogs and Ilocanos, for instance, created competition over who was considered a better workman.[51] Even though convict labor may not have been as efficient for road work in this case, convict transportation enabled officials to pit groups against each other, and the strategic insertion of the criminalized subject as negative referent for the relative degrees of freedom enjoyed by the other groups of workers was used to powerful symbolic effect.

Men like W. Cameron Forbes, Leonard Wood, and L.W.V. Kennon moved people around and forced them to work as a counterinsurgency strategy and considered it a defining feature of imperial sovereignty. Indeed, Bilibid's first warden, George N. Wolfe, imagined a revolt of some 200 detention prisoners to be caused by "lack of work".[52] When authorities captured the "inciter of a riot in Samar", Forbes suggested work as the proper cure for such rebelliousness, that he be given "good employment in Bilibid".[53] Contrary to the pronouncements of visiting officials like President McKinley's physician, Mr Rixey, who remarked that it was "a pity the whole population shouldn't serve a term in Bilibid to be built up physically and made useful laborers", the archival record is riddled with

49. *Ibid.*, p. 375.
50. *Ibid.*, pp. 376, 379.
51. *Ibid.* Kennon was quoting from Mr. Homes' 1902 report and, while reinforcing the racialized hierarchy of labor, was careful also to point out that he considered "Tao" laborers to be human, not animals.
52. George N. Wolfe, "Report of the Warden of Bilibid Prison", in *Sixth Annual Report of the Philippine Commission, 1905*, Appendix E, pp. 305–306.
53. Forbes Papers, Journals, vol. 1, January 1905, p. 136.

evidence that prisoners were starved when incapacitated and fed more when put to hard labor.[54] In 1904, the quantity and cost of rations for "native and Asiatic" prisoners inside Bilibid, for example, was valued at 0.16 of a Philippine peso, while the rations for "European and American" prisoners were more than double, 0.39. The average cost per ration for prisoners working on roads in Albay Province meanwhile was 0.28.[55] Evidently, prison administrators sought disproportionately to press downward on the social reproduction of those held in captivity.

Racial categories not only affected the quantity and cost of rations inside Bilibid, but also the type. That same year, an Executive Order had to be passed prohibiting the use of "polished rice" in government institutions due to "the relationship between a diet too largely composed of such rice and the prevalence of beriberi".[56] Here, in these reports, then, are traces not only of how racialized criminal subjects were fashioned discursively, but also how they were quite literally being made materially. Sovereign power in the prison system came to be understood not only as the monopoly on deadly violence, but as managing human life down to minute calculations of cost and caloric intake.

By the time W. Cameron Forbes took over as Governor General, he had developed a full-fledged theory of sovereign power based in his experience administering policing and prisons. It was apparent in the systems he designed for controlling the mobility of certain targeted groups, for commanding the labor of racialized criminal subjects, and for managing social and biological reproduction. Yet, it was perhaps most clearly showcased in his rationale for how he used the pardon power. Unlike the American system, "under the Spanish system the Governor General was viceroy with all the powers of the king and as such could pardon anywhere", Forbes wrote in his journal. "The Filipinos liked to have their Governor General full-powered and I took these actions without any question as to my power and without any questions raised by anyone else".[57] Likening himself to a benevolent monarch, Forbes' vision of imperial power was infused with the white-supremacist and misogynist notions of having complete discretion over those he considered beneath him.

Patriarchal self-fashioning underpinned Forbes' gendered ideology of imperial sovereignty. He took pride in being able to judge a "nice girl" from a "quarrelsome hussy", or a "very dainty pretty little Filipina" from

54. *Ibid.*, vol. 2, July 1906, pp. 39–40.
55. *Sixth Annual Report of the Philippine Commission, 1905*, pp. 324–327. For a more extended discussion, see Benjamin D. Weber, "Fugitive Justice: The Possible Futures of Prison Records from US Colonial Rule in the Philippines", *Archive Journal* (August 2017), available at: http://www.archivejournal.net/essays/fugitive-justice; last accessed 15 January 2018.
56. *Sixth Annual Report of the Philippine Commission, 1905*, p. 64.
57. Forbes Papers, Journals, vol. 3, July 1909, p. 223.

"undesirable women of the lower class", and to use his discretionary power selectively to pardon them.[58] He grabbed every chance to "ridicule men with long thumbnails", what he considered an unmanly "oriental sign of degradation" proving that they "belong to a class who does not have to work". As they "can't be of any use" to their people, Forbes wrote, "they might as well stay in jail".[59] His gendered theories cut both ways: being the wrong-looking sort of man, therefore, was reason enough for him to keep someone imprisoned rather than pardon him.

True manliness, on the other hand, was reserved only for white men according to Forbes. The creation of a penal colony was central to Forbes' convict transportation plans from the outset. He also saw it as a proving ground for his theories of manliness as management. Forbes blamed the initial failures that beset the plan to establish the penal colony on Palawan Island on a lack of strong leadership; "the success of an experiment depends on the executive capacity of its chief", he wrote.[60]

In 1905, a prison revolt of over one hundred prisoners led by Simeon Mamañgon, Bastonero Mayor, Regino Ibora, and "Moro Macalintal" led to the capture of penal colony Superintendent Dr. J.W. Madara and enabled thirty-three to escape.[61] After the escapees were hunted down, captured, or killed, Forbes chose Col. John R. White, a "manly chap", to take over and reform the penal colony. Despite its reputation for disease and violence, Forbes imagined this to be the opportunity of a lifetime: "Think of the chance for a young man, two thousand laborers absolutely at his call, twenty-two thousand acres and a virgin tropical soil [...] the world his."[62] He promised to back Col. White in his efforts to strengthen his authority, but White confidently informed him that "they would find out quick enough who was master".[63] Given the colony's chaotic start, Forbes worried that other officials like the director of public instruction might try and "emasculate" his scheme by blocking his proposal to create a hierarchy among prisoners based on heteronormative tropes of masculinity having a wife, children, and serving as an inmate-guard.[64]

According to his plan, male prisoners sent to the penal colony would be given women as a form of incentive or reward. Indeed, the list of necessities Forbes requested for Iwahig included "cattle, machinery, wives of settlers".[65] In a letter to Forbes, the new penal colony superintendent

58. *Ibid.*, vol. 5, August 1911, p. 16; *ibid.*, vol. 3, October 1909, p. 343.
59. *Ibid.*, vol. 3, October 1909, p. 51.
60. *Ibid.*, vol. 1, October 1905, p. 364.
61. *Fifth Annual Report of the Philippine Commission*, vol. 3, p. 38.
62. Forbes Papers, Journals, vol. 2, September 1906, p. 87.
63. *Ibid.*, p. 88.
64. *Ibid.*, vol. 2, October 1906, p. 140.
65. *Ibid.*, vol. 2, April 1907, p. 208.

John R. White wrote that the women he had found "prostituting" when he arrived were "allotted to the prisoners" with very satisfactory results. Given an apparent shortage of women in the colony, White also requested authority to send ex-prisoner foremen to the provinces to "collect families of prisoners and conduct them to Iwahig".[66] This was in accordance with Forbes' "General Plan for Iwahig", in which he had countenanced that "the only way of having the prisoners contented and the project a successful one is to have a fair percentage – at least thirty per cent – supplied with families".[67] Yet, Forbes also cautioned that women not be sent to the prisoners as soon as they arrived at the penal colony, but rather be used as an incentive for good behavior. In his instructions to White, Forbes recommended that women be "rigidly excluded" from the "Barrack Zone" of the penal colony, and that only married women be allowed in the "Home Zone" and "Free Zone". While he recommended that the government pay to transport women who wished to marry the prisoners, the system of *queridas*, or sweethearts, would not be tolerated. According to this scheme, men in the Barrack Zone would be allowed only occasionally to glimpse the presence of married women in the other zones and were explicitly prevented from having contact with women right away: "a prison is a prison and criminals are criminals until by good conduct extending over a period of sufficient time they have demonstrated their capacity to be citizens. For this reason it is deemed inadvisable that prisoners should be allowed to have their women and have their children during the probationary period".[68] Forbes concluded in his letter to John White: "I am convinced that with the labor at his disposal, the penalties he can inflict, and the inducements he can offer that he can practically dictate the action and conditions of the residents of the settlement".[69] Here, treating women as provisions to incentivize prisoners was considered necessary to produce a certain kind of political subject; one who would direct his energy into family rather than insurgency.

---

66. John White to W. Cameron Forbes, 8 September 1906, in Forbes Papers, Philippine Data: Dept. MS, TS, and Periodical Cuttings, 1904–1909, no. 536, p 2.
67. "General Plan for Iwahig", 8 September 1906, in W. Cameron Forbes, Confidential Letter File, Houghton Library MS Am. 1366.1, V. 3, p. 221.
68. "Letter with Plan for Penal Colony", Forbes to John R. White, 14 November 1906, in Forbes Papers, Houghton Library, Philippine Data: Dept. MS, TS, 1904–1909, v. 2, nos 288–290, "Women at the Settlement", pp. 10–12. For a comparative discussion of heteronormativity in state formation, see Margot Canaday, *The Straight State: Sexuality and Citizenship in Twentieth-Century America* (Princeton, NJ, 2011).
69. Forbes to John White, 14 November 1906, in Forbes Papers, Philippine Data: Dept. MS, TS, and Periodical Cuttings, 1904–1909, no. 296, p. 18.

CONCLUSION

Prison revolt in the Philippines served as a lightning rod for wider anti-colonial struggles against US occupation. At the end of Spanish rule, Bilibid Prison was characterized as a faucet with an unending supply of criminalized subjects flowing through it. Over the first decade of US rule, it became used as a valve for distributing revolutionary pressure around the archipelago. Mass criminalization was central to the imperialist logic, which maintained that Filipino subjects were unfit for freedom or self-rule. Through convict transportation, US officials sought to remove particular threats from their support bases, to cut off and isolate revolutionary leaders from their networks of belonging. Through mass criminalization, officials also exploited imagined cartographies of regional difference, rendering them into elaborate plans for race management. These transportation schemes relied on a theory of monarchial sovereignty as absolute power, not just to decide on the exception or hold the monopoly on violence, but to manage life by forcibly moving people around and compelling them to work. This vision of sovereignty, at once imperial, patriarchal, and white supremacist in its attempt to control all facets of social and biological reproduction, was most clearly evident in the administration of the colonial prison system.

Felipe Salvador's prophecy of a flood leading to independence can be seen in the waves of anticolonial revolutionary movement against this version of US sovereignty. First, there was the recurrent theme that imprisoned leaders – Bernardo Carpio, Andrés Bonificio, Gabriel Cortes – would return as harbingers of liberation. Next, was the growing sympathy for fugitives from law-and-order "justice" – Felipe Salvador and Julian Montalon – rooted in the collective experience of criminalization under US colonialism. Prison revolts – by Jacinto Limjap, Juan Leandro Villariño, and Arturo Baldello – were seen as triggers of widespread uprising. And, the revolution – whether Salvadorist or Aglipayan – was said to wash away established hierarchies of wealth and power.

Those alternate ideas and practices of freedom were shaped by experiences with incarceration. If, as Vicente Rafael suggests, the Philippine revolution opened a more "miraculous" experience of sovereignty as the "evanescent opening of an entirely new life", prison revolt symbolized a radical break from one condition and entrance into another state of being.[70] As symbol of anticolonial revolution, it unworked the mechanism by which

---

70. Rafael, "Afterlife of Empire", p. 352. As discussed earlier, Rafael elaborates on Apolinario Mabini's theory of sovereignty as based in *kayalaan*, which is understood to mean constant caring. He sees in this a theory of sovereignty understood in terms of "life beyond necessity" (following the philosopher George Bataille's usage of the phrase).

freedom fighters had been transformed into "outlaws"; through revolt, the imprisoned would be turned back into revolutionary leaders, thereby reversing the imperial process of criminalization.[71] Perhaps this is what the unnamed Tulisan prisoner was pointing to in his definition of *independencia* as the abolition of police, prisons, taxes, and labor.

---

71. On the ongoing legacy and interpretative stakes of efforts to undo imperial criminalization, see Weber, "Fugitive Justice".

IRSH 63 (2018), Special Issue, pp. 211–231 doi:10.1017/S0020859018000299
© 2018 Internationaal Instituut voor Sociale Geschiedenis

The "Other" at Home: Deportation and Transportation of Libyans to Italy During the Colonial Era (1911–1943)*

F R A N C E S C A   D I   P A S Q U A L E

Soprintendenza archivistica per la Sicilia
Archivio di Stato di Palermo Via Vittorio Emanuele 31
*90133, Palermo, Italy**

E-mail: francesca.dipasquale76@gmail.com

ABSTRACT: This article analyses the practices of deportation and transportation of colonial subjects from Libya, Italy's former possession, to the metropole throughout the entire colonial period (1911–1943). For the most part, the other colonial powers did not transport colonial subjects to Europe. Analysing the history of the punitive relocations of Libyans, this article addresses the ways in which the Italian case may be considered peculiar. It highlights the overlapping of the penal system and military practices and emphasizes the difficult dialogue between "centre" and "periphery" concerning security issues inside the colony. Finally, it focuses on the experience of the Libyans in Italy and shows how the presence there of colonial subjects in some respects overturned the "colonial situation", undermining the relationship of power between Italians and North Africans.

INTRODUCTION

On 23 October 1911, just twenty days after Italian troops landed in Tripoli, a massive revolt surprised the colonial soldiers in the Shara al-Shatt oasis, just outside the city. The Italians had come to Libya[1] certain of easy victory, convinced that the native population would rise up against the Turks. As a result of the revolt, the Italians in Tripoli suddenly realized that they had wrongly evaluated the colonial venture: after they had landed, the Arabs formed a coalition with the Turks and organized a common resistance to Italian occupation. Italian soldiers, caught off guard, reacted with brutality. An unspecified number of Arabs were shot in the hours following

* The research for this article is part of the project "Four Centuries of Labour Camps: War, Rehabilitation, Ethnicity", directed by the International Institute of Social History (IISH) and the Netherlands Institute for War, Holocaust and Genocide Studies (NIOD), and funded by the Netherlands Organization for Scientific Research (NWO).
1. Libya was then constituted by the Turkish-Ottoman provinces of Tripolitania and Cyrenaica.

the revolt.[2] Giovanni Giolitti, Italy's Prime Minister, ordered the immediate deportation to Italy of all "arrested rioters".[3] This deportation, which might have seemed like an exceptional measure connected to the gravity of the situation, marked the start of an enduring period of deportations and transportations of Libyans to Italy, which lasted until the end of the Italian colonial occupation of Libya in 1943. In fact, the forced removal of Libyans was not merely a corollary of the Italian colonizer's repressive measures, but an integral part of the colonial punitive system. In particular, the deportation of Libyans who had not been tried and the transportation of convicts became standard practice in managing the colony from 1911 to the 1930s.[4]

The deportation of Libyans was not the first case of Italian repressive practice in its colonial possessions. Italian colonialism developed firstly in Eastern Africa, with the invasion of Eritrea (1890–1941) and Somalia (1892–1941), thereafter in North Africa, with the military occupation of Libya (1911–1943). Finally, with the conquest of Ethiopia in 1935, the Fascist regime proclaimed the birth of the Italian Empire, which collapsed a few years later, during World War II.[5] Between 1886 and 1892, when Italy took its first steps in Eritrea, military authorities ordered the transfer to Italy of a hundred people of different origins.[6] In 1937, deportation measures struck again against natives from Italian East Africa. As part of the harsh repression that followed the attack on Viceroy Rodolfo Graziani, Governor in Ethiopia, the colonial government ordered the confinement in Italy of some 400 Ethiopians.[7]

Both in terms of the number of subjects involved and its long duration, the transfer of Libyans to Italy was the most significant deportation of colonial subjects in Italian colonial history. The reasons why the colonial authorities resorted to deportation in Libya more often than in the case of other Italian possessions still need to be clarified. In general, this issue is connected to the prison systems in each colony and, in particular, to the question of whether there were sites suitable to confine subjects considered harmful for the colony's security. In Eritrea, Nocra performed this role, with Eritrean subjects previously deported to Italy also being transferred to

2. Regarding the first month of the Italian occupation of Libya and the Shara al-Shatt revolt, see Angelo Del Boca, *Gli italiani in Libia*, 2 vols (Milan, 2013), I, pp. 96–136.

3. Telegram from Giolitti to Caneva, Commander-in-Chief in Tripoli, 24 October 1911, in Archivio Centrale dello Stato, Rome [hereafter, ACS], Carte Giolitti, folder 22, file 57.

4. Nicola Labanca, *La guerra italiana per la Libia (1911–1931)* (Bologna, 2012), p. 70.

5. For a general overview of Italian colonialism, see *idem, Oltremare. Storia dell'espansione coloniale italiana* (Bologna, 2002).

6. The deportees came from Eritrea, Ethiopia, Sudan, Somalia, Arab *jazira*, and also from Greece, as part of the Ottoman Empire. See Marco Lenci, "Prove di repressione. Deportati eritrei in Italia (1886–1893)", *Africa*, 1 (2003), pp. 1–34, 7–8.

7. Paolo Borruso, *L'Africa al confino. La deportazione etiopica in Italia (1937–39)* (Manduria, 2003).

this prison-island. As I will explain later, Italian authorities made little use of the other option open to their counterparts in other empires, namely intercolonial deportation/transportation, i.e. the possibility to transport Libyan convicts to, say, Nocra in Eritrea.

The Italian case is largely out of step with the policy regarding deportation and transportation enacted by the other European colonial powers. The history of Italian deportation and transportation chiefly concerns colonial subjects, who were transferred from colonies to the metropole. The other colonial powers in most cases resorted to penal transportation in order to remove metropolitan convicts, transferring them from the metropole to the colonies. For the most part, colonized subjects were transported to other colonial possessions.[8] The only exceptions to this were found in the French Empire. Indeed, following anti-imperial revolts, some Algerians were transferred to southern France in the nineteenth century.[9] The internment of Algerians in France decreased and finally ended when the French army succeeded in repressing the revolts. As I will explain later, the nexus between the control over the colony and the transfer of Libyans is also the key to understanding the forced removal of colonial subjects to Italy. Nevertheless, unlike the French deportations, the coerced transfers of Libyans to Italy lasted the entire colonial period, from 1911 to 1943.

This article addresses in what way the Italian case may be considered peculiar. Specifically, it analyses the practices of deportation and transportation from Libya to Italy within the imperial landscape of the twentieth century. Even if exceptional, the analysis of the Italian case integrates the study of the general theme of this volume, namely punitive relocations from a colonial perspective, and from a double viewpoint. On the one hand, it was left to the colonial "periphery" to decide whether to transfer Libyan subjects to Italy. On the other, the choice of whether to confine the majority of the prisoners in the south of Italy also originated from the "colonial" view of the southern regions, as I will explain later.

The first part of this article presents a general sketch of the deportation and transportation of Libyans. Highlighting the overlapping of the penal

---

8. For the general framework of penal transportation in Western empires, see Clare Anderson and Hamish Maxwell-Stewart, "Convict Labour and the Western Empires, 1415–1954", in R. Aldrich and K. McKenzie (eds), *The Routledge History of Western Empires* (London [etc.], 2014), pp. 102–117. For two of the most important historical instances of penal transportation, British India and French Guiana, see Clare Anderson, "Sepoys, Servants and Settlers: Convict Transportation in the Indian Ocean, 1787–1945", in F. Dikötter and I. Brown (eds), *Cultures of Confinement: A History of the Prison in Africa, Asia, and Latin America* (New York, 2007), pp. 185–220; Danielle Donet-Vincent, *De soleil et de silences. Histoire des bagnes de Guyane* (Paris, 2003); Michel Pierre, *Bagnards. La terre de la grand punition, Cayenne 1852–1953* (Paris, 2000); Peter Redfield, *Space in the Tropics: From Convicts to Rockets in French Guiana* (Berkeley, CA [etc.], 2000).
9. Sylvie Thénault, *L'Algérie, une colonie aux marges de l'archipel punitif*, available at http://convictvoyages.org/expert-essays/lalgerie; last accessed 19 January 2018.

system and military practices, here I emphasize the difficult dialogue between "centre" and "periphery" concerning security issues inside the colony. The second part focuses on the experience of the Libyans in Italy. The expulsions of the Libyans from their native soil aimed foremost to tame the resistance movements against the colonizer. But the presence of colonial subjects in Italy also entailed different outcomes to those which the Italian authorities had foreseen, including the upturning of the roles of Italians and Libyans, which subverted the colonial relationship of power.

DEPORTATION AND PENAL TRANSPORTATION WITHIN THE ITALIAN COLONIAL SYSTEM

We can divide the forced removal of Libyans to Italy into roughly three categories: collective deportations following serious military defeats for the Italian army; individual deportations of political dissidents or of supposed opponents; and transportation of convicts already detained in colonial prisons.[10]

It is difficult to establish a clear-cut division between deportations as administrative measures and deportations for political reasons. The latter were implemented over the entire colonial period; they were intended to strike against "rebels" or potential "rebels", i.e. both combatants and political figures whose presence in Libya could undermine Italian authority. Deportation was frequently ordered on the basis of very generic accusations or the mere suspicion that someone represented a potential threat. The Libyans deported for political reasons also included people acquitted by colonial courts or who had already served a term of imprisonment in Libya, but whom military authorities judged dangerous to the security of the colony.[11] The implementation of this measure has to be set in the context of Italy's "native policy" in Libya.[12] At times, certain notables were exiled as part of the so-called chiefs policy, i.e. the alliances established between the colonial authorities and some figures within the Libyan political leadership.

The lack of lists of subjects who left Libya, and the fact that an unspecified number of people died during the crossings, makes it difficult to

---

10. Since they were connected with the political appraisal by the colonial authorities, transportations and deportations had an undetermined duration.

11. Simone Bernini, "Documenti sulla repressione italiana in Libia agli inizi della colonizzazione (1911–1918)", in Nicola Labanca (ed.), *Un nodo. Immagini e documenti sulla repressione coloniale italiana in Libia* (Manduria, 2002), p. 141.

12. The same pattern also characterized Italy's native policy in Eritrea. See Antonio M. Morone, "Istituzioni, fra assimilazione e amministrazione indiretta", in Gian Paolo Calchi Novati (ed.), *Il colonialismo italiano e l'Africa* (Rome, 2011), pp. 213–235; and Isabella Rosoni, *La colonia eritrea. La prima amministrazione coloniale italiana (1880–1912)* (Macerata, 2006).

estimate the exact number of Libyan deportees in Italy during the colonial era. According to the Libyan Studies Centre,[13] the Italian authorities deported about 5,000–6,000 Libyans to Italy.[14] The scholar Mario Missori estimates that there were 4,000 deportees in Italy between 1911 and 1918.[15] All things considered, we can state with some confidence that, after World War I, deportation no longer involved large groups of subjects, but mainly individuals: notables or leading figures of the resistance movement.[16]

The main reason for collective deportations was the attempt to clear out the territory that had been the theatre of revolts and to expel as many people as possible. This happened at the beginning of the colonial occupation, after the above-mentioned Shara al-Shatt revolt, and in 1915, after the battle of Qardabiah, during the "great Arabic revolt", which forced the Italians to retreat to a few coastal outposts. Undoubtedly, deportation aimed to intimidate the colonial population. In particular, in 1911 and in 1912, the decision to deport did not correspond to any real individualized appraisal of the dangerousness of the subjects involved. After the military disaster in Adowa (Ethiopia) in 1896 – which was the most serious military defeat for any European army during the imperial age – the Italian government needed to hide the military difficulties that Italy was encountering in Libya from other European colonial powers.[17] After the Shara al-Shatt revolt, in order to stop the massacres of Libyans by Italian soldiers, which were a clear indication of the weakness of the colonial army, Giolitti, the prime minister, ordered deportations. The arrests were made en masse, which is why beggars, labourers, peasants, wealthy owners, and storekeepers were all

13. "Libyan Studies Centre" is the name with which the Libyan Jehad Centre for Historical Studies was known abroad. It was founded in 1978 to foster studies on Libyan history and in particular on the Libyan resistance (*jihad* in Arabic) to the Italian colonizer (see the Centre's website (in Arabic) at http://libsc.org.ly/mrkaz/; last accessed 19 January 2018). Between 2001 and 2005, the Libyan Centre and the Istituto Italiano per l'Africa e l'Oriente (Italian Institute for Africa and the East) directed a research project focused mainly on the Libyan deportees in Italy during the colonial era.

14. Libyan Jehad Centre for Historical Studies, Information Bulletin No. 1 (undated, but probably 1990s). Nicola Labanca also reports the same figure. See Labanca, *La guerra italiana per la Libia*, p. 71.

15. Mario Missori, "Una ricerca sui deportati libici nelle carte dell'Archivio centrale dello Stato", in *Fonti e problemi della Politica Coloniale italiana, Atti del convegno, Taormina-Messina, 23–29 ottobre 1989*, 2 vols (Rome, 1996), I, pp. 253–258.

16. These figures do not include about 5,000 Libyans transferred to two Sicilian villages, Floridia and Canicattini Bagni (Syracuse) in 1915. We will discuss this group of Libyans later.

17. Giolitti's concern emerges clearly from the first telegrams he sent to Caneva after the Shara al-Shatt revolt. In particular, Giolitti asked for precise news about what happened and the number of deaths, in order to avoid the "discredit" of Italy, both within and outside the country. See ACS, Carte Giolitti, folder 22, file 57, telegrams from Giolitti to Caneva, 24 and 29 October 1911.

captured together.[18] Old men, women, and minors were also transferred to Italian penal colonies.[19]

After Giolitti had ordered the first deportation of Libyans in 1911, all other deportations were ordered by the authorities in the colony.[20] Indeed, the Minister of the Colonies distinguished between deportees for administrative reasons and deportees who could be tried according to what the military authorities charged them with. The latter were usually accused of threatening the security of the colony and were generally defined as "rebels".[21] In 1912, the "Commission for the Prisoners of War" suggested putting all the Libyans charged with specific crimes on trial, in order to give more "legitimacy" to the deportations. The Commission highlighted all the negative effects of deportation not only for the subjects transferred to Italy, but also for those who were in Libya, because it fuelled feelings of hostility towards the Italians. However, in 1913, Italian authorities justified the suspension of their trial, maintaining that either they could be tried in a single trial for all the rebels at a later date, or they could be pardoned for fostering reconciliation in Libya. There was, in fact, an important fluidity in their legal status: although they were deported as an administrative measure, those subjects were considered prisoners of war. In fact, this group of deportees was seen as a potential bargaining chip in negotiations for a peace agreement.

Convict transportation began after the collective deportations of 1911–1912. It was the very prison rules for Libya – approved in 1913 – which established that the Libyans sentenced to penalties of more than six months' imprisonment should be transferred to Italy. In fact, the colony lacked suitable facilities for the prisons. Indeed, as late as in 1931, the colonial government had still not built new correctional facilities, and all the spaces employed as jails were insufficient and unsuitable with regard to their "juridical, disciplinary, and sanitary needs". According to Adalgiso Ravizza, the shortage of correctional facilities in Libya had convinced the governors in Libya to command the transportation of convicts to Italy.[22] Mariano D'Amelio, for his part, maintained that, since the most "fearsome

18. See Luigi Tùccari, *I governi militari della Libia (1911–1919)* (Rome, 1994), p. 264.
19. Because of the lack of lists of subjects who left Libya, it is not possible to indicate the number of women and minors deported to Italy.
20. One of the distinctive features of Italian colonial history was the colonial government's far-reaching autonomy from the central government in Rome. See Nicola Labanca, "L'internamento coloniale italiano", in Costantino Di Sante (ed.), *I campi di concentramento in Italia. Dall'internamento alla deportazione (1940–1945)* (Milan, 2001), pp. 40–67, 47.
21. See the correspondence between Bertolini, Minister of the Colonies, and the governors of Tripolitania and Cyrenaica in ACS, Ministero dell'interno, Direzione generale della pubblica sicurezza, Divisione di polizia giudiziaria, 1913–1915, published in Salaheddin Hasan Sury and Giampaolo Malgeri (eds), *Gli esiliati libici nel periodo coloniale (1911–1916). Raccolta documentaria* (Rome, 2005), pp. 50–51.
22. Adalgiso Ravizza, *La Libia nel suo ordinamento giuridico* (Padua, 1931), p. 236.

convicts" had been transferred to Italy, the penal transportation had facilitated the management of outdoor work for the prisoners, who were put to work in the penal agricultural colonies in Libya.[23]

In October 1915, the Ministry of the Colonies indicated to the colonial government that the transportation of convicts to Italy was not permitted by the Italian judicial system and was therefore "illegal".[24] In order to curb transportation to Italy, in 1915 the Ministry of the Interior set out to study the possibility of confining the Arabs who had been assigned to the motherland within Libya. The Ministry of the Colonies began searching for a site in the colony where it could build penitentiaries and exile the "rebels". The colonial government in Libya immediately put a stop to the search being undertaken by the Ministry of the Colonies.[25] The military authorities on the ground were well aware that control over the "fourth shore" was too weak and limited for Italy to plan new prisons and/or facilities for confinement in Libya itself.

In 1915, the Minister of the Colonies had proposed to the Minister of the Interior to transfer 600 Libyans who had deserted from the native troops to Sicily, in the province of Palermo.[26] Due to the war effort, there was a considerable shortage of labour in Sicily in that period. In particular, the minister thought that the Libyans could be assigned to agricultural work. The Minister of Agriculture was opposed to this labour exploitation: "it is also more dangerous the fact that in the colony, deportation is depicted as a slave trade for the farm work in Italy".[27] The minister feared that the association between deportation and slavery entailed a further weakening in the international position of Italy. Therefore, Martini, who had been

---

23. Mariano D'Amelio, "Di alcuni caratteri della legislazione penale in Libia", *Scuola Positiva*, 1–2 (1914), p. 20. The first agricultural penitentiary colonies were established in Libya in 1915, when some convicts were sent to the experimental field in Sidi Mesri, in the neighbourhood of Tripoli. Later, in 1923, the penal colony in Sghedeida, twelve kilometres from Tripoli, was founded. Two other colonies in Cyrenaica, in Coefia and Berka, were established in 1919 and 1923 respectively. See Ravizza, *La Libia nel suo ordinamento giuridico*, pp. 240–246. Adalgiso Ravizza and Mariano D'Amelio were prominent jurists who were designated judges in Libia and in Eritrea.

24. Telegram from the Ministry of the Colonies to the Governor of Tripolitania and Cyrenaica, 31 October 1915, in Archivio storico diplomatico del Ministero affari esteri, Archivio storico del Ministero dell'Africa Italiana [hereafter ASDMAE, ASMAI], folder 112/2, quoted in Bernini, "Documenti sulla repressione italiana in Libia", pp. 142–143.

25. *Ibid.*, p. 150.

26. The reports on this issue do not specify to which type of facility (penitentiary, penal colony, or other) those subjects would be transferred.

27. In Italian: "è anche più pericoloso che in colonia la deportazione sia rappresentata come una tratta di schiavi per la lavorazione delle terre in Italia". Quote from the telegram from the Ministry of Agriculture to the General Direction for Public Security, 6 June 1915, in ACS, Ministero dell'interno, Direzione generale della pubblica sicurezza, Divisione polizia giudiziaria [hereafter MI, DGPS, DPG], 1913–1915, folder 69, in Sury and Malgeri, *Gli esiliati libici nel periodo coloniale (1911–1916)*, p. 30.

Governor of Eritrea from 1897 to 1907, tried to transfer the 600 Libyans to that colony and proposed employing them in the construction of railways. Due to a large number of Eritrean workers employed as *askari* (i.e. native soldier) in Libya, there was also a shortage of labour in Eritrea. Cerrina Feroni, governor of the colony, noted that the presence of the Libyans in Eritrea would be troublesome for their surveillance and incur costs owing to the need to build barracks in the penal colony in Assab. In conclusion, he maintained that it was easier to arrange for their accommodation in Italy.

Also, in 1915, the deportees became "captives" (*ostaggi*): Tassoni, Governor of Tripolitania, banned the terms "deportations", "confinements", and other similar words from the official records concerning the forced removal of Libyans to Italy. According to Tassoni, the term "captives" did not provoke "any resentment from the native population against the government".[28] In fact, the Italian government actually intended to use the deportees as hostages: in 1916, the Minister of the Colonies bore down on the most prominent Libyan leaders confined in Italy to secure the release of Italian prisoners held by the enemy.[29] During World War I, Libya was a country "in the grip of anarchy", as Giovanni Ameglio, then Governor of Tripolitania, reported in 1917. Economic conditions in the colony were disastrous, and a significant part of the Libyan population lived in destitute circumstances. From the beginning of 1914, with Turkish support, the Libyan anti-colonial resistance inflicted severe defeats on the Italian army. During the "great Arabic revolt", as this period of hostilities in Libya was called, many Italian soldiers were taken prisoner. In August 1915, the Italian army controlled just two cities in Libya: Tripoli and Homs.

World War I was definitely the most intense and complicated period for the deportations of Libyans to Italy. The repressive measures carried out by the Italian army intensified as the siege conditions experienced by the colonizers in Libya worsened. From 1914 to 1918, deportations to Italy increased remarkably. From 1913 to 1918, most convicts were transferred to Sicily, where 2,444 Libyan "captives" arrived in its prisons and penal colonies, and 5,000 *askaris* were confined in the province of Syracuse.[30] During World War I, the Italian authorities ordered deportation from Libya as an administrative measure and for political reasons, the transportation of

---

28. In Italian: "nella popolazione indigena risentimento alcuno contro il Governo". Letter from the Governor of Tripolitania, Tassoni, to the Ministry of the Colonies, Tripoli, 28 June 1915, in *ibid.*, p. 32.

29. Tùccari, *I governi militari della Libia*, p. 265.

30. Colonial powers used the term *askaris* to refer to those African soldiers who fought in their armies in Africa. The Libyan *askaris* were transferred to Floridia and Canicattini Bagni after they had started to defect in Tripolitania. See Del Boca, *Gli italiani in Libia*, I, pp. 300–301. Concerning the deportation of Libyans in Sicily, see Francesca Di Pasquale, "I deportati libici in Sicilia (1911–1933)", in Carla Ghezzi and Salaheddin Hasan Sury (eds), *Terzo convegno sugli esiliati libici nel periodo coloniale* (Rome, 2005), pp. 137–147.

convicts who had already been incarcerated within the prisons of the colony, and even the transfer of "lunatics", to be "treated" in psychiatric hospitals in the motherland.[31]

Although the flow of deportations and transportation to Italy continually increased from 1911 to 1918, peaking during World War I, on several occasions the measure was considered counterproductive owing to its political implications in Libya. Italian authorities tried endlessly to find a balance between the need for military control of the colony and the goals of reconciliation with their Libyan counterparts. On the one hand, authorities in Italy tried to restrict the transfers to Italy, while, on the other, in Libya, military and civil governors insisted on their prolongation in order to allow them to continue applying the measure. On the whole, until the beginning of the Fascist government, the "men on the spot" prevailed and military considerations triumphed over political considerations.

The flow of convicts to the metropole was directly connected to the fact that the Italian army's control over Libyan territory was weak. When its control over the colony and its population increased, the forced removals decreased. The turning point for this shift was the so-called pacification of Libya enacted by the Fascist government from 1922. This was the recourse to very cruel repressive practices in order to permanently crush the resistance movement. In particular, in 1930–1931, Lieutenant Governor Rodolfo Graziani and Governor Pietro Badoglio ordered the confinement of the whole nomadic and semi-nomadic population of Cyrenaica, to be held in twenty concentration camps in the Sirtica region.[32] The main goal of the camps was to interrupt the resistance movement's support network among the population. All the camps were finally closed in 1934. Scholars estimate that the number of Libyan prisoners in the camps was around 100,000–120,000, and that during their internment the death toll was as high as 40,000 to 48,000.[33]

31. See the following records: the report by G. Girardi entitled *Sulle condizioni degli Stabilimenti carcerari al 30 giugno 1916 e sul lavoro dei detenuti*, in ACS, Ministero della giustizia, Direzione generale degli istituti di prevenzione e di pena, Studi per la riforma penitenziaria, folder 1, file 3 and *Prospetto degli stabilimenti penali al 9 febbraio 1915*, in *ibid.*, folder 2, file 6. Further data regarding the transfer of "lunatics" to Italy during World War I can be found in Archivio di Stato di Siracusa, Prefettura, 1916–1917, folder 2332, file "Ministero delle Colonie, trasporto dementi arabi. Esercizio 1916–17". As in the majority of other colonial contexts, in Libya the concept of mental illness was closely connected to the cultural parameters of the colonizers and, more specifically, to the necessity of building a society based on the clear racial separation between "black" and "whites".

32. Cyrenaica was de facto governed by the Senussi brotherhood, the religious and political organization leading the resistance movement against the colonizer.

33. On the camps in Libya see Labanca, "L'internamento coloniale italiano"; Gustavo Ottolenghi (ed.), *Gli italiani e il colonialismo. I campi di detenzione italiani in Africa* (Milan, 1997); and Giorgio Rochat, *Le guerre italiane in Libia e in Etiopia dal 1896 al 1939* (Udine, 2009).

The adoption of this brutal "scorched-earth policy" in Libya also marked the end of the policy of collective removal to Italy. During the Fascist era, only a few dozen Libyan notables were confined in Italy. The policy of exiling notables lay in between the ruthless repression carried out in Libya by the Fascist regime and the need to keep channels of negotiation open with exponents from elite Libyan circles. In particular, in 1930, the government in Cyrenaica ordered the deportation of thirty-one *zawia* chiefs and of Hassan Reda es-Senussi, grandson of the Chief of the Senussi brotherhood.[34] In 1927, police rules encoded the confinement (*confino*) of native citizens.[35] In particular, it established the confinement in a place of the colony or in a municipality in Italy of those who had been "cautioned or those who had committed or clearly shown the intention of committing acts to subvert" the rules and security of the colony.[36] It is noteworthy that the Fascist government employed the *confino* to banish both Libyan and Italian opponents and supposed opponents.

LIBYAN DEPORTEES IN ITALY

In 1911–1912, during the collective deportations that followed the Shara al-Shatt revolt, Libyans were initially transferred to penal colonies on the islands of Ustica and Tremiti, and subsequently also to the penal colonies on the islands of Favignana and Ponza, and to the military penitentiary in Gaeta. After this first phase, deportees who had already been sentenced in Libya were also transported to many other Italian prisons. Below is a map illustrating the twenty-one places to which Libyans were confined during the colonial era.

In broad terms, the prisoners subject to administrative measures were transferred to penal colonies, as were political opponents (or supposed political opponents). The detainees already imprisoned in the colony were sent to the prisons. However, this distinction was not very clear, because some of the Libyan notables, removed for political reasons and without trial, were also sent to prison. During the collective deportations in 1911–1912, the majority of those deported from Tripoli were sent to the penal colonies on Ustica and Tremiti, and those from Benghazi, Derna, and Homs to Gaeta and Favignana.[37] The Libyans were transferred, in fact, to the *colonie coatti*, i.e. penal colonies, where they were subject to the *domicilio coatto*, an administrative measure and "preventive" tool for public order that had been in force in Italy since 1863. In this respect, their status was the same as that of the

---

34. The *zawia* were the political, economic, and social centres constituting the Senussi brotherhood's network in Cyrenaica.
35. These rules were approved by Royal Decree, 8 May 1927, n. 884. See, in particular, articles 181–186. On this topic, see also Ravizza, *La Libia nel suo ordinamento giuridico*, pp. 106–107.
36. In Italian "ammoniti o che abbiano commesso o manifestato il deliberato proposito di commettere atti diretti a sovvertire".
37. Tùccari, *I governi militari della Libia*, p. 264.

Figure 1. A map of the places of deportation of Libyans in Italy.
Data deduced from ASDMAE, ASMAI, vol. II, folders: 112/1, 112/2, 141/1; Francesco Sulpizi and Salaheddin Hasan Sury (eds), *Primo convegno sugli esiliati libici nel periodo coloniale* (Rome and Tripoli, 2002); Sulpizi and Sury, *Secondo convegno sugli esiliati libici*; Ghezzi and Sury, *Terzo convegno sugli esiliati libici*.

Italian "undesirables", such as vagrants, the "indolent", as well as political opponents. Nevertheless, for the convicts, in terms of penal regime there was no significant difference between *colonie coatti* and prisons.[38]

As the map shows, all the places to which the Italian authorities transferred the Libyans, except for Gorgona and Florence, were located in the south of Italy. One can hypothesize that this choice was the result of the link made by the Italian authorities between southern citizens and "Arabic" citizens. As already highlighted by the literature, the policies implemented in the southern regions in the decades after Italian unification were largely influenced by an "oriental" view of the southern population, who were sometimes considered to be similar to African subjects.[39] However, before becoming the place to which Libyans were transferred, southern Italy had already been designated the favoured territory for the establishment of penal facilities. Penitentiary policy enacted by the first Italian governments located in Sicily five of Italy's eight penal colonies.[40] Thereafter, around the end of the nineteenth century, Sardinia became the preferred site for instituting penitentiary agricultural colonies.[41] At the turn of the twentieth century, the ruling classes chose southern regions for the development of penal sites as a result of a combination of considerations: the isolation of the places selected; the intention to colonize those parts of the country that were considered "virgin" and "wild", through penitentiary agricultural colonization; and, finally, the racialized vision of the southern populations, to which I have already referred. However, Sicily's proximity to the Libyan coast also played a role in the decision to transfer the majority of Libyans to this region. In particular, during World War I, the Italian authorities arranged the flow of deportees as follows: they were transferred first to Syracuse and, afterwards, male adults were destined for Favignana, "insanes" for Aversa (Caserta, Campania region), minors for Noto (Syracuse), and women for the female penitentiary in Trani (Bari, Puglia region).[42]

---

38. Daniela Fozzi, "Una 'specialità italiana'. Le colonie coatte nel Regno d'Italia", in Mario Da Passano (ed.), *Le colonie penali nell'Europa dell'Ottocento* (Rome, 2004), pp. 215–290.

39. See, among others, John Dickie, *Darkest Italy: The Nation and Stereotypes of the Mezzogiorno, 1860–1900* (New York, 1999); Silvana Patriarca, *Italianità. La costruzione del carattere nazionale* (Rome and Bari, 2010); Jane Schneider (ed.), *Italy's "Southern Question": Orientalism in One Country* (Oxford and New York, 1998).

40. Di Pasquale, "I deportati libici in Sicilia (1911–1933)", p. 142.

41. On the Sardinian penal colonies, see Franca Mele, "L'Asinara e le colonie penali in Sardegna. Un'isola penitenziaria?", in Da Passano, *Le colonie penali nell'Europa dell'Ottocento*, pp. 189–212; Vittorio Gazale and Stefano A. Tedde (eds), *Le carte liberate. Viaggio negli archivi e nei luoghi delle colonie penali della Sardegna* (Sassari, 2016).

42. See *Prospetto degli stabilimenti penali al 9 febbraio 1915*, in folder 2, file 6 in ACS, Ministero della giustizia, Direzione generale degli istituti di prevenzione e di pena, Studi per la riforma penitenziaria and Archivio di Stato di Siracusa, Prefettura, 1916–1917, folder 2332, file "Ministero delle Colonie, trasporto dementi arabi. Esercizio 1916–17".

Figure 2. Arrival of Libyan deportees on Ustica, on board the steamship "Rumania", 29 October 1911. The five guards in the foreground of the picture have been retouched by a pencil, under unknown circumstances. The Archive of the "Centro Studi Isola di Ustica" received the picture in this condition.
Archive of the "Centro Studi e Documentazione Isola di Ustica". Used by permission.

The conquest of Libya and the extensive propaganda which supported the colonial invasion contributed to developing a new national consciousness however. The colonial occupation triggered a unifying process, attenuating the regional and gender divisions that had prevailed throughout the first decades of Italian history after unification. At the same time, this process was fostered by the spread of a feeling of identity that put the Italian "race" in opposition to other "races". Therefore, the social, cultural, and gender hierarchies turned into a colonial and racist hierarchy that opposed the "white" Italian to the "black" "Arab".[43] As early as 1911, with the arrival of the Libyan deportees in Italy the majority of the population shared a sense of the "innate" superiority of Europeans over Africans. In most cases, the local communities refused to accept the Libyans who arrived. The sense of hostility towards them was also fuelled by the fact that the Libyan deportees were considered enemies

---

43. Lucia Re notes that the Libyan war fostered the unification of Italians by displacing racism from inside to outside the body of the nation and its people. See Lucia Re, "Italians and the Invention of Race: The Poetics and Politics of Difference in the Struggle over Libya, 1890–1913", *California Italian Studies*, 1:1 (2010), pp. 1–58, 6.

who had massacred Italian soldiers.[44] However, on the small islands where
the first Libyan prisoners were confined, a reversal of roles occurred, and
the local population considered the colonized peoples deported to those
penal colonies as "invaders".

The population of Ustica, in particular, strongly opposed the arrival of
the Libyans, and members of the city council resigned in protest. Certainly,
the presence of Libyans in Italy often aggravated the unstable political and
economic balance on the islands on which they were confined.[45] The sanitary situation was particularly critical. Those deported to Ustica, who were
often carriers of cholera, died in large numbers, also due to the frigid temperatures and the overcrowding at the barracks where they lived.[46] Some
infectious diseases also spread among the employees of the penal colony
and the local population. The problems connected with sanitary conditions
were the main reason behind the protest among Ustica's citizens. However,
the way in which they expressed their discomfort denoted a racist view of
Libyan prisoners, who were described as "sickening individuals and pla-
gued by thousands of infectious diseases", and as "the race considered as a
vehicle of infection".[47] In the meantime, from 1911 to 1912, a large number
of deportees died from disease and from the conditions of their imprisonment: in Ustica, 127 out of 900 Libyans died, which is about seventeen per
cent of those who were originally transferred to that penal colony; on the
islands of Tremiti, about a third of Libyans died, i.e. 437 out of 1,366
deportees.[48] In 1912, one of the physicians employed in the penal colony in
Ustica asked for some of the barracks used for the Libyans to be closed, as
they "must not be considered as shelters for human beings".[49]

Even journalists who – circumventing government censorship[50] –
denounced the conditions under which the deportees were held in the

44. Tùccari, *I governi militari della Libia*, p. 265. See also telegram from police headquarters in
Palermo to the Prefect in Palermo, 7 January 1912, in Archivio di Stato di Palermo (hereafter
ASPa), Prefettura, Gabinetto, folder 14.

45. Francesca Di Pasquale, "I libici nella colonia penale di Ustica (1911–1912)", in Sulpizi and
Sury, *Primo convegno su gli esiliati libici nel periodo coloniale*, pp. 115–123, 121–122.

46. *Ibid.*, pp. 118–119.

47. In Italian "esseri nauseabondi ed infestati da mille malattie infettive"; "la razza considerata
veicolo di infezione"; "devono essere esclusi dal numero dei rifugi per esseri umani". Quotes from
a letter by a group of Ustica citizens sent to the Prefect in Palermo, 29 November 1911, in ASPa,
Prefettura, folder 458.

48. On the death rate in Ustica see *ibid.*, p. 117; for the Tremiti islands see Claudio Moffa, "I
deportati libici alle Tremiti dopo la rivolta di Sciara Sciatt", in *Fonti e problemi della politica
coloniale italiana*, pp. 258–286.

49. See the letter from the Mayor in Ustica, Bonura, sent to the Prefect in Palermo, 9 June 1915, in
ASPa, Prefettura, Archivio Generale, folder 205.

50. In November 1911, the government prohibited journalists from visiting the Libyan deportees
in the Italian penal colonies. With regard to Ustica, see the telegram from the Ministry of Interior
to the Prefect of Palermo, 2 November 1911, in ASPa, Prefettura, Gabinetto, folder 12.

Figure 3. Photographer Giuseppe Barraco, from Ustica, with a Libyan deportee. The picture depicts the "black" servant, barefoot, and the "white" master in a typical colonial pose. *Archive of the "Centro Studi e Documentazione Isola di Ustica". Used by permission.*

penal colonies adopted at best an exotic language to describe the Libyans; in
most cases, they were explicitly racist.[51] The language adopted by the
socialist journalist Paolo Valera, a strong opponent of the colonial venture,
is particularly remarkable. In 1912, he claimed, the people confined
on Ponza Island were "muzzy", "apathetic, glassy-eyed", and showed
an "idiotic" attitude.[52] However, it is in his description of women that
Valera shared the commonest conceptions of colonial racism towards the
colonized populations. Valera wrote:

> Even here, the women who arrived and who were convoyed by the policemen and
> by the Carabinieri are, for the most part, ugly. Among [a group of about] fifty
> [females], we saw only three or four young women of a true Greek and sound
> beauty. One in particular aroused [great] admiration: she is blonde, diaphanous,
> with large, sparkling eyes a mouth made for kissing.[53]

Disparaged and reduced to objects of sexual desire, the women of the
colonized population were at the crossing of several tensions within
colonial societies. On the one hand, their control was considered essential
for their role as mothers; on the other, the colonial government tried to keep
under its control the sexual relations between "white" men and "black"
women, worrying that the ruling "race" might "mingle" and, therefore, be
"tainted" with the colonized.[54]

At the beginning of the twentieth century, this racist gaze was also fuelled
by "scientific" discourse on human "races" based on the theses of the
Positivist School. Colonial expansion had opened up a huge terrain for
examination, classification, and investigation by criminal anthropologists.
Libyans in Italy were the "other" at home: Africa within Italy's national
boundaries. Their presence aroused the interest of physicians, criminologists, and anthropologists. It offered a priceless opportunity to study the
deportees' physical traits, in order to observe the "characteristics" of the
Libyan population and their supposed inclination to crime. In the Libyan
colony, in 1912, a service for the identification and registration of detainees
by means of photographs and dactyloscopy (i.e. fingerprint identification)

---

51. See, for example, the article by Marino, entitled "Gli arabi prigionieri s'adattano al nuovo
regime", published in *Giornale di Sicilia*, 7 November 1911.
52. In Italian: "istupiditi"; "apatici, con gli occhi imbambolati"; "il loro atteggiamento è
dell'ebete", in Paolo Valera, "'Stazione sanitaria'. Gli arabi espulsi dal loro paese", *Avanti!*, 15
January 1912, published in Sury and Malgeri, *Gli esiliati libici nel periodo coloniale (1911–
1916)*, p. 45.
53. In Italian: "Anche qui le donne arrivate e scortate dai questurini e dai carabinieri sono in
maggioranza brutte. Fra una cinquantina non si sono vedute che tre o quattro giovanette di una
vera bellezza greca e sana. Una fra tutte ha sollevato l'ammirazione: bionda, diafana, con gli
occhioni pieni di faville e una bocca fatta per i baci", in *ibid.*
54. For a general overview of this topic, see Frederick Cooper and Ann L. Stoler (eds), *Tensions of
Empire: Colonial Cultures in a Bourgeois World* (Berkeley, CA, 1997).

was established.[55] Its purpose was to acquire "knowledge of the population of the new colony, knowledge that will be useful both from a scientific and from a practical standpoint".[56]

In 1915, Emanuele Mirabella, who was in charge of the health service in the penal colony in Favignana (and who had been a physician at the criminal psychiatric hospital in Aversa), examined the Libyans there. He carried out a study in order to compare their characteristics with those of ordinary Italian citizens and criminals. He highlighted "the degenerative features typical of this new population" and concluded that Libyans were inferior also to Italian criminals. After his study, Mirabella wrote a book about Libyan deportees in Favignana.[57] He dedicated the book to Enrico Ferri, one of the most prominent exponents of Italian criminal anthropology.

In that same year, about 5,000 Libyans were moved to Sicily. They were *askaris*, whom the Italian authorities transferred to the island along with their families in order to avoid them joining the resistance movement. Umberto Grabbi, an expert on exotic diseases and professor at the University of Messina, and Nello Piccioni of the National Museum of Anthropology and Ethnology in Florence studied this large group of Libyans, who had been relocated to two small villages in Sicily, namely Floridia and Canicattini Bagni (Syracuse).[58]

Starting from World War I, a number of "lunatics" were also transferred by the Italian authorities.[59] Clearly, their transfer to Italy had no punitive goal, nor was it intended to prevent the formation of rebel groups, as was the case with the deportations, the subject of the present study. Moreover, their internment in Italy reflected the interest in the mental illness of the natives expressed by the Italian government from 1912 onwards.[60] What deserves to be highlighted, instead, is that deportees, *askaris*, and "lunatics" were relevant for criminologists and anthropologists in the same way, according to a view that subsumed them within the same category, based on their "racial" identity. Since there was no mental asylum in Libya, the "lunatics" were interned in the criminal psychiatric

55. D'Amelio, "Di alcuni caratteri della legislazione penale in Libia", p. 21.

56. See Mary Gibson, *Born to Crime: Cesare Lombroso and the Origins of Biological Criminology* (London, 2002), p. 148.

57. Emanuele Mirabella, *I caratteri antropologici dei Libici in rapporto ai normali ed ai delinquenti italiani* (Rome, 1915).

58. Bernini, "Documenti sulla repressione italiana in Libia", pp. 153–157.

59. *Prospetto degli stabilimenti penali al 9 febbraio 1915*, in folder 2, file 6 in ACS, Ministero della giustizia, Direzione generale degli istituti di prevenzione e di pena, Studi per la riforma penitenziaria and Archivio di Stato di Siracusa, Prefettura, 1916–1917, folder 2332, file "Ministero delle Colonie, trasporto dementi arabi. Esercizio 1916–17". Marianna Scarfone has analysed the history of the "lunatics" transferred to the Psychiatric Hospital in Palermo in the 1930s: "La psichiatria coloniale italiana. Teorie, pratiche, protagonisti, istituzioni 1906–1952" (Ph.D., Ca' Foscari University, 2014), pp. 311–332.

60. *Ibid.*, p. 237.

hospital in Aversa. Mohamed ben Mohamed Behera, from Benghazi, was one of them. He arrived in Aversa on 26 June 1914 and died within a year, on 18 June 1915. During his internment, his brother, who was being confined in Favignana during the same period, wrote many letters to the director of the hospital in Aversa asking after Behera's health.[61] His supposed mental illness was connected to his sexual behaviour. The police in Benghazi had reported that Behera had exhibited "inappropriate" sexual behaviour – he had approached male minors, a female Jewish minor, and a Maltese girl.[62] As we have already observed, the sexual behaviour of both colonizers and the colonized was a "minefield" for colonial relationships.[63] Even within Italy, the terrain of sexuality endangered Italian dominion over North African people.

Certainly, the deportation of Libyans to Italy was a demonstration of strength over the colonized. At the same time, the presence of the colonized in the motherland in some respects overturned the "colonial situation",[64] undermining the relationship of power between Italians and North Africans. In particular, in Italy social relationships between the colonizers and the colonized were governed by rules different from the set of social norms in force in the colony. In particular, in Italy the social norms that established colonial relations and the hierarchy of colonizers over the colonized risked being subverted. This had the potential to undermine Italian prestige. And this was what happened in at least some situations involving relations between "black" men and "white" women. The presence of *askaris* in Sicily caused conflict with the local population. Indeed, the main reason why the Italian authorities decided to transfer Libyan soldiers with their families was because *askaris* had established "overly intimate" relationships with Sicilian women.[65]

During the Fascist period, Italian authorities had greater regard for the Libyan notables exiled in Italy. One can plausibly hypothesize that the Fascist government in Libya tried to secure itself potential interlocutors within Arab elite circles with whom it could establish a dialogue after military operations ceased. The main difference between exile and deportation concerned the living conditions guaranteed to the two groups of Arabs transferred to Italy. The Libyan exiles enjoyed "favourable" treatment, which made their stay in

---

61. During World War I, there was an exchange of letters among the deportees in Italy. They exchanged information, both personal and about their relatives; they reported on the treatment received in the penal colonies or in prison; and they gave instructions regarding their property or affairs in Libya. See Luciano Nisticò, "Relegati libici in Italia. Un aspetto poco noto della conquista coloniale", *Islàm Storia e Civiltà*, 4 (1989), pp. 275–285.
62. See the personal file of Mohamed ben Mohamed Behera in Archivio storico dell'Ospedale psichiatrico giudiziario di Aversa, Aversa (Caserta).
63. Ann L. Stoler, *Carnal Knowledge and Imperial Power: Race and the Intimate in Colonial Rule* (Berkeley, CA [etc.], 2010).
64. Georges Balandier, "La situation Colonial: Approche Théorique", *Cahiers Internationaux de Sociologie*, 11 (1951), pp. 44–79.
65. Bernini, "Documenti sulla repressione italiana in Libia", pp. 154–155.

Italy less burdensome than that of the majority of the other deportees. In particular, during their exile in Ustica, the *zawia* chiefs received a daily food allowance of five lire. Hassan Reda es-Senussi's exile was even more "comfortable". This notable had made a deal with the Italian government in 1929 and had accepted the colonizer's peace terms. Despite these negotiations, Graziani ordered his confinement in Italy, though he allowed him to move together with his wife, his daughter, and two "servants". Furthermore, the Italian government provided a remarkable allowance to Hassan, amounting to some 4,000 lire per month.[66]

The story of Hassan Reda es-Senussi in Italy exemplifies how the presence of natives in Italy might break the colonial order. He was exiled to Ustica in September 1930 and then, in June 1931, transferred to the Tremiti islands, owing to his "excessive familiarity" with many families in Ustica. In particular, a "distinguished person" from the island did not hesitate to promise his daughter to the Libyan notable, after he had asked to marry her – "even if he knew that Hassan was married with children" – but only on condition that es-Senussi provide a dowry of half a million lire. In the small Tremiti archipelago, some inhabitants who knew about his economic resources conned him, convincing him to spend more than he owned. In 1934, when Marshal Italo Balbo (Governor of Libya at the time) was trying to weave political alliances on Italy's "fourth shore" after the cessation of military operations, Hassan declared himself willing to negotiate with the Grand Senussi on behalf of the Italian government. In that same year, Hassan moved to Florence, where he died two years later.[67] On account of his political influence, Hassan was in the "grey area" between natives and colonizers. More generally, his experience in Italy had explicitly revealed the incompatibility of his status with the colonial hierarchy.

CONCLUSION

Italy's recourse to collective deportation was symptomatic of its weakness: the military authorities in the colony needed to expel "enemies" or potential "enemies" in order to reduce the threat posed by the resistance movement. This was what happened in particular from 1911 until World War I.[68] During the Fascist era, collective deportations ended and the regime chose to confine the nomadic and semi-nomadic populations of Cyrenaica in concentration camps in the Libyan desert. Italy deported Libyans to the motherland and not to its other colonial possessions. This was due to a combination of factors.

---

66. Eleonora Insalaco, "Confino politico nell'isola di Ustica di trentuno capi zavia e del senusso Hassan er-Reda es-Senussi dal settembre 1930", in Sulpizi and Sury, *Secondo convegno su gli esiliati libici nel periodo coloniale*, p. 124.
67. *Ibid.*, pp. 125–126.
68. Bernini, "Documenti sulla repressione italiana in Libia", p. 123.

Firstly, Italy did not have a large colonial empire with a choice of convict destinations. Secondly, Libya was much closer to Italy than to Italy's other possessions in East Africa. Thirdly, the "colonial" view of certain parts of Italy prevalent among the political authorities, and in particular concerning southern regions and the prison-islands, influenced the decision to designate Italy the favoured territory for the establishment of penal facilities. Lastly, throughout the Liberal period, Italian officials were opposed to the transfer of Libyans from one colony to another (as was the case with the removal of the *askaris* from Libya to Eritrea) and to their confinement within Libya.

Within the Italian colonial system, the deportation and transportation of convicts had exclusively punitive or preventive goals. Italy did not deport colonized peoples for labour purposes. On the contrary, the Italian authorities made every effort to dispel the association between punishment and labour exploitation. This concern arose from the weak political equilibrium that characterized the development of Italy's colonial venture, owing to the confrontation with other colonial powers but also to opposition within the colonial territories.

The peculiarity of the Italian case can also be analysed within a more general framework, which takes into consideration the imperial landscape in the nineteenth and twentieth centuries. The weakness of Italy as a colonial power arose from its position as a latecomer in the European imperial context. Italy did not embark on its colonial venture until the other main colonial powers had already become well established. In particular, in the final decades of the nineteenth century, when Italy took its first steps in acquiring its first colonial possession, Eritrea, slavery had already been abolished in most European colonies in Africa and Asia. Furthermore, Italy had no recent history of involvement in slavery.[69] All of these factors contribute to explaining the lack of connection between deportation, transportation, and forced labour in the Italian case.

With regard to the encounter between Italians and Libyans, this occasioned one of the first cases of "interracial" relationships in contemporary Italy. Italians saw Libyans through the lens of the colonial and racial hierarchy. The relationship between Libyans and Italians was marked by "new" codes in comparison with those that had been in force for centuries in the Mediterranean area and that had been characterized by uninterrupted encounters and exchanges between the two populations. Perhaps the most interesting feature of the presence of Libyan deportees in Italy concerns the manner in which the encounter with Italian society disrupted the social norms that were supposed to govern colonial relationships. This gave rise to a number of new social dynamics. Above all, it shows clearly that the history of these movements connects Libya and Italy within one and the same framework. As the case of deportation again highlights, it is impractical to elaborate a historical

---

69. Anderson and Maxwell-Stewart, "Convict Labour and the Western Empires, 1415–1954", p. 218.

analysis based on any rigid division between the colony and the motherland. As Sanjay Subrahmanyam would put it, it is much more fruitful to consider the histories of the two shores of the Mediterranean as "connected histories", where the connectedness does not erase regional, social, and cultural differences, but instead emerges from it.[70]

70. Sanjay Subrahmanyam, "Connected Histories: Notes Towards a Reconfiguration of Early Modern Eurasia", *Modern Asian Studies*, 31:3 (1997), pp. 735–762, 760. On this topic, see also Alan Lester, "Imperial Circuits and Networks: Geographies of the British Empire", *History Compass*, 4:1 (2006), pp. 124–141.